New Format

Schmidt Ink, Inc.

W9-AHJ-996

Creating Documents with Business Objects

Web Intelligence XI V3

Learn to create powerful Web Intelligence reports using Tables, Crosstabs, and Charts. Throughout the entire text there are well thought out examples on how to use these report structures to effectively transform corporate data into highly, useful information that your company can use.

Data can be presented many different ways, which can range from boring to exciting. Learn how to use Sorts, Filters, Alerters, and Ranks to get the most impact from your reports. In addition, discover how to use functions to increase the effectiveness of these presentations.

Web Intelligence offers many powerful functions that can be used to create formulas that allow for highly effective analysis of corporate data. Discover how you can use these formulas to transform everyday numbers into useful decision making tools.

Corporate data can be very large and accessed through many different universes. Learn how to build efficient queries with custom query filters, subqueries, and database ranks. Also, learn how to create multiple query documents that take advantage of these many universes.

Robert D. Schmidt
Independent Business Objects Trainer, Consultant, and Author

Schmidt Ink, Inc.
Creating Documents with Business Objects Web Intelligence XI V3.1

Published by
Schmidt Ink, Inc.
San Diego, CA 92131

Printed in USA

Schmidt Ink, Inc.
Phone: (858) 405-9317
www.schmidtink.com

Other Schmidt Ink, Inc. Publications:
Creating Documents with BusinessObjects: Desktop Intelligence XI R2 (978-0-9722636-7-2)
Creating Documents with BusinessObjects XI R2 - CBT (978-0-9722636-4-1)
Creating Universes with Designer XI V3 - CBT (978-0-9722636-2-7)
Creating Universes with Designer XI R2 - CBT (978-0-9722636-3-4)

0-9828352-0-5 (978-0-9828352-0-3)

I dedicate this book to my loving wife and family.

I also dedicate it to all the readers who trust my books to help further their knowledge and careers. I appreciate your trust and thank you for the motivation that you give me.

Introduction

Thank you for purchasing Creating Documents with Business Objects Web Intelligence XI V3.1. I hope that this book provides you with the reference and training that will help you to become a Business Objects professional. In this book we will examine many topics on creating documents and reports. Most of these topics will reference a database called SI Data V3.

The SI Data V3 database is available on our web site: www.SchmidtInk.com. You may use this database directly, or import it into a relational database. The database contains data from an investment company that had a one-year portfolio fund. In this fund there were six portfolios that traded stocks from their respective industries. The data also includes calls to clients and the daily prices of included stocks.

The universe for this book is also available on our web site: www.SchmidtInk.com. The universe is called SI Data V3, and there are several versions of the universe. There is a version for MS SQL Server and for Oracle. There may be others as demand requires.

In the previous versions of this book, I included a CBT to help people understand the examples better. In this version, the CBT is not included and will be available through our web site, after this book is published.

If your company has many people to train in Business Objects Designer, Web Intelligence, and/or Desktop Intelligence, then you may be interested in the Corporate Training Package. This package gives a company limited rights to reproduce the manuals in order to train their employees. Please contact us at RSchmidt@SchmidtInk.com for more information. You may also contact me at this address, if you have any questions on any of the exercises in the book. Please also send any comments and suggestions that you may have.

Sincerely,
Robert D. Schmidt
www.SchmidtInk.com

Table of Contents

Chapter 1: Web Intelligence Introduction

In this chapter, we are going to be introduced to Web Intelligence. Since there are two ways to access Web Intelligence, we are going to discuss both the InfoView Thin Client and the Rich Client applications. Most of the differences between these two versions are in the start-up of the applications. The thin client version is accessed through InfoView and the rich client is accessed through the Windows Start menu. After discussing how to access the applications, the two products become almost identical, so we will stop referring to the specific version of Web Intelligence, unless the topic can only be accomplished with only the Rich Client or the Thin Client version.

Introduction

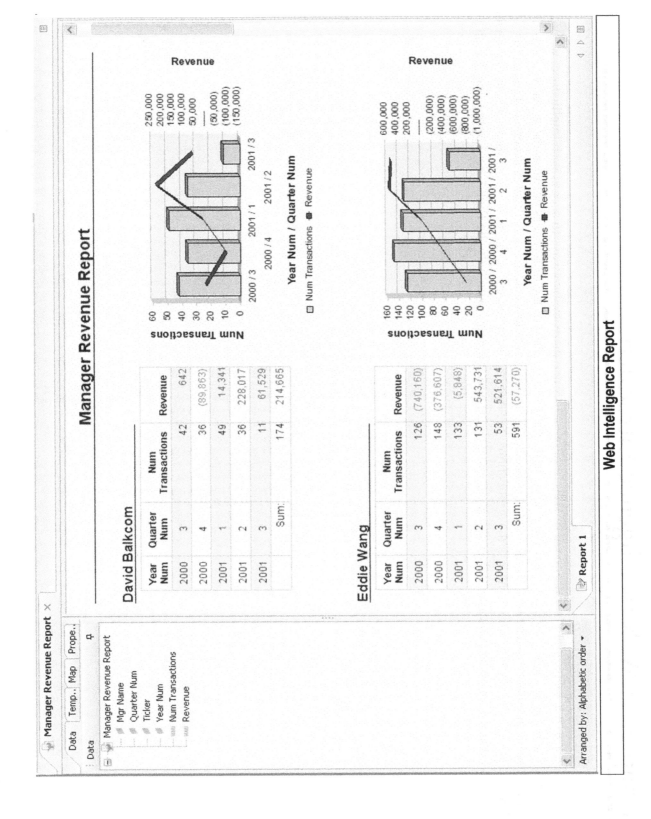

Introduction

Web Intelligence is a dynamic reporting environment that allows for reports to be created, viewed, and analyzed through a web interface.

Reports are basically formatted data that should expose information that is necessary to the function of a company. Many companies have large amounts of data stored on databases throughout the businesses in the company. This data, while important, is not useful, unless it is formatted and targeted to an audience. There are many ways to format and target data, and most companies use several - dashboards, spreadsheets, presentations, and reports. In this book, we are going to discuss Web Intelligence reports.

Reports need at least two things to make them useful - access to data and accessibility by the employees of the company. Web Intelligence provides both.

The data in a Web Intelligence report usually comes from a Business Objects universe. These universes are mappings of databases that allow visual and structured access to data. Through a universe, Web Intelligence report designers create data providers by selecting objects that represent data in a database. These objects can represent fields in a table, formulas, or even constant values. The advantage to universes is that all of the relationships between the tables have been mapped, so they offer a consistent interface to the data, which allows consistent results in different reports.

Web Intelligence reports are stored in a repository, referred to as the CMS. Employees have access to the CMS through various applications, one of which is Web Intelligence. Therefore, anybody with access to the CMS and Web Intelligence can open reports.

In the graphic above, you can see the data objects in the document's data provider, on the left pane of the report. The report is on the right pane. Together the data and the report make up the document.

Notes

Dimension Objects

Portfolio Name	Ticker	Year Num
Finance	C	2000
Finance	C	2001
Finance	GS	2000
Finance	GS	2001
Media	DIS	2000
Media	DIS	2001
Media	FOX	2000
Media	FOX	2001

Table of Dimension Objects

Portfolio Name
Finance
Media

Portfolio Name Context

Portfolio Name	Ticker
Finance	C
Finance	GS
Media	DIS
Media	FOX

Portfolio Name - Ticker Context

Portfolio Name	Ticker	Year Num
Finance	C	2000
Finance	C	2001
Finance	GS	2000
Finance	GS	2001
Media	DIS	2000
Media	DIS	2001
Media	FOX	2000
Media	FOX	2001

Portfolio Name - Ticker - Year Num Context

Dimension Objects

Dimensions create the context for a report, in much the same way that the frame of your house provides support for your walls and roof. Without the frame of your house, your home would just be a pile of wood, glass, and a few sinks thrown about. Without dimensions in a data set, our reports would just be a collection of meaningless numbers. Dimensions create the rows in a data set by providing unique combinations of values.

In the table of dimension objects, shown in the graphic, there are no two rows containing the same combination of dimension values. Some of the values repeat, such as Finance, but the other dimension values on the row make each row unique. Therefore, the context of this table is created by the Portfolio Name, Year Num, and Ticker dimensions.

Each dimension in a table will add to the context of the table and will usually create more rows within a table. For example, a table containing only the Portfolio Name will contain two rows - one for Finance and one for media. If we add Ticker to the table, then the rows will have to increase to display all of the possible Portfolio Name - Ticker combinations. Now, if we add Year Num to the table, then the context will change and the rows will once again have to increase to accommodate the new combinations of values.

Notes

Measure Objects

Portfolio Name	Ticker	Year Num	Num Transactions
Finance	C	2000	9
Finance	C	2001	11
Finance	GS	2000	5
Finance	GS	2001	15
Media	DIS	2000	11
Media	DIS	2001	7
Media	FOX	2000	14
Media	FOX	2001	19

Num Transactions Measure Object

Portfolio Name	Ticker	Num Transactions
Finance	C	20
Finance	GS	20
Media	DIS	18
Media	FOX	33

Measure Adjusts when Year Num is Removed

Select PorfolioName, Ticker, YearNum, Sum(NumTransactions)

From PortfolioTransactions

Group By PorfolioName, Ticker, YearNum

Measures Usually Create Summary Queries

Measure Objects

Measure objects do not create contexts, as do Dimensions. They usually conform to contexts through a preassigned aggregate function. In this example, Num Transactions is the measure and Sum is its predefined function. Notice the measure in the Num Transactions Measure Object graphic does not add any rows to the table.

Business Objects populates tables in a report using a dataset defined from selected objects. Tables in the report can display the entire dataset, or a subset of the data. The context of a table will change when a dimension object is removed from a table. For example, when Year Num is removed, the remaining values of Portfolio Name and Ticker will consolidate to form unique rows, as shown in the graphic. The measures in the table must conform to the new context. Num Transactions conforms, by summing the yearly values in the dataset for each ticker.

Measure objects usually cause a query to return summarized data, which basically means that only unique combinations of dimension values will be returned, and the measure will contribute an aggregated value to each row in the dataset. This can be seen in the following SQL:

Select PorfolioName, Ticker, YearNum, Sum (NumTransactions)
From PortfolioTransactions
Group By PorfolioName, Ticker, YearNum

The Group By clause instructs the database to only return distinct rows based on the values of the columns stated in the clause. Notice that the Group By clause is also the context of the dataset.

Notes

Detail Objects

Data Set 1

Dimension	Measure
Mgr Name	Revenue
David Balkcom	214,665
Eddie Wang	(57,270)
Kathy James	(78,540)
Maria Castro	79,426
Robert Denning	67,462
Sean Wilkenson	1,351,453

Data Set 2

Dimension	Detail
Mgr Name	Mgr Phone
David Balkcom	5555551900
Eddie Wang	5555552003
Kathy James	5555552000
Maria Castro	5555551278
Robert Denning	5555552002
Sean Wilkenson	5555551276

Combined Data Set 1 & 2

Dimension	Detail	Measure
Mgr Name	Mgr Phone	Revenue
David Balkcom	5555551900	214,665
Eddie Wang	5555552003	(57,270)
Kathy James	5555552000	(78,540)
Maria Castro	5555551278	79,426
Robert Denning	5555552002	67,462
Sean Wilkenson	5555551276	1,351,453

Data Set 1

Dimension	Measure
Mgr Name	Revenue
David Balkcom	214,665
Eddie Wang	(57,270)
Kathy James	(78,540)
Maria Castro	79,426
Robert Denning	67,462
Sean Wilkenson	1,351,453
Sum:	1,577,196

Data Set 3

Dimension	Dimension
Mgr Name	Ticker
David Balkcom	CPST
David Balkcom	FCEL
Eddie Wang	CIEN
Eddie Wang	PSFT
Kathy James	AOL
Kathy James	VIA
Maria Castro	DGX
Maria Castro	GENZ
Robert Denning	JPM
Robert Denning	LEH
Sean Wilkenson	AA
Sean Wilkenson	JPM
Sean Wilkenson	MMM

Combined Data Set 1 & 3

Dimension	Dimension	Measure
Mgr Name	Ticker	Revenue
David Balkcom	CPST	214,665
David Balkcom	FCEL	214,665
Eddie Wang	CIEN	(57,270)
Eddie Wang	PSFT	(57,270)
Kathy James	AOL	(78,540)
Kathy James	VIA	(78,540)
Maria Castro	DGX	79,426
Maria Castro	GENZ	79,426
Robert Denning	JPM	67,462
Robert Denning	LEH	67,462
Sean Wilkenson	AA	1,351,453
Sean Wilkenson	JPM	1,351,453
Sean Wilkenson	MMM	1,351,453

Detail Objects

A Detail object is an attribute of a Dimension object. It has only one value for each of its dimension's values. For example, an employee ID dimension should only have one employee name detail value.

In the graphic, we have data set 1 and data set 2. Data set 1 consists of a dimension (Mgr Name) and a measure (Revenue). The context of data set 1 is Mgr Name. Data set 2 consists of a dimension (Mgr Name) and a detail (Mgr Phone). The context of data set 2 is also Mgr Name. Data set 1 has a measure that should not be multiplied by duplicating the rows in the table. For example, if we were to repeat each row of the table, then the total of the table would be two times larger than it should be. Therefore, it is very important to not change the context of the table by adding objects that would cause the rows to repeat. If we were to combine data sets 1 & 2, then the number of rows would not increase, because there is only one Mgr Phone detail value for each Mgr Name value. This is why Mgr Phone can be defined as a detail.

The context of data set 1 is Mgr Name, because Mgr Name is the dimension. The context of data set 3 is Mgr Name and Ticker, because they are both dimensions. Notice that the Ticker object causes the Mgr Name to repeat, and thus creates more rows, than if Mgr Name were the only dimension in the table. If we were to combine data set 1 & 3, than the context of data set 1 would change to accommodate for the new Ticker dimension. This change in context would cause the Revenue values to repeat for each ticker owned by the manager, as can be seen in the graphic (Combined Data Set 1 & 3), and thus fan (repeat) the revenues across the repeated Mgr Name values, which may make it appear that the total revenue were much higher than the actual total.

Therefore, it is safe to bring a detail object into any context, as long as its related dimension is also present in the context. Dimensions that will change the context of a data set should not be allowed into the set, because it may cause the revenues to fan (repeat) across the new dimension's values.

Notes

Web Intelligence Objects (Summary)

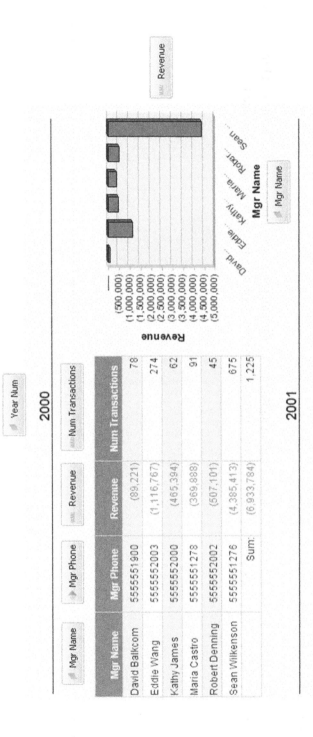

Year Num

2000

Mgr Name	Mgr Phone	Revenue	Num Transactions
David Balkcom	5555551900	(89,221)	78
Eddie Wang	5555552003	(1,116,767)	274
Kathy James	5555552000	(465,394)	62
Maria Castro	5555551278	(369,888)	91
Robert Denning	5555552002	(507,101)	45
Sean Wilkenson	5555551276	(4,385,413)	675
	Sum:	(6,933,784)	1,225

2001

Mgr Name	Mgr Phone	Revenue	Num Transactions
David Balkcom	5555551900	303,886	96
Eddie Wang	5555552003	1,059,497	317
Kathy James	5555552000	386,854	58
Maria Castro	5555551278	449,314	93
Robert Denning	5555552002	574,563	75
Sean Wilkenson	5555551276	5,736,866	816
	Sum:	8,510,980	1,455

Objects in a Report

Web Intelligence Objects (Summary)

Business Objects represents the different types of objects with icons, as shown in the graphic. Dimensions are blue planes, details are green pyramids, and measures are orange rulers. While a document is being created, the document designer will select the different query objects to supply the data source for the document with data. A document can have multiple data sources defined with different sets of query objects.

Once the data sources for a document are defined and the queries are executed, the objects are arranged to create different types of report structures. Documents can contain a single report or multiple reports, each defined on a different report tab in the document. The report in the graphic is called a Section report, because it is divided into sections based on the Year Num dimensions values. This is a typical use for a dimension - creating sections on a report.

Each section contains a table and a chart. The context of the table is Year Num and Mgr Name, because these are the dimensions that define the calculation context for the measures - Revenue and Num Transactions. Notice that Mgr Phone has no effect on the calculations or the number of rows in the table. If the Mgr Phone column were removed from the table, then nothing would change, except the phone number would be missing from the table, which is how we expect detail objects to behave

The chart is defined with the Mgr Name on the X-axis and Revenue on the y-axis. The context of the chart is the same as the context for the table: Year Num - Mgr Name. The context is the same, because no new dimensions are added to the chart's definition. Therefore, each column in the chart is a graphical representation of the values in the Revenue column in the table.

Notes

_____

Start Web Intelligence Rich Client

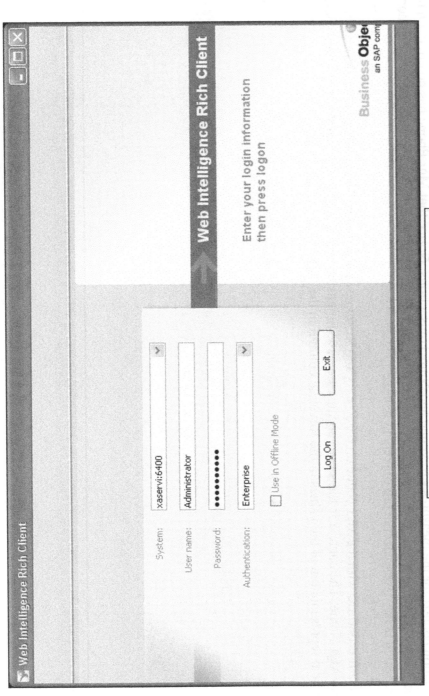

Web Intelligence Rich Client Log In Screen

Authentication Types

Windows XP Desktop Icon

Windows XP Start Menu

Start Web Intelligence Rich Client

Business Objects has several versions of reporters. We will be using the Rich Client version, which is very similar to the Java Report Panel in InfoView. All of the examples in this book can be accomplish with either the Rich Client or Java Report Panel versions of Web Intelligence.

To start the Rich Client application, select Start>All Programs>BusinessObjects XI 3.1>Business Objects x>Web Intelligence Rich Client, where the x defines the version of Business Objects, such as enterprise or edge.

When the application starts, you will probably be greeted by a log in screen. The first field asks for the system. You may be able to click the down arrow button associated to the System edit to select a system. If not, then you should ask your Business Objects administrator for the system name and port number. The port number may or may not be necessary, so if you cannot identify the port number, then you can try the system name without the associated port number. The system name is usually the server where the Business Objects application is installed.

Next, enter your user name and password, if necessary. There are many ways to install Business Objects security. Some systems expect a user name and password, and others just use Windows security to identify the user name and password.

There are several Authentication methods. Enterprise expects a User Name and Password to be entered into the respective fields. LDAP, Windows AD, and Windows NT will use the user information assigned to these systems to assign the user name and password. Standalone logs into no system and opens the application in unsecured mode. In this mode you can create documents with unsecured universes and open unsecured documents. Usually, these unsecured universes and documents must be saved with the *save for all users* option selected.

The Use in Offline Mode will allow you to log in to the application with the same rights that you had in the previous online login. This will allow you to open and create documents that you have access to. However, you will not be able to access the repository to retrieve documents or universes.

Once all of the fields have been properly filled out, you may click the Log On button to log into Web Intelligence Rich Client.

Notes

Start Web Intelligence Thin Client

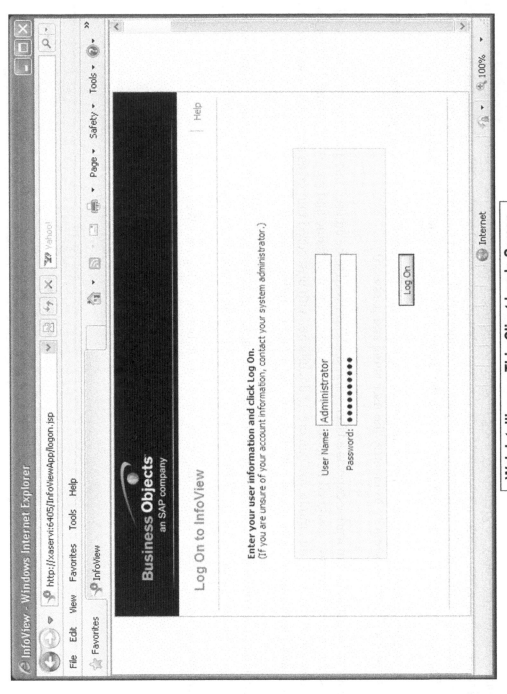

Web Intelligence Thin Client Log In Screen

Web intelligence URL: **http://*webserver:portnumber*/InfoViewApp/logon.jsp**
BusinessObjects Enterprise Java InfoView

Start Web Intelligence Thin Client

The thin client version of Web Intelligence runs in an Internet browser, such as Internet Explorer. To start the application, you just need to enter the correct URL into the browser's address bar. Usually, the URL is in the following format:

http://*webserver:portnumber*/InfoViewApp/logon.jsp

Where webserver is the name of the server where Web Intelligence is installed. In my case, the server name is xaservi. The port number is the port where the Business Objects server accepts log ins. In my case the port number is 6405. The log in screen for your Web Intelligence may differ from the one shown in the graphic.

BusinessObjects Enterprise users can select BusinessObjects Enterprise Java InfoView from the Business Objects Enterprise submenu in the Windows Start menu.

Once all of the fields have been properly filled out, you may click the Log On button to log into Web Intelligence Thin Client.

Notes

Creating a Data Source

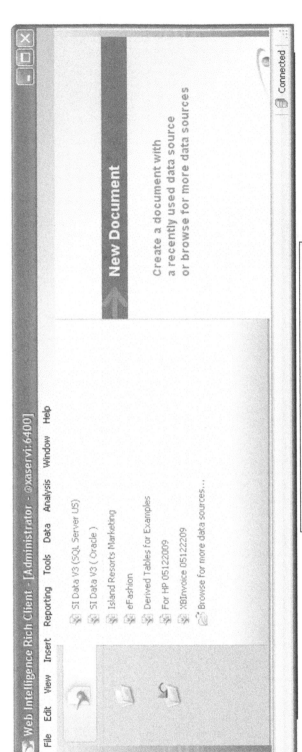

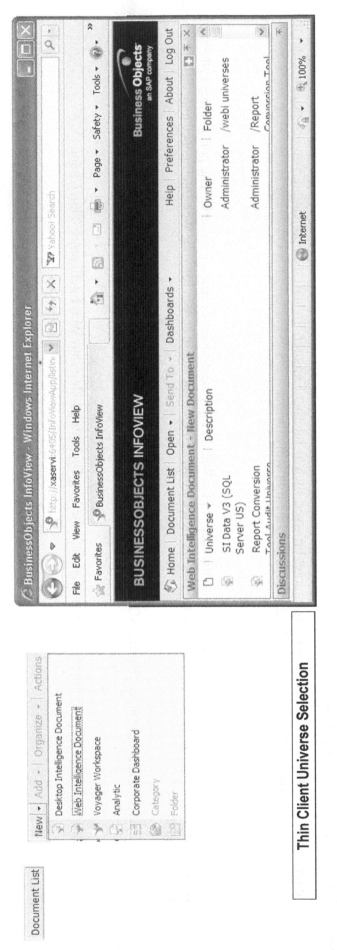

Rich Client Universe Selection

Thin Client Universe Selection

Creating a Data Source

Since Rich and Thin client are very similar, we will continue to show both until the examples are independent of the Web Intelligence version.

After we log into Rich client, we can create a data source for a document. We do this by clicking on the top icon in the New Document screen, which will display the available universes. Universes allow us to select objects to create reports. In this course, we are going to use the SI Data V3 (SQL Server US) universe.

After logging into InfoView, we need to click the *Document List* button to put the application in document mode, and then click on the *New* button to display the available document applications. Then, click the Web Intelligence Document item in the list, as shown in the graphic. A list of all available universes will be displayed. In this course, we are going to use the SI Data V3 (SQL Server US) universe.

With the InfoView Thin Client, we can only create documents using universes. With the Rich Client, we can local data sources, such as csv's or MS Excel files. We will learn how to use local data sources later in this book.

Notes

Query Panel

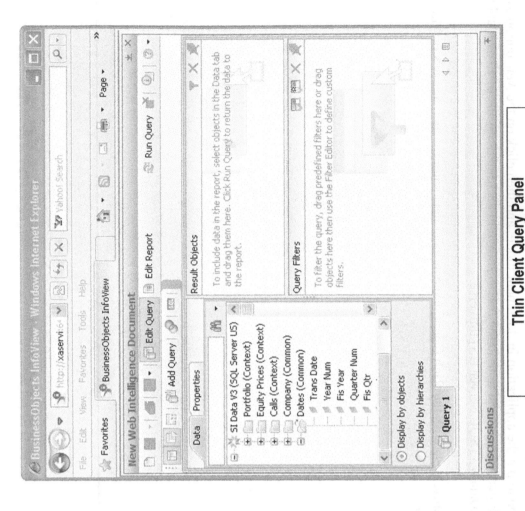

Rich Client Query Panel

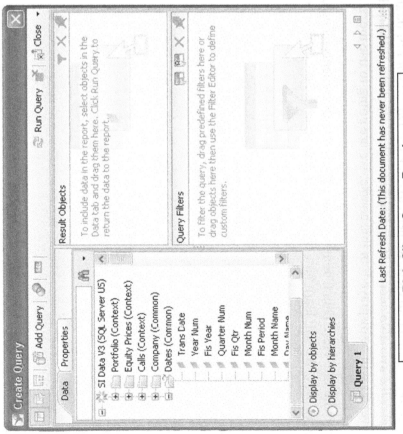

Thin Client Query Panel

Query Panel

As you can see from the graphic, the Rich and Thin client versions of Web Intelligence are very similar, so this is where we will stop comparing the two versions. Previously, we selected a universe from a list. After we select a universe, Web Intelligence will display the query panel for the selected universe. The query panel organizes the Dimension, Detail, and Measure objects into folders, known as classes.

To create a data source, we simply browse the folders to locate objects of interest. Then, we place the desired objects in the Result objects section of the panel.

Notes

Selecting Objects for a Data Source

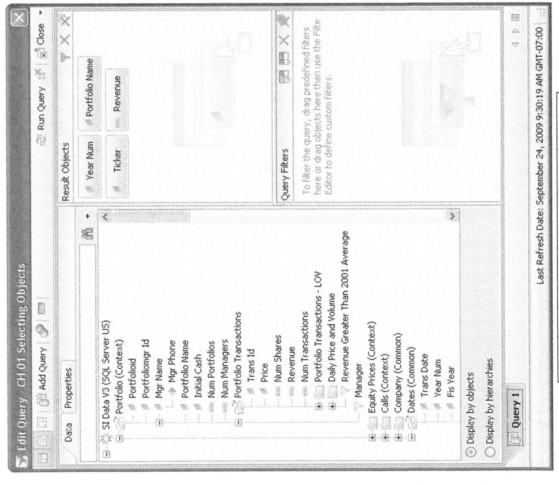

Selected Objects in Query Panel

Resulting Table

Year Num	Portfolio Name	Ticker	Revenue
2000	Alternative Energy	ACPW	(17,569)
2000	Alternative Energy	APWR	2,809
2000	Alternative Energy	BLDP	(16,380)
2000	Alternative Energy	CPST	7,635
2000	Alternative Energy	FCEL	9,343
2000	Biotech	AMGN	(126,995)
2000	Biotech	CHIR	(47,800)
2000	Biotech	GENZ	(51,588)
2000	Biotech	MRK	14,812
2000	Biotech	PFE	(29,257)
2001	Alternative Energy	ACPW	37,217
2001	Alternative Energy	APWR	811
2001	Alternative Energy	BLDP	31,378
2001	Alternative Energy	CPST	45,220
2001	Alternative Energy	FCEL	81,232
2001	Biotech	AMGN	129,101
2001	Biotech	CHIR	66,756
2001	Biotech	GENZ	86,978
2001	Biotech	MRK	(19,002)
2001	Biotech	PFE	30,200
		Sum:	234,901

Selecting Objects for a Data Source

To create a data source from a Business Objects universe, we select objects in the class folders and place them in the Result Objects section of the query panel.

When selecting objects, we must consider the context that will be created by the selected dimensions. In this example, we have selected the Year Num, Portfolio Name, and Ticker dimensions. These dimension objects will create a context that will divide the selected measure's values by properly distributing the amounts to the unique rows created by the dimension values.

The table in the graphic has been formatted and filters have been placed on it to limit its size. In the table, we can see how the revenue gets distributed to each row in the table, and how each row is defined by a unique combination of dimension values.

Notice that the column names are the same as the object names in the query, and that the columns are in the same order as the objects. This is the default table that is created when a query is first executed. If there are additional objects added to the query after the default table is created, then the new objects will not automatically be added to the default table. The new objects can be manually added to the table, and the table can be modified and formatted to highlight the purpose of the report. We will discuss formatting over the next few chapters.

Notes

Saving Documents with Thin Client Web Intelligence

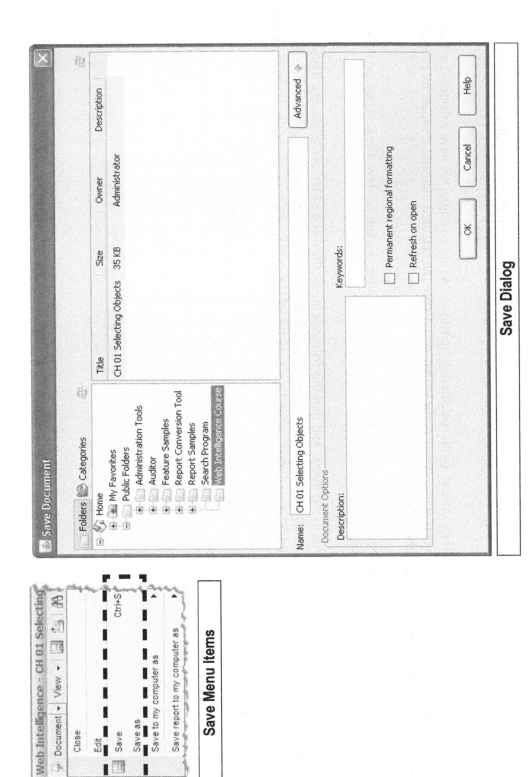

Save Menu Items

Save Dialog

Saving Documents with Thin Client Web Intelligence

Thin client Web Intelligence saves documents to the repository, also known as the CMS. The CMS is a database that stores documents and the data contained in the documents. The documents are organized into folders that may have differing levels of security applied to them. For example, if you write a report for the finance group, then you will probably save that document in a folder that the finance group has rights to. Then, when the finance group wants to open a document, they will browse their folders to locate it.

Notice that I used the terms report and document to refer to the document. We write reports in a document. Therefore, many people will refer to a document has a report. Few people will say, "Get me the Quarterly document." Most people will say, "Get me the Quarterly report," even though the report is contained in a document. A document can hold several reports, and each report can be represented by a different tab, or all reports can be on the same tab.

Notice that there are several fields available in the Advanced section of the dialog. You can give your documents descriptions, which will help others to understand the purpose of the document. You can also give your document Keywords, which will help people to locate the document through keyword searches.

The *Refresh on Open* will cause the document to refresh each time it is opened. While this may be important to keep the document current, consideration must be given to this option, since it may frustrate people for the document to refresh each time it is opened, especially, if they just opened it a few minutes prior.

Formatting of time, dates and numbers may vary from region to region. If the document is to retain the current regional formats, then click the *Permanent regional formatting* option.

Notes

Opening Documents with Thin Client Web Intelligence

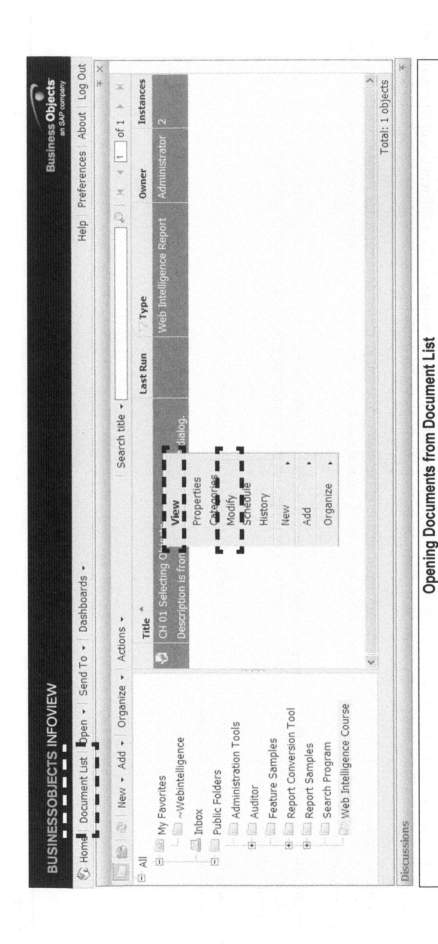

Opening Documents from Document List

Opening Documents with Thin Client Web Intelligence

With Web Intelligence, you can open documents for viewing of for modifying. The Viewer application is usually different from the modifying application. If a document is opened to view, then it will use one of two Web applications - Web Viewer or Interactive Viewer, or will open the document in a PDF format, which uses Adobe Acrobat reader. You cannot modify the document with Web Viewer or Adobe Acrobat. The Interactive viewer will allow modifications, but it is not as robust as the Thin or Rich Client versions of the editor.

If the document is opened for modification, then one of four applications can be used. The Advanced Thin Client editor (The one we are using in this class), the Interactive Viewer, the Rich Client editor (Also used in this class), or Web Accessibility. The Advanced version needs Java 2 installed and the Rich Client editor must be downloaded to use.

The main difference between the Advanced version and the Rich Client version is that the Advanced (we refer to as Thin Client) version works with documents on the server, and there are no files involved. The Rich client downloads the file to work on it.

To View or Modify a document, click the Document List button to display the available documents, and then, right-click on a document and select View or Modify from the pop-up menu.

Notice the ~Webintelligence folder in the My Favorites folder. This folder was created by Business Objects when Web Intelligence Thin Client timed-out, which it will do after a specified number of minutes. The folder was created to hold the document that was in the Thin client application when it timed-out. Business Objects did not do this in version R2, so a lot of people got frustrated when the application timed-out and they lost some of their work. Now, the file is stored in this temporary folder upon time-out.

Notes

Selecting Viewing and Modifying Peferences

BUSINESSOBJECTS INFOVIEW

Home | Document List | Open ▾ | Send To ▾ | Dashboards ▾

Help | Preferences | About | Log Out

Business Objects
an SAP company

Preferences - Administrator

▲ General

▲ Change Password

▶ Web Intelligence

Select a default view format:

- ◉ Web (no downloading required)
- ○ Interactive (no downloading required)
- ○ PDF (Adobe AcrobatReader required)

When viewing a document:

- ○ Use the document locale to format the data
- ◉ Use my preferred viewing locale to format the data

Select a default creation/editing tool:

- ◉ Advanced (Java 2 required)
- ○ Interactive (no downloading required)
- ○ Desktop (Web Intelligence Rich Client required) [Install Now]
- ○ Web Accessibility (508 Compliant)

Select a default Universe:

No default universe [Browse ...]

Selecting Viewing and Modifying Peferences

When we select View or Modify, Business Objects will open the selected document in a default application. This default application is set in the InfoView Preferences, in the Web Intelligence section. The viewers are Web, Interactive, and PDF. Each has an advantage, so they are all available for you to select.

The editors are Advanced, which is the application we are referring to as Thin Client. We are calling it Thin Client, because it does not run on your local machine. The pages are generated on the Web Intelligence server and then viewed on your local machine. You need to have Java 2 installed for the application to run on your machine.

Interactive is another thin client application, but it does not need Java installed. However, it is not as powerful as the Advance thin Client editor.

The Desktop option is the Rich Client editor, which is the other editor that we are using in this class. This editor was not available in Business Objects R2. The Desktop Rich Client needs to be installed on your local machine, and does not need to see the CMS in order to open and refresh documents. It also does not time-out, as the Thin client does.

Notes

Saving Documents with Rich Client Web Intelligence

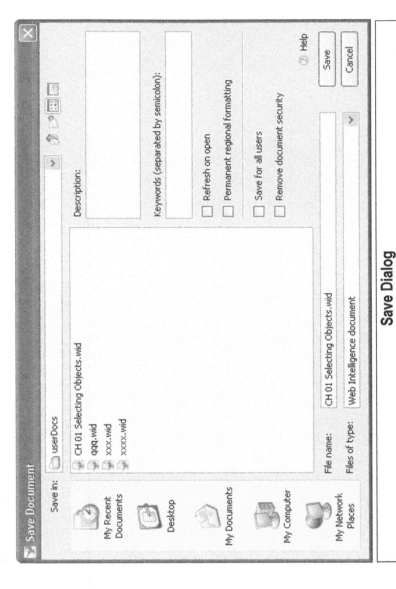

Save Dialog

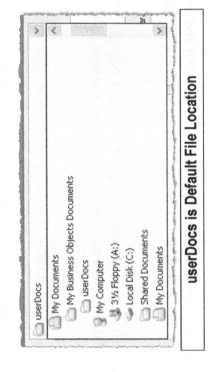

userDocs is Default File Location

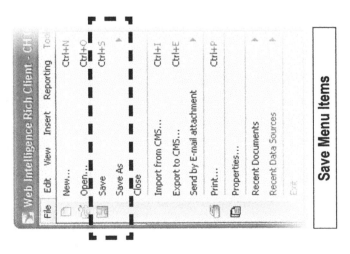

Save Menu Items

Saving Documents with Rich Client Web Intelligence

On the previous topic, we learned that Web Intelligence Thin Client only saves Web Intelligence documents to the CMS. Rich client is different, because it saves documents to the file system, as a * .wid file. This is an actual file that can be emailed, saved to a USB drive, or anything else that can be done to a file on a computer.

Rich client documents that are saved as files can only be accessed by browsing to the directory where the document is saved. Documents can be saved in a shared directory on the network, so that they can be available to multiple users.

Rich client documents have the same options that Thin clients have - *Description, Keywords, Refresh on open,* and *Permanent regional formatting.* However, Rich client documents have a couple extra options in the Save dialog - *Save for all Users* and *Remove Document Security.* The *Save for all users* option allows any user in the same user group to open the document. The *Remove Document Security* allows the document to be opened by anybody with Web Intelligence Rich Client. This option is usually used when emailing documents to people outside of your Business Objects system, such as a technical support person. The reason Rich Client has these options and Thin client does not, is because Thin Client documents must have security in order for the documents to be saved in the CMS. Rich client documents can be saved on the hard drive, so sometimes they do not need the security.

Notes

Exporting Documents with Rich Client Web Intelligence

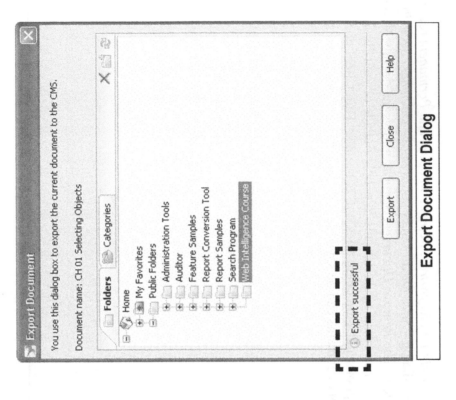

Export Document Dialog

Export to CMS Menu Item

Can Overwrite Documents in CMS

Exporting Documents with Rich Client Web Intelligence

Rich client Web Intelligence works with files on your hard drive. Thin client works with documents on the Web Intelligence server, and there is no actual file with thin client. However, thin client can open and modify rich client documents. In order for thin client, or other Business Objects applications to access documents created with rich client, the document must be exported to the CMS. The CMS is a common repository that stores documents and their data.

To export a document, select *File>Export to CMS…* from the menu. The Export Document dialog allows you to export to any folder that you have rights to. Each folder has its own security, and usually we export to a folder so that other users with similar rights can access the documents.

Notes

Opening Documents with Rich Client Web Intelligence

Open Dialog (userDocs is Default File Location)

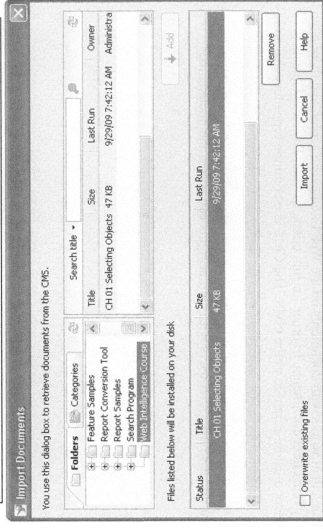

Open Dialog (userDocs is Default File Location)

Open Toolbar Button

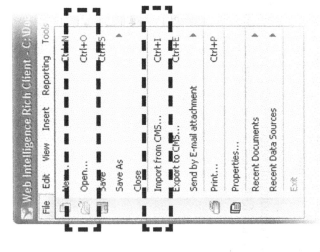

Open & Import Menu Items

Opening Documents with Rich Client Web Intelligence

Web Intelligence rich client works with files on our hard drive. The files can be there because they were created there, or because they were imported from the CMS.

Earlier, we saw that both thin client and rich client can save files to the CMS. These files can be there because they were created there, or because they were imported to your hard drive through the rich client interface, regardless of which application created them. To import a document, simply select *File>Import from CMS...* from the menu. This selection will cause the Import Documents dialog to be displayed. With this dialog, we can locate documents in the folders and mark them for download by clicking the *Add* button. The Search title control can also be used to help locate documents. Once the documents are marked for download, click the *Import* button and the document files will be downloaded to you userDocs directory.

To open Web Intelligence documents, we just select *File>Open...* from the menu to display the Open dialog. By default the Open dialog will display all of the rich client documents in the userDocs directory. Rich client documents have the *.wid extension.

Working with files has an advantage over the thin client documents, as we can open them even when we are not connected to the network or cannot see the CMS. This allows us to view documents while on a plane, or show documents to clients while at their place of business.

Notes

_____

Document Properties

Document Properties Pane

Document Properties

Document Information

Created by:	Administrator
Last modified by:	Administrator
Creation date:	September 24, 2009 9:40:39 AM GMT-07:00
Name:	CH 01 Selecting Objects
Description:	Description is from the Save Document dialog.

Keywords: Keywords are from Save Document Dialog.

Locale: English

Data Tracking: Off

Document Options

- ☐ Refresh on open
- ☐ Enhanced viewing
- ☐ Use query drill
- ☐ Permanent regional formatting

Data Synchronization Options

- ☑ Auto-merge dimensions
- ☐ Extend merged dimension values

Report Order

Report 2 (1)

Document Properties Pane

Properties Menu Item

Year Num	Portfolio Name	Ticker	Revenue
2000	A		(17,569)
2000	A	Set as Section	2,809
2000	A	Insert	(16,380)
2000	A	Copy as text	7,635
2000	A	Clear	9,343
2000	A	Remove	(26,995)
2000	B	Turn To	(47,800)
2000	B	Format Text…	(51,588)
2000	B	Formula Toolbar	14,812
2000	B	Format	(29,257)
2000	B	Hyperlinks	37,217
2001	A	Sort	811
2001	A	Order	31,378
2001	A	Align	45,220
2001		Document Properties	

Properties Menu Item

Document Properties

When we saved a document with either Rich or Thin client, we were able to assign a Description and Keywords. We can see these properties in the Document Properties pane, which is the same for Rich or Thin client. To display the pane, right-click on the document, and then select *Document Properties* from the pop-up menu.

We cannot change the properties in the Document Information section of the pane. However, there are options that we can change. These modifiable options are the Document Options, Data Synchronization Options, and Report Order. It is really too soon to talk about many of these options, but we will give a brief description of each, and then discuss them in further detail within the proper context.

Document Options:

Refresh on Open: Will cause a document to refresh each time it is opened. This option is used mainly to keep documents current.
Enhanced Viewing: Documents can be viewed onscreen or printed. When viewed onscreen, it is not necessary to have the same margins, headers and footers as the printed versions. Enhanced viewing changes these properties for onscreen viewing.
Use Query Drill: Drilling allows for summaries to be drilled into displaying more detailed information. After drilling into a value, you can also drill back up to the summary values. Web Intelligence will simply re-aggregate the detail values into the summary values, which will not work well with aggregates, such as average. Use Query Drill causes the query to be refreshed at each level of drill.
Permanent Regional Formatting: Keeps the current format of Dates, Numbers, and Time, even when opened in a different region.

Data Synchronization Options:

Auto-merge Dimensions: When a document contains more than one data provider, dimensions from the same universe, with the same name will be merged.
Extend Merged Dimension Values: When merging data providers, Web Intelligence wants to join on dimension values that are in both data providers. If one data provider has only a subset of the values, then the merged data set will only contain the subset values. If you want to report on all dimension values, even if they are not in both data sets, then select this option.

Notes

Summary

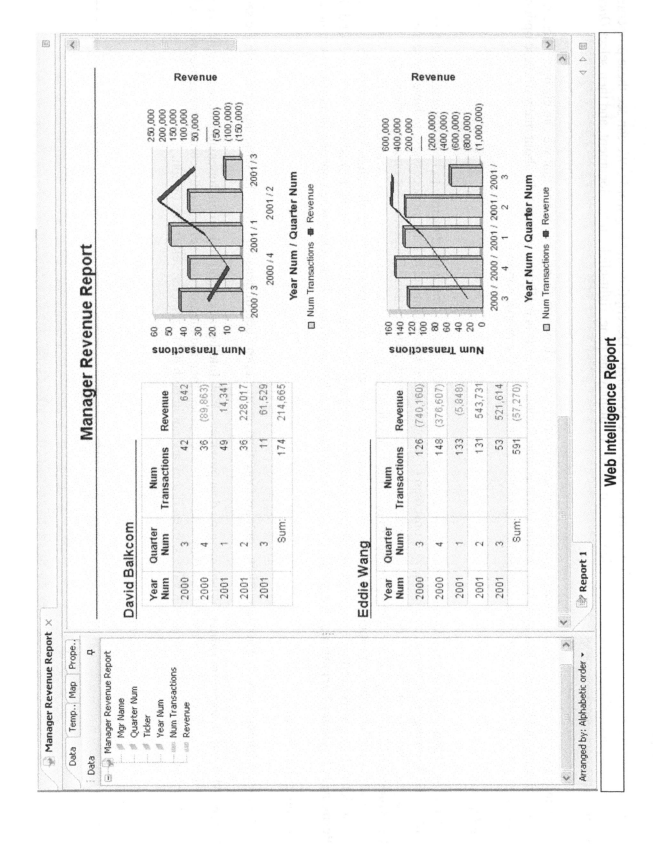

Summary

In this chapter, we learned that there are two versions of Web Intelligence - a thin client and a rich client. We learned that the thin client can only save Web Intelligence documents in the CMS and not on a hard-drive. The reason for this is that the Web Server does not run on your local machine, and it may not be able to access your hard-drive. The rich client can save on a local drive and export to the CMS.

We also learned about the data objects in Web Intelligence. Knowing about these objects and how they behave will help you to write powerful reports with them. Remember that Dimensions create contexts, Measures conform to contexts, and Details do not create contexts (if there parent Dimension is in the report structure).

We will use the skills that we were introduced to in this chapter, throughout this entire book. Please always keep in mind how the objects behave and how this behavior can help you to create the reports that you need to help analyze your business.

Notes

Chapter 2: Report Structures

In this chapter, we are going to learn how to use report structures to create effective reports.

Introduction

Manager Report
May 20, 2010

Total Transactions: 2,660
Total Revenue: 1,577,196

Year Num	Quarter Num	David Balkcom		Eddie Wang		Kathy James	
		Num Trans	Revenue	Num Trans	Revenue	Num Trans	Revenue
2000	3	42	642	126	(740,160)	31	(267,653)
2000	4	36	(89,863)	148	(376,607)	31	(197,741)
2001	1	49	14,341	133	(5,848)	23	52,981
2001	2	36	228,017	131	543,731	27	112,154
2001	3	11	61,529	53	521,614	8	221,719
Sum:		174	214,665	591	(57,270)	120	(78,540)

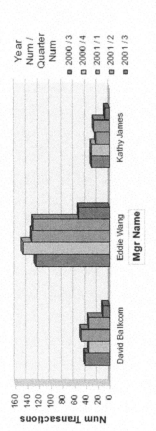

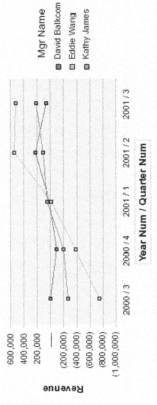

Introduction

There are many ways to structure a report. Many of us have viewed reports and know that some reports are very effective, while others are just too confusing. Before we talk about how to structure a report, we should discuss the purpose of a report. Reports are supposed to communicate to the viewer of the report some important information. For example, Quarterly Financial Reports communicate the state of a company.

Reports should concisely communicate this information. Most viewers of reports are interested in obtaining usable information, such as "Did we have a gain or a loss last quarter?" "If we had a loss, then where did we lose money?"

Notes

Structure Types

Table

Mgr Name	Year Num	Quarter Num	Num Transactions	Revenue
David Balkcom	2000	3	42	642
David Balkcom	2000	4	36	(89,863)
David Balkcom	2001	1	49	14,341
David Balkcom	2001	2	36	228,016
David Balkcom	2001	3	11	61,529
Eddie Wang	2000	3	126	(740,160)
Eddie Wang	2000	4	148	(376,607)
Eddie Wang	2001	1	133	(5,848)
Eddie Wang	2001	2	131	543,731
Eddie Wang	2001	3	53	521,614

Crosstab

	2000	2000	2001	2001	2001	Manager
	3	4	1	2	3	Sum
David Balkcom	642	(89,863)	14,341	228,016	61,529	214,665
Eddie Wang	(740,160)	(376,607)	(5,848)	543,731	521,614	(57,270)
Kathy James	(267,653)	(197,741)	52,981	112,154	221,719	(78,540)
Maria Castro	(400,996)	31,108	(119,552)	273,348	295,519	79,426
Robert Denning	(292,493)	(214,608)	77,166	253,014	244,383	67,462
Sean Wilkenson	(2,578,025)	(1,807,388)	330,350	1,340,450	4,066,066	1,351,453
Quarter Sum:	(4,278,686)	(2,655,098)	349,438	2,750,713	5,410,828	1,577,196

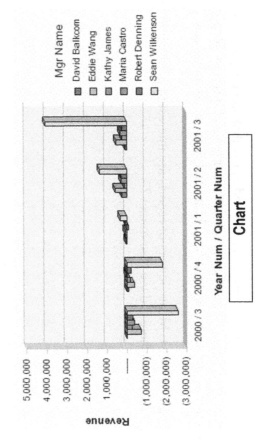

Chart

Mgr Name
- David Balkcom
- Eddie Wang
- Kathy James
- Maria Castro
- Robert Denning
- Sean Wilkenson

Revenue

5,000,000
4,000,000
3,000,000
2,000,000
1,000,000
—
(1,000,000)
(2,000,000)
(3,000,000)

2000 / 3   2000 / 4   2001 / 1   2001 / 2   2001 / 3

Year Num / Quarter Num

Structure Types

When a document is created it will contain a default report, which is usually a table representation of the dataset contained in the document. Tables are interesting, because they contain data of interest, but tables by themselves are not usually effective portrayers of information. Therefore, we must use a variety of structures and formats to highlight the information that is significant in a report. In Business Objects, we do this with tables, cross tables, and charts.

Each report structure is very useful and each type has its advantages and disadvantages. As you become more advanced, you will use report structures to create more and more powerful reports. A powerful report is one that allows viewers of the report to understand exactly what you are trying to show them.

Notes

Tables

Mgr Name	Year Num	Quarter Num	Num Transactions	Revenue
David Balkcom	2000	3	42	642
David Balkcom	2000	4	36	(89,863)
David Balkcom	2001	1	49	14,341
David Balkcom	2001	2	36	228,016
David Balkcom	2001	3	11	61,529
Eddie Wang	2000	3	126	(740,160)
Eddie Wang	2000	4	148	(376,607)
Eddie Wang	2001	1	133	(5,848)
Eddie Wang	2001	2	131	543,731
Eddie Wang	2001	3	53	521,614
		Sum:	765	157,395

← Header Row

← Table Body

← Footer Row

Table

My Table's Revenue: $ 157,395				
Mgr Name	Year Num	Quarter Num	Num Transactions	Revenue
David Balkcom	2000	3	42	642
David Balkcom	2000	4	36	(89,863)
David Balkcom	2001	1	49	14,341
David Balkcom	2001	2	36	228,016
David Balkcom	2001	3	11	61,529
Eddie Wang	2000	3	126	(740,160)
Eddie Wang	2000	4	148	(376,607)
Eddie Wang	2001	1	133	(5,848)
Eddie Wang	2001	2	131	543,731
Eddie Wang	2001	3	53	521,614
		Sum:	765	157,395

Table with Title and Calculation in Header

Mgr Name	Year Num	Quarter Num	Num Transactions	Revenue
David Balkcom	2000	3	42	642
David Balkcom	2000	4	36	(89,863)
David Balkcom	2001	1	49	14,341
David Balkcom	2001	2	36	228,016
David Balkcom	2001	3	11	61,529
Eddie Wang	2000	3	126	(740,160)
Eddie Wang	2000	4	148	(376,607)
Eddie Wang	2001	1	133	(5,848)
Eddie Wang	2001	2	131	543,731
Eddie Wang	2001	3	53	521,614
		Sum:	765	157,395
		Quarter Average:	76.5	15,739
		Manager Average:	382.5	78,697

Table with Multiple Footer Rows

Tables

Tables consist of rows of information, and each row is defined by unique combinations of Dimension objects. For example, the table in the graphic has rows that are defined by Mgr Name, Year Num, and Quarter Num. Therefore, the context of the table is Mgr Name, Year Num, and Quarter Num. The rows are almost never defined by Detail objects, because detail objects are usually associated with a dimension object that is defining the context. If a detail is present in a table without its associated dimension object, then the detail will also define the context.

The measures in a table do not define contexts. They simply conform to the contexts created by the dimensions in the table. As dimension columns are deleted or added to a table, the context of the table will change and the measures should conform to the new contexts.

Most tables have a header row, as shown in the graphic. The header row usually is used to hold column header labels. However, the header row can also contain titles and/or calculations. In the graphic, we added a title row and inserted a formula to display the title - My Table, and a calculation for the total revenue in the table.

Tables can also have a footer, as shown in the graphic (Table). Footers are usually used to hold summaries for the detail rows in the table. In our example, the footer is displaying the total Revenue and Num Transactions. A table can also have multiple footer rows, as shown in the graphic (Table with Multiple Footer Rows).

When a document is created, the default report is usually a table with a single header row. The default table does not usually have a footer row, because calculations may not be required for the table.

Notes

Inserting Tables

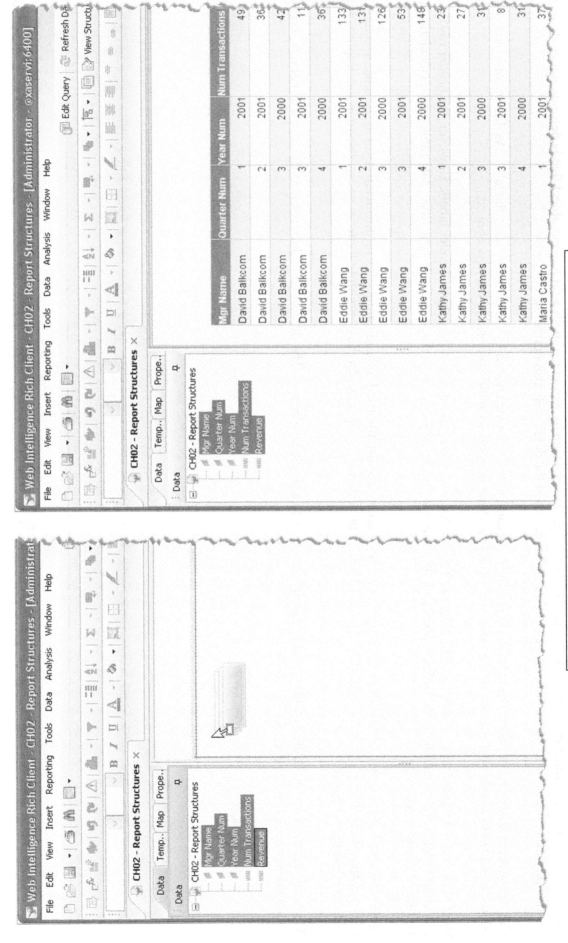

Creating a Table

Inserting Tables

Along the left-side of the application, there are four tabs (Default). One of these tabs is the Data tab. The Data tab shows all of the variables contained in the report. Variables are objects that are supplied by the query and objects that are created within the document. To create a table on a report, select the desired objects by clicking on the first of the objects, and then, while holding down the [CTRL] key, selecting the rest of the objects.

After selecting the objects, drag them unto the report and drop them. This will create a table populated with the selected objects, as shown in the graphic.

Exercise: Create a Table

1. Create a query with Mgr Name, Year Num, Quarter Num, Num Transactions, and Revenue.
2. This will create a default report with a table created from the objects in the query.
3. Along the bottom of the document, there should be a tab called *Report 1*. Right-click on this tab and select *Insert Report* from the pop-up menu. This will insert a blank report into the document. A document can contain many report tabs.
4. If the Data tab is not visible in the reporting environment, then click the configure view button, and then select Data. Click on the Mgr Name object to select it, and then hold down the [CTRL] key while selecting the remaining objects. Lastly, drag the objects unto the report to create the table.

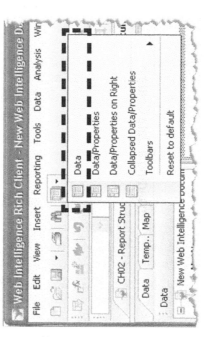

Notes

Removing and Inserting Columns

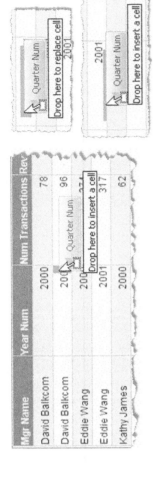

Inserting a Data Column

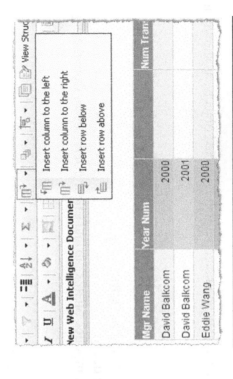

Inserting an Empty Column

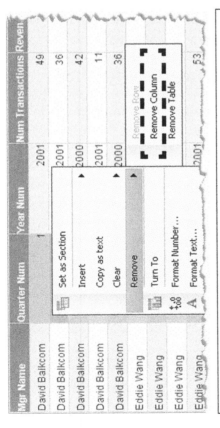

Removing a Column

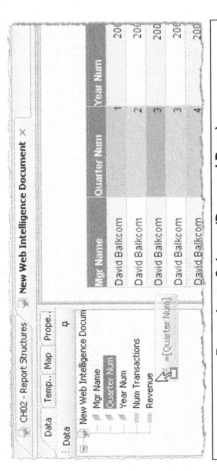

Removing a Column (Drag and Drop)

Removing and Inserting Columns

There are basically two ways to remove a column from a report. The first is to right-click on the column and select *Remove>Remove Column* from the pop-up menu. The other method is to click on the header cell or a body cell in the column, and then drag it to the Data tab. Both methods are shown in the graphic.

Notice that when a dimension column is removed from a table, the measure columns must re-calculate to conform to the new context. Sometimes these re-calculations can be incorrect, depending on the nature of the calculation. For example, if the calculations are averages, then the re-calculation of the averages may be incorrect, if the measures try to average the existing average values. Sums will almost always be correct, because the sums can simply be added to conform to the newer condensed context. When the measure objects are created in the universe, the Designer defines how the measures will conform to the new context. Sometimes, the report must be refreshed for the measures to conform. If this is the case, then #TOREFRESH will be displayed in the cells until the report is refreshed.

To insert a data cell, select a cell from the Data tab and drag it to the desired location in the table. The object can be dropped on the left, or right, side of a cell to insert the object into the respective position. If an object is dropped in the lower portion or upper portion of a cell, then a new row will be added to the table. If the object is dropped into the center of a cell, then the current object in the column will be replaced with the dropped object. If an empty column is desired, then click on the column to select it, and then click on the Insert toolbar button. You can also select *Insert>Row...* or *Insert>Column...* from the menu.

Exercise: Remove and Insert a Table Column

1. Remove the Quarter Num Column
   a. Right-click on the Quarter Num column.
   b. Select *Remove>Remove Column* from the pop-up menu.
2. Insert Quarter Column
   a. Click on Quarter Num in the Data tab
   b. Drag it to the right-side of a Year Num cell in the table and drop it.

Notes

Moving and Sizing Columns

Mgr Name	Quarter Num	Year Num	Num Transactions
David Balkcom	1 =[Year Num] Drop here to replace cell	2001	4
David Balkcom		2001	3
David Balkcom		2000	4
David Balkcom	3	2001	1
David Balkcom	4	2000	3
Eddie Wang	1	2001	13
Eddie Wang	2	2001	13
Eddie Wang	3	2000	12

Swap Column Locations

Mgr Name	Quarter Num	Year Num	Num Transactions
David Balkcom	1 =[Year Num] Drop here to insert a cell	2001	49
David Balkcom		2001	36
David Balkcom		2000	42
David Balkcom	3	2001	1
David Balkcom	4	2000	36
Eddie Wang	1	2001	133
Eddie Wang	2	2001	131
Eddie Wang	3	2000	120

Insert Column to a New Location

Mgr Name	Quarter Num	Year Num	Num Transactions
David Balkcom	1	2001	49
David Balkcom	2	2001	36
David Balkcom	3	2000	42
David Balkcom	3	2001	1
David Balkcom	4	2000	36
Eddie Wang	1	2001	13
Eddie Wang	2	2001	13
Eddie Wang	3	2000	12

Sizing a Column

Mgr Name	Quarter Num	Year Num	Num Transactions
David Balkcom	1	2001	49
David Balkcom	2	2001	36
David Balkcom	3	2000	42
David Balkcom	3	2001	1
David Balkcom	4	2000	36
Eddie Wang	1	2001	133
Eddie Wang	2	2001	13
Eddie Wang	3	2000	120

Sizing a Row

Moving and Sizing Columns

Many times when we insert a table, the columns are not in the order that we want them to be. To arrange the columns, simply click on a column drop in the desired location in the table. If you drop it on either side of a cell, then it will be inserted into that location, as seen in the graphic (Insert Column to a New Location). If you drop the selected column into the middle of a cell, then it will swap positions with the column, as seen in the graphic (Swap Column Locations).

A default table usually has a columns and rows the same size. For example, Mgr Name is much wider than Year Num. Since most reports get printed onto a standard size of paper, it is very important not to have columns wider than need be. To size a column, just place the cursor over the right-hand side of the column (the cursor should turn into the sizing cursor), and then just click to grab hold of the border and drag it to the desired width. You also can double-click on the border with the sizing cursor and the column will size to accommodate the widest contents in any cell of the column, including the header cell. However, be careful when double-clicking to size columns in large reports, because it may take quite a long time - a minute or two.

You can also size rows in the same manner, by placing the cursor over the lower border of a row. When a data row is sized, than all rows in the body of the table will also be sized. Sometimes we want to size a row because it has a large data cell, but not increase the heights of the other rows in the body. We can do this by selecting Wrap text and Autofit Height in the properties for the row. I will show this on the next page.

Exercise: Swap Columns in Table

1. If Quarter Num is to the left of Year Num in the table, then swap Year Num and Quarter Num.
   a. Click on Quarter Num and drop it on the center of Year Num.

Notes

Format Header Cells

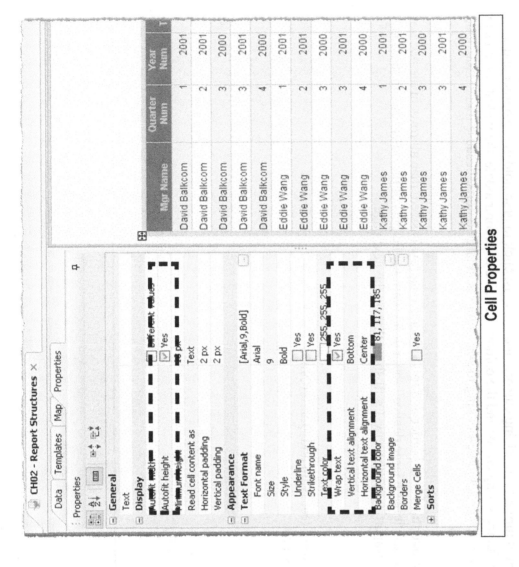

Table Properties

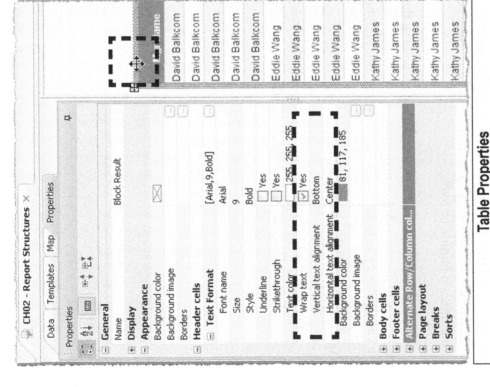

Cell Properties

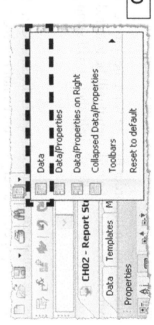

Configure Display

Format Header Cells

We can format the header cells in a table by first selecting the table. We select a table by placing our cursor over the edge of the table, and then when the cursor changes into the four way cursor, clicking on the edge of the table. Once the table is selected, the properties will display properties for the table. Within the Appearance group there is a section for Header Cells. This will allow us to access most of the properties for the header cells.

The Header cells properties within the Table properties is good for most cases, but sometimes we want to change some properties that are not available in this section. If we select all of the header cells, by first clicking on any of them and then by holding down the [CTRL] key and selecting the remaining header cells, we can then set the properties for the specific cells in the header row. This will allow us to Wrap Text (For multi-row header cells), Horizontal Text Alignment - Center, and Autofit Height (In the Display section).

If the Properties pane is not visible, then you can use Configure Display toolbar button to select the state of the pane. I usually just select Data, and then activate the Properties tab by clicking on it.

Also notice that we can format the Body Cells and the Footer Cells in the same manner.

Exercise: Format Table Header

1. Click on the Mgr Name header cell to select it.
2. Hold down the [CTRL] key and click on the remaining header cells.
3. If the Properties tab is not visible, then select *Data* from the *Configure Display* toolbar button.
4. Click on the Properties tab to activate it.
5. In the *Appearance>Text Format* section
    a. Set *Wrap Text* to *Yes.*
    b. Set *Horizontal Text Alignment* to *Center.*
6. In the Display section
    a. Set *Autofit Height* to *Yes.*

Notes

Formatting Cell Contents (Number)

Number Format

Format type:
- Default
- Number
- Currency
- Date/Time
- Boolean
- Custom

Properties:
- 1,234.57
- 1.234567E3
- 1235
- 1235; (1235)
- 1234.57
- 1,235

☑ Custom

Positive	Negative	Equal to Zero	Undefined
#,##0[Blue]	(#,##0)[Red]	\-\-\-	n/a

OK   Cancel   Add   Help

Number Format

Format type:
- Default
- Number
- Currency
- Date/Time
- Boolean
- Custom

Properties:
- true, false

☑ Custom

True	False	Undefined
On	Off	

OK   Cancel   Add   Help

Number Format

Format type:
- Default
- Number
- Currency
- Date/Time
- Boolean
- Custom

Properties:
- $1,235; $-1,235
- €1,234.57
- €1,234.57; €-1,234.57
- €1,235
- €1,235; €-1,235
- ¥1,235

☑ Custom

Positive	Negative	Equal to Zero	Undefined
€#,##0.00	€-#,##0.00[Red]		

OK   Cancel   Add   Help

Year Num	Quarter Num	Num Transactions
		42
		36
		49
		36
		11
		126
		148
		133
		131
		53
		765

Set as Section
Insert
Copy as text
Clear
Remove
Turn To
Format Number...
Format Text...
Formula Toolbar
Format
Hyperlinks

Format Number Menu Item

Formating Cell Contents (Number)

Web Intelligence allows us to define the format of numbers in cells. The three number types are Number, Boolean, and Currency. To format a number, we can select an existing format or define one using the *Custom* Option.

Number: Numbers have four states - Positive, Negative, Zero, and undefined. We can select a predefined format from the *Properties* list, which usually defines one or two of the states. Undefined states use the default format. Each state has it formatting characters. For example, positive has '#', '0', and ','. The '#' represents a digit in a number. The '0' also represents a digit. The difference is that if there is no digit in the number's spot, then a '0' will display a 0, where a '#' will display nothing. The comma is a place holder for the thousandths spot. For example:

Number	Format	Result
123	####	123
123	0000	0123
1000	#,##0	1,000
23	0	23
0	#	
0	0	0

Boolean: Is a two state number - either it is zero, which is false, or it is non-zero, which is true.

Number	Format	Result
100	True = On; False = Off	On
0	True = On; False = Off	Off

Currency: This format is similar to Number, but we include a currency symbol. Business Objects has provided us with three symbols, but if we need more we will have to find the symbol and cut and paste it into the custom format fields. I usually search the web and find the character. I find some on http://www.xe.com/symbols.php.

Notes

Formatting Cell Contents (Date)

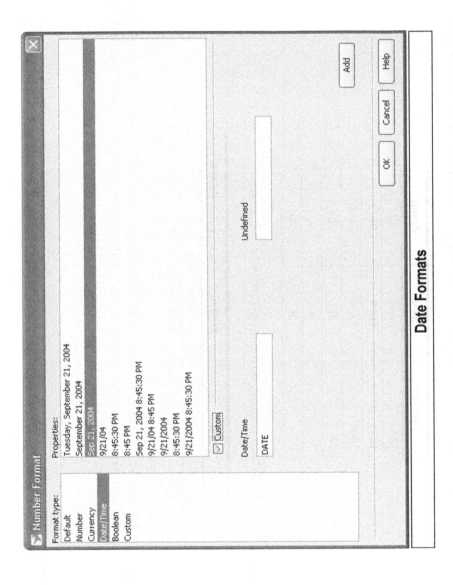

Date Formats

Formatting Cell Contents (Date)

When we formatted numbers, we used format masks, such as `#,##0`. When we format dates, we could use masks, such as Mmm dd, yyyy. However, these format masks are a little confusing to most, since if capital y's were used, then the output would be: Mmm dd, YYYY = Sep 21, YYYY. This means that the case of the characters in the mask is considered when formatting the output.

Therefore, Web Intelligence provides keywords, such as DATE. Where Date = Mmm dd, yyyy. Later, when you learn to use the functions, you will find that these keywords also work better than the masks. Below, is a list of the available date masks:

Keyword	Mask	Result
FULL_DATE	Dddd, Mmmm, yyyy	Tuesday, September, 2004
LONG_DATE	Mmmm d, yyyy	September 4, 2004
DATE	Mmm d, yyyy	Sep 4, 2004
SHORT_DATE	m/d/yy	9/4/04
TIME	h:mm:ss A	12:04:00 AM
SHORT_TIME	h:mm A	12:04 AM
DATE_TIME	Mmm d, yyyy h:mm:ss A	Sep 4, 2004 12:04:00 AM
SHORT_DATE_TIME	m/d/yyyy h:mm A	9/4/2004 12:04 AM
INPUT_DATE	m/d/yyyy	9/4/2004
INPUT_TIME	h:mm:ss A	12:04:00 AM
INPUT_DATE_TIME	m/d/yyyy h:mm:ss A	9/4/2004 12:04:00 AM

Notes

Formatting Cell Contents (Text and Colors)

Ti392 l5: 4:03:05 PM

Time Is: 4:03:05 PM

Format String: Time Is: h:mm:ss A

Format String: Ti\me l\s: h:mm:ss A

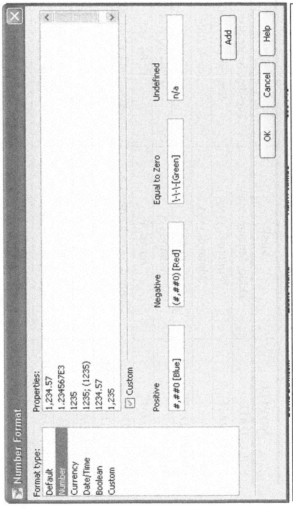

Number Format with Colors and Escape Characters

Formatting Cell Contents (Text and Colors)

Sometimes we want to use colors or text in our formats to help clarify or emphasize the data. To use colors, we enclose the name of the color in square brackets after the format string in the Number Format dialog. Available colors are [Red], [Blue], [Green], [Yellow], [Gray], [White], [Dark Red], [Dark Blue], [Dark Green].

To place text in the format, we just type in the desired text. This works in most cases, but when one of the characters is also a format character, then the character will be read as a format character, which may make the label look a little strange, as seen in the graphic. In this case, we are formatting a Date/Time and we want the label: *Time Is:*. The only problem is that the 'm', 'e', and 's' are also format characters, so they get the value instead of the text: m=3, e = 92, and the s= 5, therefore *Time Is:* returns *Ti392 I5:*. To tell Web Intelligence that we want to use the literal value of the format character and not the translated value, we place a backslash (\) prior to the character in the format string. This will make our format string: *T\im\e I\s:*.

If we use the Format Number dialog to place text in a field, then it will have no effect on the sort. This is one of the advantages to using the Format Number dialog to do such formatting. For example, suppose we used the following formula to format the time:

> = *"Time Is: " + FormatDate([Date Obj]; "h:mm:ss A"),*

which will convert the time to a text string. It will now lose all of its time characteristics, including sorting chronologically. It will now sort 1:00, 12:00, 2:00, and so forth.

Notes

Moving and Copying Tables

Mgr Name	Quarter Num	Year Num	Num Transactions	Revenue
David Balkcom	1	2001	49	14,341
David Balkcom	2	2001	36	228,016
David Balkcom	3	2000	42	642
David Ball/David Balkcom		2001	11	61,529
David Ball/David Balkcom		2000	36	(89,863)
David Ball/Eddie Wang		2001	133	(5,848)
David Ball/Eddie Wang		2001	131	543,731
David Ball/Eddie Wang		2000	126	(740,160)
Eddie Wa/Eddie Wang		2001	53	521,614
Eddie Wa/Eddie Wang		2000	148	(376,607)
Eddie Wa/Kathy James		2001	23	52,981
Eddie Wa/Kathy James		2001	27	112,154
Eddie Wa/Kathy James		2000	31	(267,653)

Moving a Table

Mgr Name	Num sactions	Revenue
David Balkcom	49	14,341
David Balkcom	36	228,016
David Balkcom	42	642
David Balkcom	11	61,529
David Balkcom	36	(89,863)
Eddie Wang	133	(5,848)
Eddie Wang	131	543,731
Eddie Wang	126	(740,160)
Eddie Wang	53	521,614
Eddie Wang	148	(376,607)

Cut
Copy
Copy as text
Paste
Clear All table cells
Remove
Turn To
Format
Order
Align
Document Properties
4   2000

Copying a Table

Moving and Copying Tables

In the previous example, we learned to select a table by clicking on the edge of the table. To move a table, we click on the edge of the table and drag it to a new location on the report.

We often want to copy an existing table, for the following and other reasons: to place filters to limit the data in a table, to transform tables into other report elements, such as charts and crosstabs, and to remove columns from detail tables to create summaries. To copy a table, we can click and move the table to a new location on the report, but before releasing the mouse button, we hold down to [CTRL] key. This will copy the table to the new location. We can also right-click on the edge of a table and then select *Copy* from the pop-up menu. Then we can right-click on the report where the copy is to be placed, and then select Paste from the pop-up menu. We can also click on the report where the table is to be placed and then press the key combination: [CTRL]-V.

Exercise: Copy a Table

1. Click on the edge of a table to select it.
2. Press the key combination [CTRL]-C.
3. Click the report to the right of the table, and press the key combination [CTRL]-V.

Notes

Table Properties

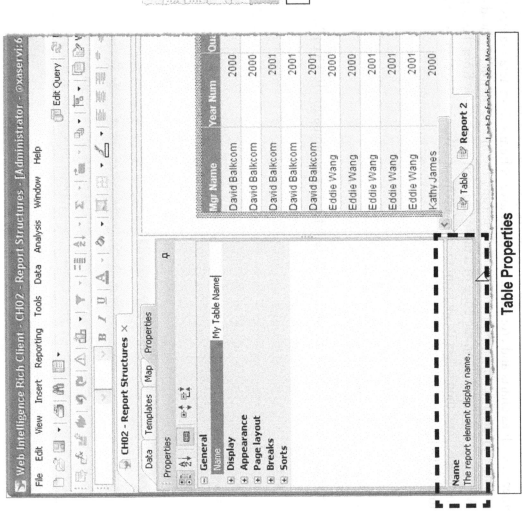

Table Properties

Configure Display

Table Properties

We have used the Table Properties earlier in this chapter, but now we will look at all of the properties that are available. Table properties allow us to set and view much of the property behavior of a table. These properties allow us to make our tables more powerful information displayers.

There are six property sections: General, Appearance, Page Layout, Breaks, and Sorts. Each section may have subsections, so we will discuss one section on each of the next pages.

The General section for a table only has one property - Name. The Name property allows us to name the tables in a report. Most of the time this is not necessary, especially if there is only one table. However, there are times that we may have multiple tables placed on a report and it may become necessary to name them to help identify the tables.

Exercise: Name a Table

1. Click on the edge of the table that we created in the previous exercise to select it.
2. Click the Properties tab to activate it.
   a. If the Properties tab is not visible, then click the *Configure Display* toolbar button and select one of the configurations. I often select the Data configuration, because it places all of the available tabs along the left-side of the environment.
   b. If you do not see the properties shown in the graphic, then make sure that you have properly selected the table by clicking on the edge of the table when the cursor switches to the four way cursor.
3. Click on the plus (+) sign in front of the General section.
4. Enter a name for the table in the Name property field and press [Enter].

Notes

Table Display Properties

Table Display Properties

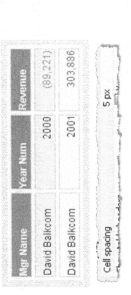

Table Display Properties

The Display properties allow you to modify what is displayed in a table.

Cell Spacing: Allows the space between the cells to be increased/decreased.

Show Table Headers/Footers: Shows or hides the header or footer of a table. Sometimes we want to hide the table header, because the breaks within a table have headers, and the table header is redundant. We can create a summary for a column by showing the table footer and copying a cell from the measure column into the footer. We do not always need an aggregate function, such as Sum ([x]), because many measures have a default function.

Avoid Duplicate Row Aggregation: Earlier, we found that Dimensions will always aggregate to form unique rows within a table. To turn off this behavior and display all of the detail rows, we use this property. We often use this property when debugging a report, because it allows us to see any details that may form a summary, when a column is deleted from the table.

Show Rows with Empty Measure/Dimension Values: Sometimes there are no measure values associated with certain combinations of dimension values within a table. This option will allow you to hide the rows with such NULL measure values. In addition, sometimes there are no Dimensions associated with a measure value in a table. For example, the total measure value for all NULL dimension values. This option will allow you to hide the rows with no dimension values. Notice that the default is to hide the rows with empty dimension values.

Show when Empty: Sometimes there is no data returned to a table at all. In these cases, you can hide the table if this is the case.

Exercise: Display footer and insert a total

1. Click on the edge of the table that we created in the previous exercise to select it.
2. Click the Properties tab to activate it.
3. Click on the plus (+) sign in front of the Display section.
4. Check the *Show Table Footers* option.
5. Click on any value in the Revenue column of the table, hold the [CTRL] key down, and drag the cell into the newly exposed footer. (This should copy the Revenue object into the footer. The Revenue object will automatically aggregate by summing.)

Notes

Table Appearance Properties

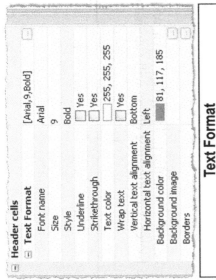

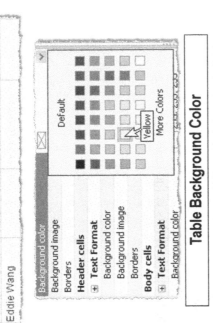

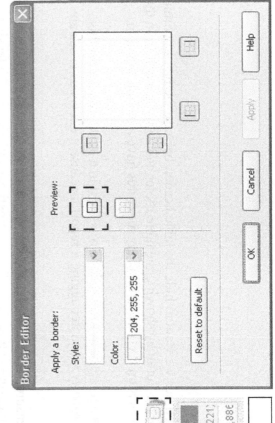

Table Background Color

Border Editor

Text Format

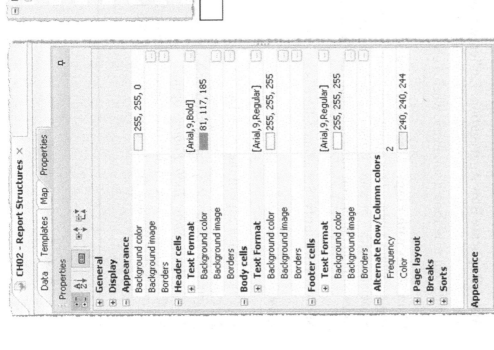

Selected Objects in Query Panel

Table Border Format

Table Appearance Properties

The Appearance properties control how the Background Color/Image and Borders will appear in a table. Remember that these are table properties and not individual cell properties, so these will only apply to the table as a whole.

Background Color: This is the color behind the table, and it is only visible if cells are missing from the table. For example, if there are breaks in the table, as seen in the graphic (Table Background Color).

Borders: This is the format for the border for the entire table and not the cells within the table, as seen in the graphic (Table Border Format).

Header/Body/Footer Cells: With these sections, we can format all of the cells in a specific region, of a table, with the same format. For example, we can wrap text in all of the Table Header Cells.

Alternate Row/Column Colors: This property allows you to set row color for every nth row. Many people like to lightly color every other row, because it is easier to follow a row across a report. If the table is a horizontal table, then the color for every nth column can be set.

Exercise: Set Table Appearance Properties

1. Click on the edge of the table that we created in the previous exercise to select it.
2. Click the Properties tab to activate it.
3. Click on the plus (+) sign in front of the Appearance section.
4. Click the (...) button next to the Borders property, to display the Border Editor dialog.
5. Select a style from the *Style* drop list. Select a color from the *Color* drop list. Click on the *Border* button.
   a. Notice that the only the table's perimeter border changes.

Notes

Table Page Layout Properties

Mgr Name	Quarter Num	Year Num	Num Transactions	Revenue
David Balkcom	1	2001	49	14,341
David Balkcom	2	2001	36	228,016
David Balkcom	3	2000	42	642
David Balkcom	3	2001	11	61,529
David Balkcom	4	2000	36	(89,863)

Mgr Name	Quarter Num	Year Num	Num Transactions	Revenue
Eddie Wang	1	2001	133	(5,848)
Eddie Wang	2	2001	131	543,731
Eddie Wang	3	2000	126	(740,160)
Eddie Wang	3	2001	53	521,614
Eddie Wang	4	2000	148	(376,607)

Relative Position

Place the upper-left of this table/chart/cell

from the 20 px Left edge of Report 2

from the 10 px Bottom edge of Dave

OK   Cancel   Apply   Help

Relative Position Sets Distance Between Report Elements

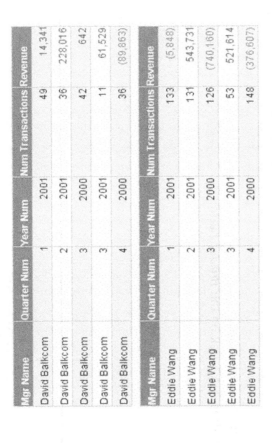

CH02 - Report Structures

Data Templates Map Properties

Properties

General
Name — Block Result

Display

Appearance

Page layout

Relative Position — 23 px;23 px
  Left edge — 23 px
  Top edge — 23 px
  Start on new page — ☐ Yes
  Repeat on every new page — ☐ Yes
  Avoid page break in table — ☐ Yes
  Repeat header on every page — ☑ Yes
  Repeat footer on every page — ☐ Yes

Breaks

Sorts

Page layout

Page Layout Properties

Table Page Layout Properties

The Page Layout properties allow you to determine how report elements will appear on a page.

Start on a New Page: If there are multiple structures on a page, this property will make the selected structure start on the page after the current structure finishes. This ensures that the selected structure will appear at the start of a new page in the report.

Repeat on Every Page: This will cause the selected report structure to appear on each page of a report. We can use this property to show a summary table at the top of each page, or to display report headers on every page in a report.

Avoid Page Break in Table: If there are multiple tables on a page, and a page break occurs in one of the tables, other than the first on the page, then this property will cause the table to start on the next page.

Repeat Header/Footer on Every Page: Many tables continue through several pages. With these longer tables, it is usually best to repeat the table header on each new page in the report. Repeating the footer on every page may be confusing to many viewers, because people assume that the footer occurs at the bottom of a table. However, the repeat table footer option is often used to repeat information on each page, such as specifications.

Relative Position: Many times we place tables above other tables on a report. At the time of placement, the report looks very good, because the tables are a comfortable distance from one another. However, after the report is refreshed, the top table can grow smaller or larger, and thus increasing the distance between the tables, or even worse, writing over the lower table and making it impossible to read. This property allows you to set a constant distance between two structures on a report.

Exercise: Set Relative Distance for Two Tables

1. Click on the Mgr Name column and click the filter button, then select David Balkcom and click OK.
2. Copy the table to a location just below the table. You should now have two tables placed vertically on the report.
3. Click on the edge of the first table and expand the General section on the Properties tab. Name the table *Dave*.
4. Click on the edge of the second table to select it, and then click on the plus sign (+) in front of the Page Layout section.
5. Click on the (...) button in the Relative Position property to display the Relative Position dialog.
6. Set the table 10 px from the bottom edge of Dave, and then click OK.

Notes

Table Templates

Form Table

Year Num	2000
Mgr Name	David Balkcom
Num Transactions	78
Revenue	(89,221)

Year Num	2000
Mgr Name	Eddie Wang
Num Transactions	274
Revenue	(1,116,767)

Crosstab Table

	2000	2001	Sum:
David Balkcom	(89,221)	303,886	214,665
Eddie Wang	(1,116,767)	1,059,497	(57,270)
Kathy James	(465,394)	386,854	(78,540)
Maria Castro	(369,888)	449,314	79,426
Robert Denning	(507,101)	574,563	67,462
Sean Wilkenson	(4,385,413)	5,736,866	1,351,453
Sum:	(6,933,784)	8,510,980	1,577,196

Vertical Table

Mgr Name	Year Num	Num Transactions	Revenue
David Balkcom	2000	78	(89,221)
David Balkcom	2001	96	303,886
Eddie Wang	2000	274	(1,116,767)
Eddie Wang	2001	317	1,059,497
Kathy James	2000	62	(465,394)
Kathy James	2001	58	386,854

Horizontal Table

Mgr Name	David Balkcom	David Balkcom	David Balkcom	David Balkcom	David Balkcom
Year Num	2000	2000	2001	2001	2001
Quarter Num	3	4	1	2	3
Num Transactions	42	36	49	36	11
Revenue	642	(89,863)	14,341	228,016	61,529

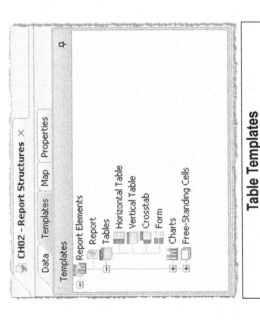

Table Templates

CH02 - Report Structures ×

Data | Templates | Map | Properties

Templates

Report Elements
- Report
- Tables
  - Horizontal Table
  - Vertical Table
  - Crosstab
  - Form
- Charts
- Free-Standing Cells

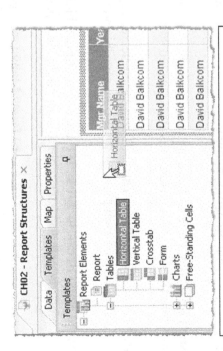

Dragging a Template

CH02 - Report Structures ×

Data | Templates | Map | Properties

Templates

Report Elements
- Report
- Tables
  - Horizontal Table
  - Vertical Table
  - Crosstab
  - Form
- Charts
- Free-Standing Cells

Horizontal Table

Mgr Name	Year
David Balkcom	
David Balkcom	
David Balkcom	
David Balkcom	

Table Templates

The default table is a vertical table. If a different type of table is desired, then click on the Templates tab, and then drag a table template on top on the table. This will transform the vertical table into one of the other three types of tables available.

Horizontal Table: This table is a table that has been rotated ninety degrees counter-clockwise. This places the header in the left (first) column, and each subsequent row, as a column. Instead of going down the page, this table goes across the page. Therefore, it is usually best not to have too many data columns, because they will travel past the right-hand margin.

Crosstab: This is a summary table with dimensions along the top and left sides of the table. This allows for both the rows and columns to contain a summary. Notice, in the graphic both dimensions Mgr Name and Year Num has totals. Each of the body cells (Not the Headers), is translated from a row in a vertical table. Therefore, this six row crosstab is created from a twelve row table (6 rows * 2 columns). This allows us to fit a vertical table that may span several pages on a single page, by placing one or more of the dimensions as a row across the column header.

Form Table: The form table creates a record from each row in a vertical table. This is useful for smaller reports, but with large reports the records become difficult to locate. I like to create this type of report with the horizontal table and sections, which I will discuss later.

Exercise: Using Table Templates

1. Create a table with Mgr Name, Year Num, Quarter Num, Num Transactions, and Revenue
2. Drag the Horizontal Table template on the table. Notice that it creates a very wide table that spans many pages. Click the Page Layout button to see the pages. This type of report is usually not useful, unless it is combined with sections. We will demonstrate sections later in this chapter.
3. Drag and drop the Form template onto the Horizontal table. Notice that it creates records out of each column in the horizontal table. It is vertically arranged, so it spans vertical pages.
4. Drag and drop the Vertical Table template on the Forms. This will bring back the original vertical table.
5. Create a report with Mgr Name, Year Num, and Revenue.
6. Drag the Crosstab template onto the vertical table. This should create a crosstab with Year Num in the first column and Mgr Name across the top row. There are only two years and six managers, which makes the crosstab shallow and wide.
7. Click on any Mgr Name cell and drag it on top of any Year Num cell. This will cause the headers to swap, and Year Num will now be across the top row. This creates a crosstab that is deep and narrow.

Notes

Crosstabs

Mgr Name	Year Num	Revenue
	Drop here to create a crosstab	(89,221)
David Balkcom	2001	303,886
David Balkcom	2000	(1,116,767)
Eddie Wang	2001	1,059,497
Eddie Wang	2000	(465,394)
Kathy James	2001	386,854
Kathy James	2000	(369,888)
Maria Castro	2000	

Drag a Dimension Column Over a Table

	2000	2001
David Balkcom	(89,221)	303,886
Eddie Wang	(1,116,767)	1,059,497
Kathy James	(465,394)	386,854
Maria Castro	(369,888)	449,314
Robert Denning	(507,101)	574,563
Sean Wilkenson	(4,385,413)	5,736,866

To Create a Crosstab

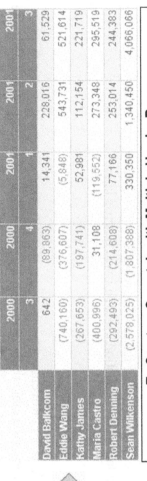

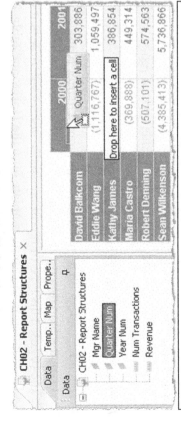

Drag a Dimension into the Header

	2000 3	2000 4	2001 1	2001 2	2001 3
David Balkcom	642	(89,863)	14,341	228,016	61,529
Eddie Wang	(740,160)	(376,607)	(5,848)	543,731	521,614
Kathy James	(267,653)	(197,741)	52,981	112,154	221,719
Maria Castro	(400,996)	31,108	(119,552)	273,348	295,519
Robert Denning	(292,493)	(214,608)	77,166	253,014	244,383
Sean Wilkenson	(2,578,025)	(1,807,388)	330,350	1,340,450	4,066,066

To Create a Crosstab with Multiple Header Rows

Drag a Measure into the Body

	2000		2001	
David Balkcom	78	(89,221)	96	303,886
Eddie Wang	274	(1,116,767)	317	1,059,497
Kathy James	62	(465,394)	58	386,854
Maria Castro	91	(369,888)	93	449,314
Robert Denning	45	(507,101)	75	574,563
Sean Wilkenson	675	(4,385,413)	816	5,736,866

To Create a Crosstab with Multiple Measures

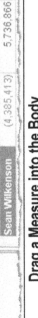
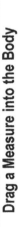

Crosstabs

The Crosstab template is useful, but if we want better control over the dimension placement, we can just drag a dimension over the table to create a crosstab. It is important to drop the dimension in the *crosstab rectangle* that becomes visible when the dimension is placed over the table, because if the dimension is placed too high over the table, then a section report will be created.

Many times, we need multiple column headers. For example, if we want to display quarter numbers, it is good to also place year in the header to display which year the quarter belongs to. This can be seen in the *Drag a Dimension into the Header* graphic. Later, we will use breaks or sections to separate the years into year groups.

Crosstabs can have several measures in the body. In the graphic, we have both Revenue and Num Transactions in the body. We did this by dragging the Num Transactions measure to the right side of the Revenue column.

Exercise: Creating Crosstabs

1. Create a table with Mgr Name, Year Num, and Revenue.
2. Drag any cell from the Year Num column up to the Crosstab rectangle, and then drop it.
3. Copy the Crosstab.
   a. Click on the edge of the crosstab, drag it to a new position, and hold the [CTRL] key while releasing the mouse button.
4. Create a multiple header crosstab
   a. Drag Quarter Num from the Data tab to the lower portion of the Year Num Column header.
5. Create a multiple measure crosstab
   a. Drag the Num Transactions data object to the right-side of the Revenue column, as shown in the graphic.

Notes

Crosstab Properties

Data | Templates | Map | Properties

Properties

General
Name: Block Result

Display
Cell spacing: 0 px
Show object name: ☐
Show top header: ☑ Yes
Show left header: ☑ Yes
Show table footers: ☐
Avoid duplicate row aggregation: ☐ Yes
Show rows with empty measure values: ☑ Yes
Show columns with empty measure values: ☑ Yes
Show rows/columns with empty dimension values: ☐
Show when empty: ☑ Yes

Appearance
Background color
Background image: ☒
Borders

☐ Header cells
☐ Body cells
☐ Footer cells
☐ Alternate Row/Column colors
☐ Page layout
☐ Relative Position: 23 px;23 px
Start on new page: ☐ Yes
Repeat on every new page: ☐ Yes
Avoid page break in table: ☐ Yes
Repeat header on every page: ☑ Yes
Repeat footer on every page: ☐ Yes

☐ Breaks
☐ Sorts

Crosstab Properties

Table Display Properties

Display
Cell spacing: 0 px
Show table headers: ☐ Yes
Show table footers: ☐ Yes
Avoid duplicate row aggregation: ☐ Yes
Show rows with empty measure values: ☑ Yes
Show rows with empty dimension values: ☐ Yes
Show when empty: ☑ Yes

Table Display Properties

Year Num	2000	2001
Mgr Name	Revenue	Revenue
David Balkcom	(89,221)	303,886
Eddie Wang	(1,116,767)	1,059,497
Kathy James	(465,394)	386,854
Maria Castro	(369,888)	449,314
Robert Denning	(507,101)	574,563
Sean Wilkenson	(4,385,413)	5,736,866

Show object name: ☑ Yes

	2000	2001
	Revenue	Revenue
	(89,221)	303,886
	(1,116,767)	1,059,497
	(465,394)	386,854
	(369,888)	449,314
	(507,101)	574,563
	(4,385,413)	5,736,866

Show left header: ☐ Yes

Year Num	2000	2001
Mgr Name	Revenue	Revenue
David Balkcom	(89,221)	303,886
Eddie Wang	(1,116,767)	1,059,497
Kathy James	(465,394)	386,854
Maria Castro	(369,888)	449,314
Robert Denning	(507,101)	574,563
Sean Wilkenson	(4,385,413)	5,736,866

Show table footers: ☑ Yes

Crosstab Properties

Since a crosstab is a table, many of the crosstab properties are the same as the table properties. However, since crosstabs have both column and row headers, there are a few extra Display properties, as seen in the graphic.

Show Object Name: This will display the object name, similar to the header in a vertical table. This is very helpful for crosstabs will multiple measures in the body.

Show Top/Left Header: Hiding a vertical table may make sense, because in a vertical table, the headers are usually text fields that identify the data in the columns below it. In a crosstab, the headers are actually dimension data, so hiding the headers in a crosstab is necessary, so this option is available.

Show Table Footers: In a crosstab there are two footers - a footer for both the column and row summaries. These footers allow you to have three totals - totals across the crosstab, totals down the crosstab, and in the intersection of these two footers, which is a grand summary for the entire crosstab.

Show Columns with Empty Measure Values: This will allow you to hide columns with no measure values.

Exercise: Crosstab Properties

1. Create a table with Mgr Name, Year Num, and Revenue.
2. Drag the Year Num column to the crosstab rectangle above the table, to create a crosstab
3. Click on the edge of the crosstab to select it.
4. Activate the Properties tab and check the *Show Table Footers* option.
5. Click on any measure cell in the body of the crosstab, hold down the [CTRL] key and drag the measure into the newly exposed footer.
    a. Notice that you will have to drag the measure cell to three places in the footer - The right footer, the bottom footer, and the intersection of the two.
5. Drag the Num Transactions object to the right-side of a Revenue cell in the body of the crosstab.
6. Click on the edge of the table to select it.
7. Check the *Show Object Name* property, in the Display section.
8. Notice that there is now an empty space in the footer for the Num Transactions total. Drag the Num Transactions object into the footer.

Notes

Breaks in Tables and Crosstabs

Apply Breaks

Insert | Reporting | Ta...
- Row
- Column
- Filters...
- **Breaks**
- Sorts
- Calculations

Insert Calculation

Insert | Reporting | Tools | Data | Analysis | Win...
- Row
- Column
- Filters...
- Breaks
- Sorts
- Calculations

Σ	Sum
Χ̄	Average
n	Count
✕	Minimum
✕	Maximum
Σ%	Percentage
Σ	Default

Σ	Sum
n	Count
Χ̄	Average
✕	Min
✕	Max
Σ%	Percentage
Σ	Default aggregation

Break on Mgr Name

Mgr Name	Year Num	Revenue
David Balkcom	2000	(89,221)
	2001	303,886
		214,665
Eddie Wang	2000	(1,116,767)
	2001	1,059,497
		(57,270)
Kathy James	2000	(465,394)
	2001	386,854
		(78,540)
...		
Sean Wilkenson	2000	(4,385,413)
	2001	5,736,866
		1,351,453
	Sum:	1,577,196

Breaks on Mgr Name and Year Num

Mgr Name	Year Num	Quarter Num	Revenue
David Balkcom	2000	3	642
		4	(89,863)
David Balkcom	2000		(89,221)

Mgr Name	Year Num	Quarter Num	Revenue
	2001	1	14,341
		2	228,016
		3	61,529
David Balkcom	2001		303,886
			214,665

Mgr Name	Year Num	Quarter Num	Revenue
Eddie Wang	2000	3	(740,160)
		4	(376,607)
Eddie Wang	2000		(1,116,767)

Mgr Name	Year Num	Quarter Num	Revenue
	2001	1	(5,848)
		2	543,731
		3	521,614
Eddie Wang	2001		1,059,497
			(57,270)

Crosstab Break on Year Num

	2000			2001				Report
	3	4	Total	1	2	3	Total	Total
David Balkcom	642	(89,863)	(89,221)	14,341	228,017	61,529	303,886	214,665
Eddie Wang	(740,160)	(376,607)	(1,116,767)	(5,848)	543,731	521,614	1,059,497	(57,270)
Kathy James	(267,653)	(197,741)	(465,394)	52,981	112,154	221,719	386,854	(78,540)
Maria Castro	(400,996)	31,108	(369,888)	(119,552)	273,348	295,519	449,314	79,426
Robert Denning	(292,493)	(214,608)	(507,101)	77,166	253,014	244,383	574,563	67,462
Sean Wilkenson	(2,578,025)	(1,807,388)	(4,385,413)	330,350	1,340,450	4,066,066	5,736,866	1,351,453
Total	(4,278,686)	(2,655,098)	(6,933,784)	349,438	2,750,713	5,410,828	8,510,980	1,577,196

Breaks in Tables and Crosstabs

For many tables, a single total at the bottom is not sufficient. Therefore, Business Objects allows for breaks to be placed within a table. Breaks allow for summaries to be placed for each of the dimension values within a column or row. Notice the *Break on Mgr Name* graphic, this table has a total for each Manager, in addition to the table total in the footer.

Tables can have multiple breaks on different dimensions. Look at the Breaks on *Mgr Name and Year Num* graphic. This table has totals for each manager and totals for each Year Num within Mgr Name. These are not the totals for each Year Num, but the yearly totals for each manager.

The crosstab break has a break on Year Num in the row header. This allows the crosstab to show yearly summaries for each manager. Notice, the crosstab shows yearly and manager totals. The vertical table only allowed for manager totals and yearly totals within each manager.

To apply a break, we just select a dimension in the table by clicking on it, and then we click the *Insert Break* button from the menu. We can also select the menu item *Insert>Breaks*. To insert the sums, we can just place the measure object into the footers created by the break. We can also click the *Insert Calculation* button on the toolbar, and then select the *Sum* menu item, as shown in the graphic.

Exercise: Create a Table with Breaks

1. Create a query with Mgr name, Year Num, Quarter Num, and Revenue.
2. Set a break on Mgr Name
   a. Select any value in the Mgr Name column.
   b. Click the *Insert/Remove Break* button.
3. Insert totals on Revenue
   a. Click on any cell in the Revenue column.
   b. Click the *Insert Sum* button.

Notes

Break Properties

Break Properties

Data	Templates	Map	Properties	Input Controls

Properties

General
Text	=[Mgr Name]

Display
Autofit width	☐ Yes
Width	96 px
Autofit height	☑ Yes
Height	22 px
Read cell content as	Text
Horizontal padding	2 px
Vertical padding	2 px

Appearance
Text Format	[Arial,9,Regular]
Background color	☐ 255, 255, 255
Background image	
Borders	
Merge Cells	Not applicable

Breaks
Show break header	☑ Yes
Show break footer	☑ Yes
Remove duplicate values	☑ Yes
Center values across break	☐ Yes
Apply implicit sort to values	☑ Yes

Page layout
Start on new page	☐ Yes
Avoid page breaks in table	☐ Yes
Repeat header on every page	☐ Yes
Repeat break value on new page	☑ Yes

Sorts
Sort	None

Break Header ⟶

Break Footer ⟶

Table Footer ⟶

Mgr Name	Year Num	Quarter Num	Revenue
David Balkcom	2000	3	642
	2000	4	(89,863)
	2001	1	14,341
	2001	2	228,017
	2001	3	61,529
David Balkcom		Sum:	214,665

Mgr Name	Year Num	Quarter Num	Revenue
Eddie Wang	2000	3	(740,160)
	2000	4	(376,607)
	2001	1	(5,848)
	2001	2	543,731
	2001	3	521,614
Eddie Wang		Sum:	(57,270)
		Sum:	157,395

Break Headers and Footers

Duplicate Values have been Removed

	2000			2001			2001	Report
	3	4	Total	1	2	3	Total	Total
David Balkcom	642	(89,863)	(89,221)	14,341	228,017	61,529	303,886	214,665
Eddie Wang	(740,160)	(376,607)	(1,116,767)	(5,848)	543,731	521,614	1,059,497	(57,270)
Kathy James	(267,653)	(197,741)	(465,394)	52,981	112,154	221,719	386,854	(78,540)
Maria Castro	(400,996)	31,108	(369,888)	(119,552)	273,348	295,519	449,314	79,426
Robert Denning	(292,493)	(214,608)	(507,101)	77,166	253,014	244,383	574,563	67,462
Sean Wilkenson	(2,578,025)	(1,807,388)	(4,385,413)	330,350	1,340,450	4,066,066	5,736,886	1,351,453
Total	(4,278,686)	(2,655,098)	(6,933,784)	349,438	2,750,713	5,410,828	8,510,980	1,577,196

Year Num Values Centered Across Break

Break Properties

Break properties allow you to define how the break will behave.

Show Break Header/Footer: Each table has a table header at the top of the table. If there are breaks present, then you can show the headers at the break level. This allows for each break to have it own header, which makes it easier to determine when each break begins. Usually, when the break headers are displayed, then the table header is hidden, as seen in the graphic. If there are totals, then the break footers will contain the break totals, and the Table Footer will contain the table totals.

Remove Duplicate Values: This option allows for only the first row of a break to contain the break value, as seen in the graphic.

Center Value Across Break: This option centers the break value across the break, as seen in the crosstab in the graphic.

Apply Implicit Sort to Values: Breaks are applied whenever a value in the break column changes values. This option sorts the values before applying the break, which allows for grouping of the values. With this option cleared, there is a chance that there may be several breaks for the same value.

Exercise: Create a Crosstab with Breaks

1. Create a query with Mgr name, Year Num, Quarter Num, and Revenue.
2. Drag Year Num from the table, and drop it just above the table to create a crosstab with Year Num in the Header row.
3. Drag Quarter Num from the crosstab and drop it in the lower part of a Year Num header cell, to create a multi-row header.
4. Click on any Year Num cell in the crosstab, and then click the *Insert/Remove Break* button to insert a break on Year Num.
5. Center Year Values Across Break
   a. Click on any Year Num cell to select it.
   b. Click on the Properties tab to display properties.
   c. In the Breaks section, click *Center values across breaks.*

4. Center the Quarter Num values, by selecting a cell and then clicking the *Align Center* button.
5. Total the Revenues, by first clicking on any Revenue cell, and then by clicking the *Insert Sum* button.
6. Chage the Sum labels, by double-clicking on them and changing the text to *Total.*
7. Double-click on the empty cell above the rightmost total and enter the text *Report.*
8. Center all total headers.

Notes

Breaks and Page Breaks

Page layout

Start on new page	[ ] Yes
Avoid page breaks in table	[ ] Yes
Repeat header on every page	[ ] Yes
Repeat break value on new page	[✓] Yes

Page Layout Properties

Mgr Name	Year Num	Quarter Num	Revenue
Robert Denning	2000	3	(292,493)
	2000	4	(214,608)

Mgr Name	Year Num	Quarter Num	Revenue
	2001	1	77,166
	2001	2	253,014
	2001	3	244,383
Robert Denning		Sum:	67,462

Repeat Header Turned On

Repeat Break Value Turned Off

Mgr Name	Year Num	Quarter Num	Revenue
Robert Denning	2000	3	(292,493)
	2000	4	(214,608)

Robert Denning	2001	1	77,166
	2001	2	253,014
	2001	3	244,383
Robert Denning		Sum:	67,462

Repeat Header Turned Off

Repeat Break Value Turned On

Mgr Name	Year Num	Quarter Num	Revenue
David Balkcom	2000	3	642
	2000	4	(89,863)
	2001	1	14,341
	2001	2	228,017
	2001	3	61,529
David Balkcom		Sum:	214,665

Mgr Name	Year Num	Quarter Num	Revenue
Eddie Wang	2000	3	(740,160)
	2000	4	(376,607)
	2001	1	(5,848)
	2001	2	543,731
	2001	3	521,614
Eddie Wang		Sum:	(57,270)

Start on a New Page

Breaks and Page Breaks

Since many reports will span more than a single page, it is important to define page break behavior.

Start on a New Page: This option will start each new break in a column on a new page. This option is good for segregating break values onto different pages, thus making it easier to locate new break values and easier to distribute the break sections to different recipients, such as departments.

Avoid Page Breaks in Table: Starts a break on a new page, but only starts on a new page when the entire break cannot fit on the reminder of a page.

Repeat Header on every Page: When a page break does occur in a break, then the header will be repeated on the next page. This is an important option, since most people are uncomfortable with tables without headers.

Repeat Break Value on Every Page: If the Remove duplicates option is used, then the break value will only appear in the first row of the break. This means that if a page break occurs in a break section that the break value will not be seen on the new page. The Repeat Break Value option repeats the break value on the new page when a page break occurs.

Notes

Horizontal Tables

Mgr Name	David Balkcom	David Balkcom	David Balkcom	David Balkcom	Eddie Wang	Eddie Wang	Eddie Wang	Eddie Wang
Year Num	2000	2000	2001	2001	2000	2000	2001	2001
Quarter Num	3	4	1	2	3	4	1	2
Revenue	642	(89,863)	14,341	228,017	(740,160)	(376,607)	(5,848)	543,731
Num Transactions	42	36	49	36	126	148	133	131

Horizontal Tables Often are Too Long to Fit on a Page

Mgr Name	David Balkcom	David Balkcom	David Balkcom	David Balkcom	David Balkcom
Year Num	2000	2000	2001	2001	2001
Quarter Num	3	4	1	2	3
Revenue	642	(89,863)	14,341	228,017	61,529
Num Transactions	42	36	49	36	11

Horizontal Tables Should Have Limited Rows

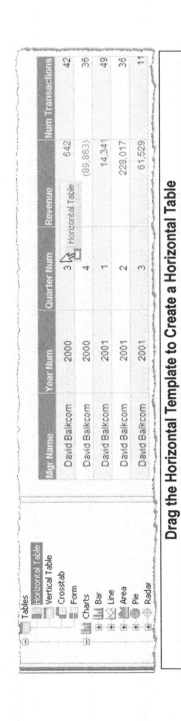

Mgr Name	Year Num	Quarter Num	Revenue	Num Transactions
David Balkcom	2000	3	642	42
David Balkcom	2000	4	(89,863)	36
David Balkcom	2001	1	14,341	49
David Balkcom	2001	2	228,017	36
David Balkcom	2001	3	61,529	11

Tables
- Horizontal Table
- Vertical Table
- Crosstab
- Form

Charts
- Bar
- Line
- Area
- Pie
- Radar

Horizontal Table

Drag the Horizontal Template to Create a Horizontal Table

Horizontal Tables

Horizontal tables rotate a table to display the rows as columns. This type of report is useful when displaying data as records. For example, employee or product information may be better viewed in this manner. However, if there are too many rows in a table, then usually it runs off the right side of a page. We should always try our best not to let data run off the side of a page, because it makes it very difficult to view the data. People are used to tables continuing vertically to a new page, but are uncomfortable with tables continuing off the side of a page onto a new page.

To create a horizontal table, we just drag the Horizontal Table template on to a report structure. In the case of the graphic, we are dropping the template on to a vertical table, but we could also drop it on a crosstab or a chart.

In the two upper graphics, one table has too many rows and the other does not. The data in the limited rows graphic has been limited by placing a filter on the table that only allows for David Balkcom to be displayed. Another way to limit data, is to create sections on a report for one of the grouping dimensions in a table. In this case, the grouping dimension is Mgr Name. We will learn how to create sections in a few pages, after we discuss Form tables.

Exercise: Create a Horizontal Table

1. Create a query with Mgr Name, Year Num, Quarter Num, Revenue, and Num Transactions.
   a. If you already have the query from previous exercises, then simply insert a new Report, and drag the objects from the Data tab on to the new report to create a vertical table.
2. Click on the Templates tab to activate it, and drag the Horizontal Table template onto the vertical table.

Notes

Form Tables

Mgr Name	Year Num	Quarter Num	Revenue	Num Transactions
David Balkcom	2000	3	642	42
David Balkcom	2000	4	(89,863)	36
David Balkcom	2001	1	14,341	49
David Balkcom	2001	2	228,017	36
David Balkcom	2001	3	61,529	11
Eddie Wang	2000	3	(740,160)	126

Report Elements
- Report
- Tables
  - Horizontal Table
  - Vertical Table
  - Crosstab
  - Form
- Charts
  - Bar
  - Line

Drag the Form Template to Create a Form Table

Mgr Name	David Balkcom
Year Num	2000
Quarter Num	3
Revenue	642
Num Transactions	42

Mgr Name	David Balkcom
Year Num	2000
Quarter Num	4
Revenue	(89,863)
Num Transactions	36

Mgr Name	David Balkcom
Year Num	2001
Quarter Num	1
Revenue	14,341
Num Transactions	49

Mgr Name	David Balkcom
Year Num	2001
Quarter Num	2
Revenue	228,017
Num Transactions	36

Mgr Name	David Balkcom
Year Num	2001
Quarter Num	3
Revenue	61,529
Num Transactions	1

Mgr Name	Eddie Wang
Year Num	2000

Form Table

Form Tables

Form tables are similar to Horizontal tables, but instead of rotating the entire table, form tables turn each row in a data set into a horizontal record. Many people try to create labels with this format. While this is possible, it is difficult to place the forms on each label or envelope when printing. There is an example on how to do this in the CH02 - Report Structures example document.

While viewing data in forms may be interesting, this format is a little awkward to work with, because we have little control over the form's format and it is difficult to locate forms of interest. The next page will introduce sections in a report. With sections, we can make reports that look similar to forms, but we can control how the forms are placed and what information they will contain.

Exercise: Create a Form Table

1. Create a query with Mgr Name, Year Num, Quarter Num, Revenue, and Num Transactions.
   a. If you already have the query from previous exercises, then simply insert a new Report, and drag the objects from the Data tab on to the new report to create a vertical table.
2. Click on the Templates tab to activate it, and drag the Form template on to the vertical table.

Notes

_____

Sections in Reports

Creating Sections with Mgr Name

=[Mgr Name]

	Num	Quarter Num	Revenue	Num Transactions
David Balkcom	2000	3	642	42
David Balkcom	2000	4	(89,863)	36
David Balkcom	2001	1	14,341	49
David Balkcom	2001	2	228,017	36
David Balkcom	2001	3	61,529	11
Eddie Wang	2000	3	(740,160)	126
Eddie Wang	2000	4	(376,607)	148

Drop here to create a section

Sections on a Report

David Balkcom

Year Num	Quarter Num	Revenue	Num Transactions
2000	3	642	42
2000	4	(89,863)	36
2001	1	14,341	49
2001	2	228,017	36
2001	3	61,529	11
Sum:		214,665	174

Eddie Wang

Year Num	Quarter Num	Revenue	Num Transactions
2000	3	(740,160)	126
2000	4	(376,607)	148
2001	1	(5,848)	133
2001	2	543,731	131
2001	3	521,614	53
Sum:		(57,270)	591

Horizontal Table in Sections

David Balkcom

Year Num	2000	2000	2001	2001	2001
Quarter Num	3	4	1	2	3
Revenue	642	(89,863)	14,341	228,017	61,529
Num Transactions	42	36	49	36	11

Eddie Wang

Year Num	2000	2000	2001	2001	2001
Quarter Num	3	4	1	2	3
Revenue	(740,160)	(376,607)	(5,848)	543,731	521,614
Num Transactions	126	148	133	131	53

Kathy James

Year Num	2000	2000	2001	2001
Quarter Num	3	4	1	2	3

Section Navigation Map

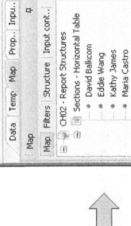

CH02 - Report Structures

Data | Temp. | Map | Prop... | Inpu...

Map

Map | Filters | Structure | Input cont...

CH02 - Report Structures
- Sections - Horizontal Table
  - David Balkcom
  - Eddie Wang
  - Kathy James
  - Maria Castro
  - Robert Denning
  - Sean Wilkenson

Sections in Reports

Sections seem to be similar to breaks, as they both group. However, breaks group data in a single table, which have a single table header and table footer. Sections create sections on a report and multiple report structures can be placed in sections. In the examples above, we simply have a table in the sections. Each section is defined with a Dimension object from the data source. In our case, this dimension is Mgr Name. For each value in the dimension, a section is created on a report. In our example, the sections are defined by the values of Mgr Name. Then, each structure in a section will only contain values for the value of the section dimension. For example, the David Balkcom section only contains rows of data where Mgr Name equals David Balkcom. Later in this chapter, we will include both a table and a chart in the sections.

One of the great advantages of sections is that Business Objects provides a map to the sections. The map is a list of links to each section in a report. All we have to do is to click on a dimension value in the Map and the report will jump to that section. This feature is also available when the report is saved into PDF format. Therefore, the map feature can also be available in Adobe Acrobat documents created by saving a Web Intelligence document as a PDF.

Notice how much better the Horizontal table looks when combined with sections on a report. Not only are the widths of the tables manageable, each section is easily located through the section map.

Exercise: Create a Report with Sections

1. Create a query with Mgr name, Year Num, Quarter Num, Revenue, and Num Transactions.
2. Drag Mgr Name from the table, and drop it above the table, above the create crosstab area, to create a section report with Mgr Name defining the sections.

Notes

Sections are Filtered Containers

All Managers

Year Num	Quarter Num	Revenue	Num Transactions
2000	3	(739,518)	168
2000	4	(466,471)	184
2001	1	8,493	182
2001	2	771,748	167
2001	3	583,143	64
	Sum:	157,395	765

David Balkcom

Year Num	Quarter Num	Revenue	Num Transactions
2000	3	642	42
2000	4	(89,863)	36
2001	1	14,341	49
2001	2	228,017	36
2001	3	61,529	11
	Sum:	214,665	174

Eddie Wang

Year Num	Quarter Num	Revenue	Num Transactions
2000	3	(740,160)	126
2000	4	(376,607)	148
2001	1	(5,848)	133
2001	2	543,731	131
2001	3	521,614	53
	Sum:	(57,270)	591

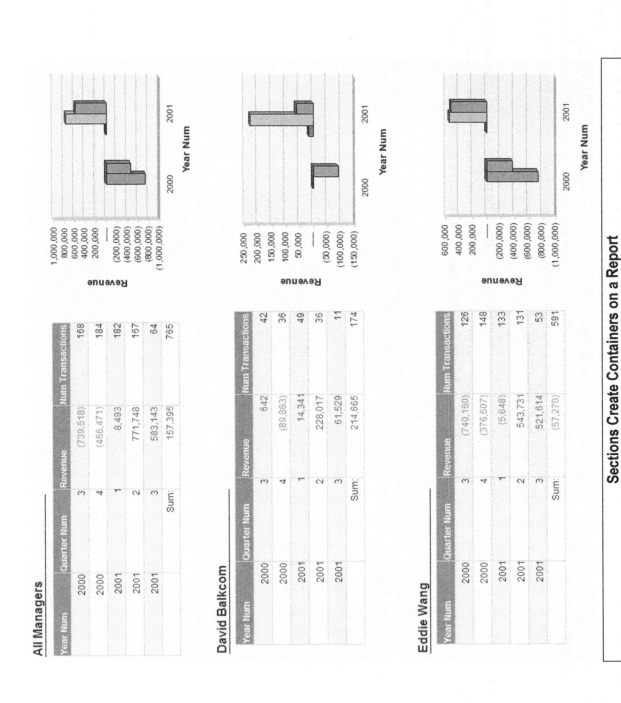

Sections Create Containers on a Report

Sections are Filtered Containers

Section reports create containers on a report page. Each container is filtered by the value of the Dimension used to create the sections. In the graphic, Mgr Name has been used to create the sections.

Since sections create filtered containers, we can place multiple report structures in the containers. In the graphic, we have a table, a chart, and a freestanding cell to display the section value. This report has two sections - David Balkcom and Eddie Wang. The All Managers table and chart are not contained in a section, and therefore represent all values in the report. The All Managers table is placed above the first section container. It could also have been placed after the last container to display report totals.

Notes

Structure Mode

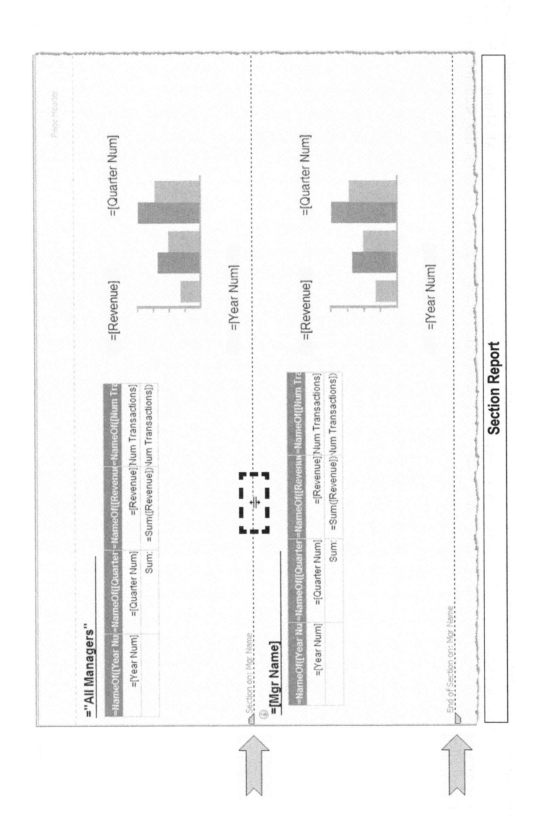

Section Report

Structure Mode

Structure mode allows report designers to see the structure of a report, which includes the section boundaries. In the report, in the graphic, there is one section defined with Mgr Name. We can see this definition by looking at the left side of the dashed delimiter line, where it says *Section on: Mgr Name*. There will be one section for each of the values of Mgr Name in the report. If we look at the top table, above the Mgr Name section, we will see another table and chart. These two structures are located outside of the sections, and will contain the data for all of the Mgr names in the report. Therefore, these top structures represent report summaries, since the data is for all Mgr Names.

We can size the sections on the report, by dragging the dashed delimiters. Notice the sizing mouse cursor when the cursor is placed over the delimiter. Also, notice the small *i* placed above the Mgr Name cell in the section. This small *i* is letting the designer know that there is a filter placed on the section. To see the filter, simply click on the *i*.

Exercise: Create the Section Report in the Graphic

1. Create a query with Mgr name, Year Num, Quarter Num, Revenue, and Num Transactions.
2. Drag Year Mgr Name from the table, and drop it above the table to create the Mgr Name Sections. (Be sure to drag it high enough so it doesn't create a crosstab.)
3. Click the *View Structure* button in the Reporting toolbar.
4. Create the Chart
   a. Click on the table and drag it to the right of itself, then before releasing the mouse button, hold down the [CTRL] key.
   b. Delete the Num Transactions column from the newly copied table.
   c. Click on the Template tab in the Data section of the reporting environment.
   d. Drag the Vertical Grouped template on to the copied table.
5. Create the report level table and chart
6. Drag the Blank Cell template from the Free-Standing section of the Templates tab, and place just above the table in the report level area.
7. Double-click on the cell and enter *All Managers*.
8. Click the *View Results* button in the Reporting toolbar.

   a. Drag the upper section delimiter down to create room for the report level table and chart.
   b. Copy the table and chart into the enlarged header area, created by dragging the upper delimiter. Be sure to leave room for the All Managers cell.

Notes

Multiple Section Report

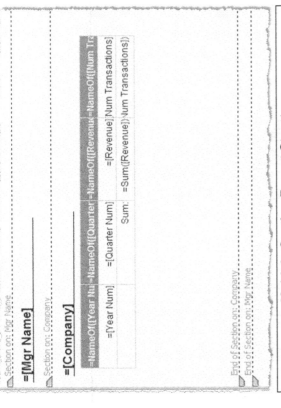

Drag Company into Mgr Name Section to Create Subsection

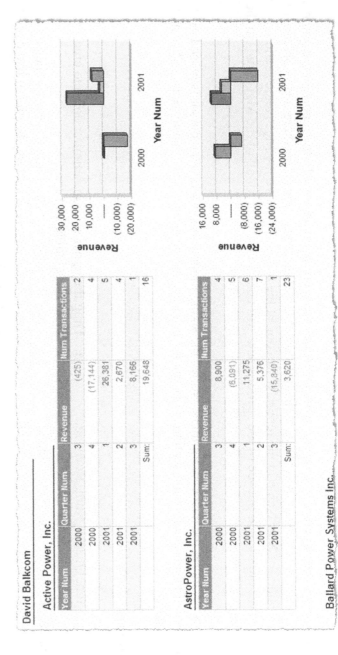

Multiple Section Report Structure

Multiple Section Map

Multiple Section Report

In the previous example, we had sections on the report for each manager. This is a good report, if we are interested in a high level summary of how each manager performed. However, if we want to know how each manager did with each company that they trade, then we can add a new sub-section for Company.

The Map in the graphic displays the sections in a hierarchical structure that allows the sections to be easily navigated.

To remove a section, just drag the cell containing the section filter value from the section. You can also delete the cell. Business Objects will then prompt if you want to delete the section. Click *Yes*, to delete the section. By the way, if you click *No*, then the cell will be removed without removing the section. This means that you can have sections on the report without displaying the section filter cell. We will discuss this behavior on the next page.

Exercise: Create the Multiple Section Report in the Graphic

1. Edit the query from the previous example
    a. Click the Edit Query button in the upper right of the reporting environment, to display the Query Editor.
    b. Add the Company dimension from the Company folder.
    c. Click *Run Query*.
2. Click the *View Structure* button.
3. Drag the Company object from the Data tab into the Mgr Name Section. (This will create a sub-section for Company within Mgr Name).
    Click the *View Results* button.

Notes

Multiple Section Variations

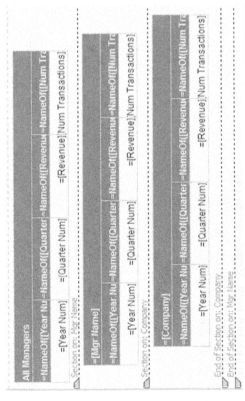

Structure Mode Shows Sections

Multiple Section Variation 1
- David Ballkom
  - Active Power, Inc.
  - AstroPower, Inc.
  - Ballard Power Systems Inc.
  - Capstone Turbine Corporation
  - Electric Fuel Corporation
  - FuelCell Energy, Inc.
  - H Power Corp.
  - Plug Power Inc.
- Eddie Wang

Section Map

All Managers

Year Num	Quarter Num	Revenue	Num Transactions
2000	3	(4,278,686)	588
2000	4	(2,655,098)	637
2001	1	349,438	645
2001	2	2,750,713	643
2001	3	5,410,828	167

David Ballkom

Year Num	Quarter Num	Revenue	Num Transactions
2000	3	642	42
2000	4	(89,863)	36
2001	1	14,341	49
2001	2	228,017	36
2001	3	61,529	11

Active Power, Inc.

Year Num	Quarter Num	Revenue	Num Transactions
2000	3	(425)	2
2000	4	(17,144)	4
2001	1	26,381	5
2001	2	2,670	4
2001	3	8,166	1

AstroPower, Inc.

Year Num	Quarter Num	Revenue	Num Transactions
2000	3	8,900	4
2000	4	(6,091)	5
2001	1	11,275	6
2001	2	5,376	7
2001	3	(15,840)	1

Table in Header, Mgr Name Section, and Company Section

Multiple Section Variations

When we create sections on a report, the sections create containers. When we create subsections, the subsections are contained within a section container. The subsection is in the context - Section - Subsection. In this case, Mgr Name - Company. Above and below the sub section, there is an area for the header and footer, respectively. These headers and footers allow us to place report structures that are in the context of the section. In this case, Mgr Name. Since they are in the same context as the section, we are able to create summary level information, simply by placing a report structure in the header or footer. In this report, we have three levels of summary - All Managers, Manager, and Company (within manager).

When we make such reports, we size the sections by dragging them to create appropriate distances between the different context levels.

Exercise: Create the Multiple Section Report with a Header Summary

1. Create a Query with Mgr Name, Company, Year Num, Quarter Num, Revenue, and Num Transactions.
2. Create sections for Mgr Name, by dragging Mgr Name from the table and dropping it above the table.
3. Create sub sections for Company by, dragging Company from the table and dropping it to the right, but not on top, of Mgr Name in the section.
4. Click the View Structure button.
5. Delete the Mgr Name cell by clicking on it and pressing the [Delete] key. Answer *No* to the delete section dialog.
6. Make the Mgr Name section larger by dragging the top of the Company section down.
7. Copy the table from the Company section into the Mgr Name section.
8. Click on any cell in the header of the newly copied table in the Mgr Name section, and insert a row above.
9. Double-click on the leftmost cell in the newly added header row and type the following: = *[Mgr Name]*. Click on the Mgr Name cell that you just added, and then while pressing the [CTRL] key, click on the remaining cells in the row. Then, click the *Merge Cells* button.
10. Make the report header area larger by dragging down the Section on: Mgr Name section delimiter.
11. Copy the Company Table into the newly enlarge header area. Click on any cell in the header and insert a row above. Double-click on the leftmost cell in the newly added header row, and type *All Managers*. Select all of the cells in the row and click the *Merge Cells* button.
12. Delete the Company section cell, by clicking on it and pressing the [Delete] key. Answer *No* to the delete section dialog.
13. Double-click on the leftmost cell in the newly added header row and type the following: = *[Company]*. Click on the Company cell that you just added, and then while pressing the [CTRL] key, click on the remaining cells in the row. Then, click the *Merge Cells* button.
14. Adjust the position of the tables and tighten up the sections by dragging the delimiters. Click *View Results.*

Notes

Section Properties

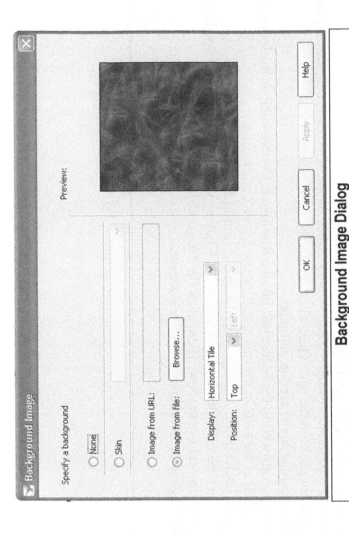

Section Properties

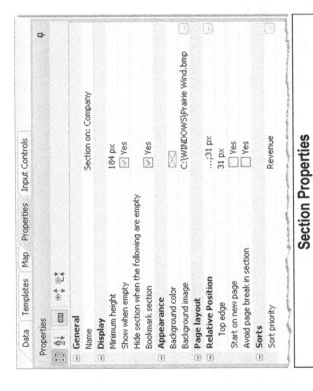

Background Image Dialog

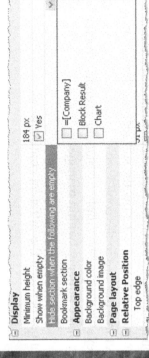

Hide Section Property

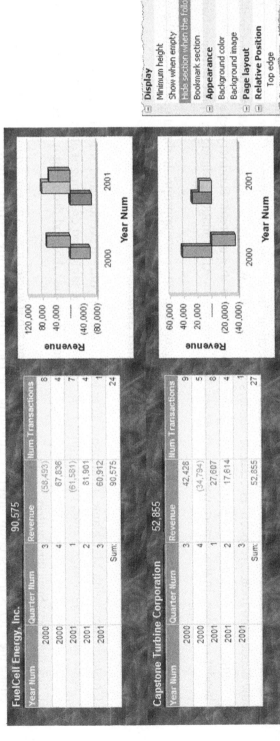

Bitmap Background and Inverse Sort on Revenue

Section Properties

Section properties allow us to control how our sections behave and appear.

General: We can change the *Name* of a Section, but it is usually a good idea to leave the default, since it identifies the dimension on which the section is defined.

Display: We can define the *Minimum Height* of a section. If there is no data in the section, we can hide the empty section by unchecking the *Show when Empty* option. We can also *Hide Section When the Following are Empty*, by selecting which report structure(s) in the section will cause the section to be hidden. If we do not want the section to appear in the Section Map or with links in an Acrobat file, then we can clear the *Bookmark Section* property.

Appearance: We can set the *Background Color* or *Background Image* of a section. This property helps to distinguish sections in multiple section reports. This property will not work for watermarks, as the table cells are not transparent. However, you can modify the DefaultConfig.xml file to make the cells transparent, which will allow the background image to show through the tables in the section.

Page Layout: We can set the *Relative Position* relative to the Top Edge of the structures placed above it in a report. We can also *Start on a New Page* to start every new section on a new page, or we can *Avoid Page Break in Section* to start any sections that won't fit on a reminder of a page on the next page.

Sorts: The default sort for a section is the Dimension on which the section is defined. However, if we place a freestanding cell with an object, such as Revenue, in the section, we can then sort the sections based on the contents of this freestanding cell. This allows us to sort sections defined on a dimension by a measure object.

Notes

Charts

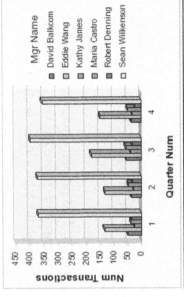

Pie Chart Illustrating Percentages

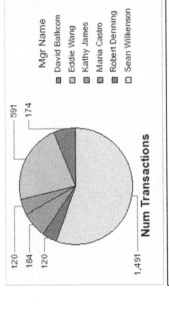

Mgr Name	Num Transactions	Percentage
David Balkcom	174	6.49%
Eddie Wang	591	22.05%
Kathy James	120	4.48%
Maria Castro	184	6.87%
Robert Denning	120	4.48%
Sean Wilkenson	1,491	55.63%
Percentage:		100.00%

Table Displaying Percentages

Vertical Grouped Bar Illustrating Magnitudes

	1	2	3	4
David Balkcom	49	36	53	36
Eddie Wang	133	131	179	148
Kathy James	23	27	39	31
Maria Castro	37	45	54	48
Robert Denning	34	32	33	21
Sean Wilkenson	369	372	397	353

Crosstab Displaying Magnitudes

Charts

Tables and crosstabs display numerical information, which is precise, but not easy to digest. For example, in the table, in the graphic, we have to scan the percentage column to find the largest and/or smaller values. We have to remember all of the numbers and compare them to the other numbers in the column. So, if we are analyzing the numbers to find outliers (numbers which are significantly different from the others in the column), or just trying to spot trends in the numbers, then tables are difficult to use for this purpose. If we look at the Pie chart in the upper-right of the graphic, we will notice that we can quickly find the largest percentage and the smallest percentage. We also added data labels, so we can see the magnitude of the number representing the percentage.

The crosstab displays the number of quarterly trades by each manager. It is difficult to compare the different managers, because we must constantly scan the crosstab and perform calculations in our head. The vertical grouped chart displays this same data graphically, which makes it very easy to compare the quantities. A quick look at the two charts and we can see that Sean Wilkenson had the most trades each quarter and the most of all managers.

Therefore, the purpose of charts is to allow viewers of a report to quickly observe how dimension values compare to one another through their associated measure magnitudes.

Exercise: Create the Report Structures in the Graphic

1. Create a query with Mgr name, Quarter Num, and Num Transactions.
2. Create two tables by copying the resulting table to under the table.
3. Create the upper table and Pie Chart
   a. Remove the Quarter Num Column from the upper table.
   b. Copy the upper table to the right of itself.
   c. Click on any value in the Num Trasactions column of the left-upper table, and then select *Percentage* from the *Calculation* menu.
   d. Activate the Templates tab and drop the Pie Chart template on the upper-right table.
4. Create the lower crosstab and bar chart.

   a. Create the crosstab by dragging Quarter Num to just above the table (the tooltip should say Drop here to create crosstab), and then drop it in the crosstab rectangle.
   b. Copy the crosstab to the right of itself.
   c. Create the bar chart by dropping the Vertical Grouped Bar Chart template on the newly copied crosstab.

Notes

Modify Charts

=[Quarter Num]
Year Num
Drop here to insert a cell

Add Year to Chart Axis

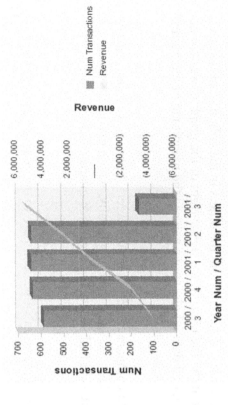

Revenue

3,000,000
2,000,000
1,000,000
—
(1,000,000)
(2,000,000)
(3,000,000)

Num Transactions
Revenue

800
700
600
500
400
300
200
100
0

Num Transactions

1   2   3   4
Quarter Num

Graph Shows Forth Quarter Down

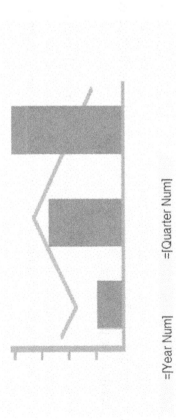

Revenue

6,000,000
4,000,000
2,000,000
—
(2,000,000)
(4,000,000)
(6,000,000)

Num Transactions
Revenue

700
600
500
400
300
200
100
0

Num Transactions

2000 / 2000 / 2001 / 2001 / 2001 /
3   4   1   2   3
Year Num / Quarter Num

Graph Now Shows Positive Trend

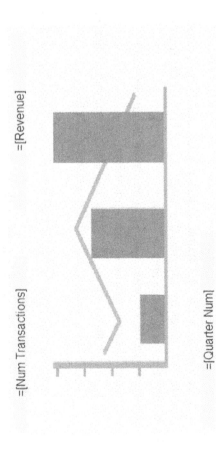

=[Num Transactions]

=[Revenue]

=[Quarter Num]

Structure Mode Shows Axis Objects

=[Num Transactions]

=[Revenue]

=[Year Num]   =[Quarter Num]

Graph Now Has Year Num / Quarter Num on Axis

Modify Charts

In the previous example, we graphed Num Transactions, Mgr Name and Quarter. This report was not accurate, because it grouped quarters for both years in the report. Therefore, each quarter could contain data from 2000 and 2001. However, we made no mention of that in our report. In the chart in the upper-left of the graphic, we can see that from first the second quarter we had an upward trend, but after that the trend was negative. If we published that graph, we would be incorrect. In the chart in the lower-right of the graphic, we have added Year Num to correctly distribute the quarterly values for Revenue. Now, the trend is positive for all quarters.

To modify an existing chart, we enter Structure Mode, by clicking on the *View Structure* button. This particular chart has two measure series: Num transactions and Revenue, as can be seen at the top of the chart. Num Transactions uses the left Y-axis and Revenue uses the right Y-axis, which can be seen by their relative placement in the structure. The X-axis originally only had the Quarter Num dimension. We added the Year Num dimension by dropping it on the upper portion of the Quarter Num object in the structure.

Exercise: Modify an Existing Chart

1. Create a Query with Year Num, Quarter Num, Num Transactions, and Revenue.
2. Delete the Year Num Column and make sure that the Num Transactions column is before the Revenue column.
3. Drop the Vertical Grouped and Line Bar Chart template on the table.
   Notice that the revenue line is in a downward trend.
4. Click the View Structure button to enter Structure mode.
5. Drag Year Num from the Data tab and place it in the upper portion of the Quarter Num dimension in the chart.
6. Click the View Results button.
   Notice that the trend is now positive, and accurately reflects the data.

Notes

Moving, Copying and Sizing Charts

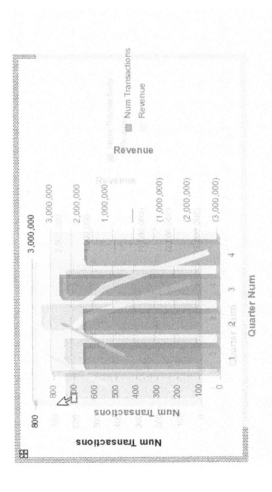

Moving a Chart

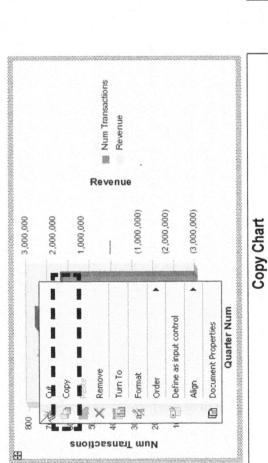

Copy Chart

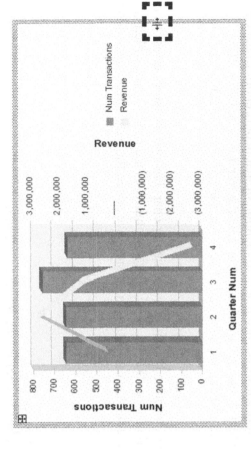

Size Cursor

Move Cursor

Chart Templates (Bar)

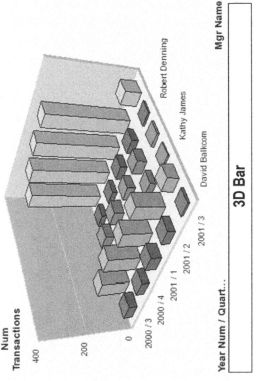

Vertical Grouped

Mgr Name
- David Balkcom
- Eddie Wang
- Kathy James
- Maria Castro
- Robert Denning
- Sean Wilkenson

Revenue

Year Num / Quarter Num

2000 / 3 2000 / 4 2001 / 1 2001 / 2 2001 / 3

5,000,000
4,000,000
3,000,000
2,000,000
1,000,000
—
(1,000,000)
(2,000,000)
(3,000,000)

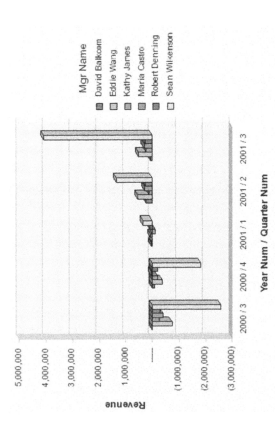

Bar and Line

Num Transactions
Revenue

Revenue

6,000,000
4,000,000
2,000,000
—
(2,000,000)
(4,000,000)
(6,000,000)

Num Transactions

700
600
500
400
300
200
100
0

Year Num / Quarter Num

2000 / 3 2000 / 4 2001 / 1 2001 / 2 2001 / 3

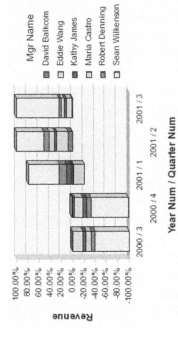

3D Bar

Num Transactions

400

200

0

Year Num / Quart...

2000 / 3 2000 / 4 2001 / 1 2001 / 2 2001 / 3

Mgr Name

Robert Denning
Kathy James
David Balkcom

Mgr Name
- David Balkcom
- Eddie Wang
- Kathy James
- Maria Castro
- Robert Denning
- Sean Wilkenson

Vertical Percent

Revenue

100.00%
80.00%
60.00%
40.00%
20.00%
0.00%
-20.00%
-40.00%
-60.00%
-80.00%
-100.00%

Year Num / Quarter Num

2000 / 3 2000 / 4 2001 / 1 2001 / 2 2001 / 3

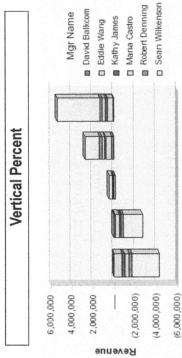

Mgr Name
- David Balkcom
- Eddie Wang
- Kathy James
- Maria Castro
- Robert Denning
- Sean Wilkenson

Vertical Stacked

Revenue

6,000,000
4,000,000
2,000,000
—
(2,000,000)
(4,000,000)
(6,000,000)

Year Num / Quarter Num

2000 / 3 2000 / 4 2001 / 1 2001 / 2 2001 / 3

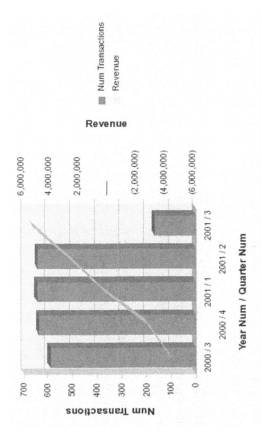

Moving, Copying and Sizing Charts

Charts do not grow in size, as more data is reflected in a chart, as tables do. Chart elements just get denser. For example, the columns get closer and narrower. Therefore, we need to size the chart to accommodate the estimated quantity of data. For example, a chart with 12 months on the X-axis should be wider than a chart with only 4 quarters on the X-axis. We size a chart by placing the mouse cursor over one of the container borders, and when the cursor changes to the size cursor, we click and drag the border to a new position.

We often want to copy charts on a report. We may do this, because we want to place different filters on the same chart, or we may want to copy a chart into the report summary area above a section. To copy a chart, we just right-click on the chart and then select *Copy* from the pop-up menu. Then, we just right-click on the report where we want the upper-left corner of the copied chart to be place, and then select *Paste* from the pop-up menu.

To move a chart, we just place the mouse cursor over the chart, and then when the mouse pointer changes to the Move cursor, we click and drag the chart. We do not have to place the cursor over the border of the chart, as we do when moving tables.

Notes

Chart Templates (Bar)

Bar charts allow us to compare dimensions based on their related measure values. We can use bar charts to compare quarterly totals, as seen in the Bar and Line chart. We can also use them to compare the manager's quarterly totals, as seen in the Vertical Grouped chart. These two examples use the time dimension, but bar charts don't need to include time. For example, we can compare the total games won across the teams in a sports league.

Vertical Grouped: This chart has two dimension axes - one for X-axis distribution and one for grouping. In the graphic the managers are grouped by quarter. This allows us to compare the quarterly performances of the managers.

Bar and Line: This chart has two measure series that allows us to see how one measure changes relative to the other. In the graphic, we have Num Transactions as the column and Revenue as the line.

Vertical Stacked: Allows us to view the total magnitude of a measure and how each of a dimension's values contributed to the total. In the graphic, we can see the total revenue for each quarter and how the managers contributed to the totals.

Vertical Percent: Allows us to see the percentage of a dimension's values to the total magnitude of a measure. Each column represents 100% of the measure's magnitude. In the graphic, we can see each manager's percentage contribution to the total revenue for the quarter.

3D Bar: Is similar to the Vertical Grouped, but instead of grouping a dimension's values, it spreads them out across the Z-axis. In the graphic, the managers are distributed across the Z-axis, and we can compare each manager's series to the other managers. This type of graph is not usually used for analytics, because it is difficult to compare the magnitudes, as the base of the chart is not level. Many people take advantage of the unlevel base, by placing their results on the higher-right side, and their competitors to the left of them. This gives the appearance that they are doing better, even when the magnitudes are about the same.

Notes

Chart Templates (Line)

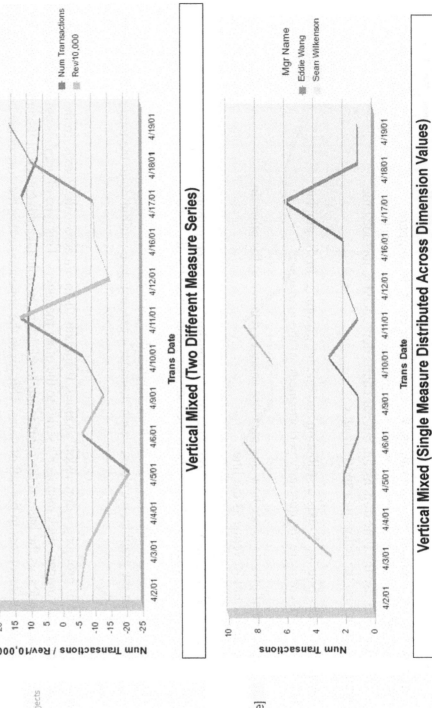

Vertical Mixed (Single Series Across Time)

=[Revenue]

=[Trans Date]

Place dimension objects here (optional).

Revenue

Legend: Revenue

Vertical Mixed (Two Different Measure Series)

=[Num Transactions]
=[Rev/10,000]

=[Trans Date]

Place dimension objects here (optional).

Num Transactions / Rev/10,000

Legend: Num Transactions, Rev/10,000

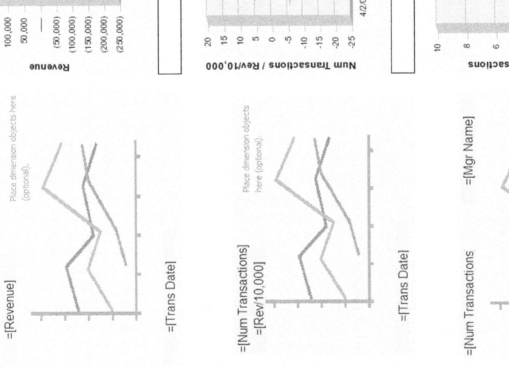

Vertical Mixed (Single Measure Distributed Across Dimension Values)

=[Num Transactions]
=[Mgr Name]

=[Trans Date]

Num Transactions

Legend: Mgr Name — Eddie Wang, Sean Wilkenson

Chart Templates (Line)

Line charts allow us to view measure values across a continuous dimension, where a bar chart allowed us to view across discrete dimension values. Line charts allow us to compare several measure series or a measure series across dimension values. For example, if we were a manager of a shoe store, we could compare number of sales versus the revenue generated by the sales. We could also, compare the daily total sales of the sales people.

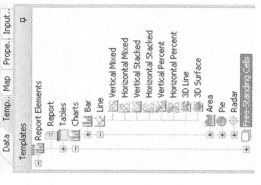

Vertical/Horizontal Mixed: The line magnitudes in Series Mixed charts are independent of one another. This allows each line to be compare to the other lines in the chart. As seen in the graphic, we can have a line for each measure in the chart definition. This allows us to compare several different measures. Many times, if we are only comparing two measures, then we should consider the Bar and Line chart in the previous example. We can also have a line for each of a dimension's values, which can also be seen in the graphic. This dimension is very similar to the grouping dimension for the bar chart.

Vertical/Horizontal Stacked: Stacked charts are additive, meaning that each line forms the base for the next, and each next line is the total of its magnitude and the magnitudes of the lines below it. This type of chart can be very deceiving and it could appear that the upper lines are performing much better than the lower lines, since the upper lines are the total of all lines beneath them. It is probably better to use a stacked area chart, since the stack is more obvious.

Vertical/Horizontal Percent: This chart is similar, but the lines will now add up to 100%. Again, it is deceiving, because the top line will appear to have 100% of the magnitude. The Area Percent chart is probably better.

Notes

Chart Templates (Area)

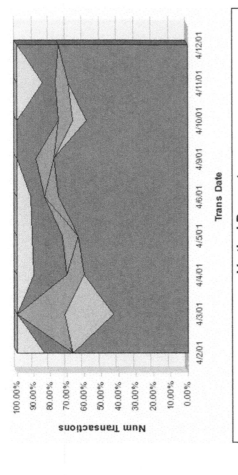

Vertical Absolute

Num Transactions

Trans Date

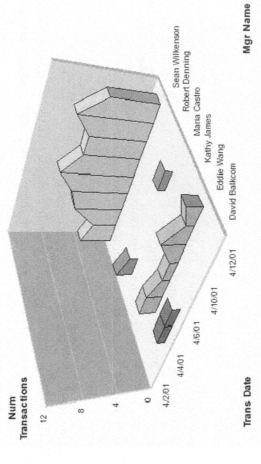

Vertical Percent

Num Transactions

Trans Date

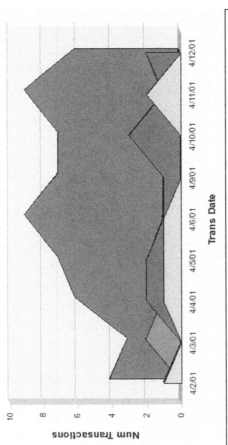

Vertical Stacked

Num Transactions

Trans Date

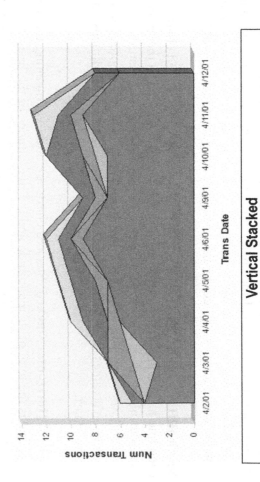

3D Area

Num Transactions

Trans Date

Mgr Name

Sean Wilkenson
Robert Denning
Maria Castro
Kathy James
Eddie Wang
David Balkcom

Chart Templates (Area)

Area charts are very similar to Line charts. However, the space below the line is also filled in, thus creating a solid area between the X-axis and the magnitude of the line. With Line charts, we can see lines when they dip below another line. With an Area chart, we cannot always see the other series when they dip below series that are placed in front of them. Thus, the Vertical Absolute chart is rarely used. However, the Stacked Area chart is very useful, because it shows the total combined magnitude of all of the series in the chart, and their relative contributions to the magnitude. The Percent chart is also useful, as it shows the percent contribution of each member of the series to the total magnitude.

Vertical Absolute: This chart is very similar to a Line chart. However, the series are solid from the magnitude of the line to the X-axis.

Vertical Stacked: Combines the magnitudes of all members in a series, thus allowing the magnitude to reflect the total of all lines. It also shows the relative contributions of all members in the series.

Vertical Percent: Displays the percentage contribution of all members in a series.

3-D Area: Spreads the members of a series over the Z-axis, thus creating a separate area chart for each member.

Notes

Chart Templates (Pie)

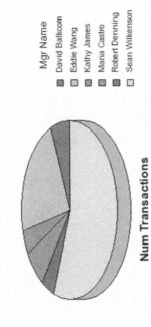

Num Transactions

3D Pie

Mgr Name
- David Balkcom
- Eddie Wang
- Kathy James
- Maria Castro
- Robert Denning
- Sean Wilkenson

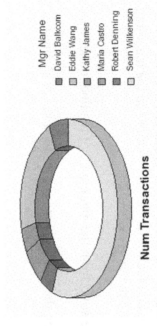

Num Transactions

3D Pie

Mgr Name
- David Balkcom
- Eddie Wang
- Kathy James
- Maria Castro
- Robert Denning
- Sean Wilkenson

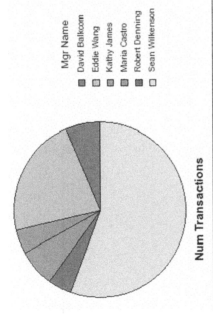

Num Transactions

Doughnut

Mgr Name
- David Balkcom
- Eddie Wang
- Kathy James
- Maria Castro
- Robert Denning
- Sean Wilkenson

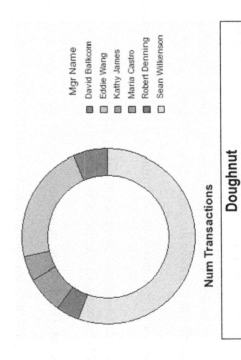

Num Transactions

3D Doughnut

Mgr Name
- David Balkcom
- Eddie Wang
- Kathy James
- Maria Castro
- Robert Denning
- Sean Wilkenson

Chart Templates (Pie)

Pie charts are best when showing how one Dimension's share of a measure compares to the total measure value for all Dimension values. We usually do not compare the pieces of the pie to one-another, as a bar chart does this more effectively and pie charts can be a little deceiving. In the charts, in the graphic, we can see that Sean Wilkensen had most of the transactions, as Sean's piece of the pie represents more than half the pie. However, when looking at the smaller slices, it is difficult to see which is largest. Have a look at the upper-left chart in the graphic and try to guess which slices are the smallest. This is why in many pie charts, we also display the magnitudes of the slices in the data labels.

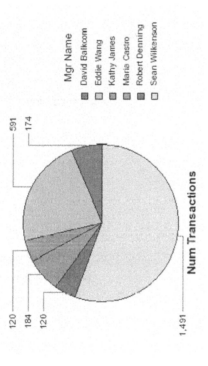

Earlier, did you guess which pieces were the smallest? Look at this graphic and see if you were correct. We use the Chart properties to display these labels, as we will see in the next few pages.

Notes

Chart Templates (Radar)

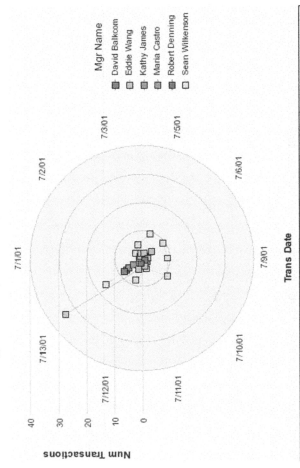

Radar Line (Daily Manager Transactions)

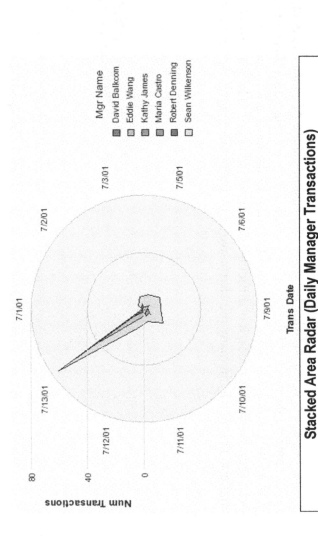

Stacked Area Radar (Daily Manager Transactions)

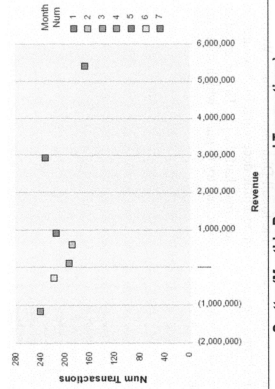

Polar (Monthly Revenue and Transactions)

Scatter (Monthly Revenue and Transactions)

Chart Templates (Radar)

Radar charts are used to process large sets of data points. Usually, we are looking for patterns in the data or points that are outliers.

Radar Line: This chart allows for two dimension values and a measure. One dimension is represented by lines that extend perpendicular to the center of the chart in a radial pattern. The measure magnitude bands radiate from the center. It is similar to a Line chart that has been dragged in a 360 degree arc while keeping the origin (0, 0) pinned. This allows us to fit many more data points, than with a line chart. In the graphic, we can see in the Radar line chart that most of the data points fit within the 10 valance band. We can also see that there are two outliers on 7/13/2001. These two outliers should be investigated.

Stacked Area Radar: As seen in the line radar chart, we can find individual points that are outliers. However, what if the total magnitude of many events on a single day is significant, while the individual events are not? If this is the case, then we can use the Stack Area Radar chart to find the total of multiple events on an axis point. We can see that the combination of the events on 7/13/2001 was around 60 transactions, where the largest individual was less than 30, as seen in the radar line chart.

Polar: Polar charts allow us to not only see the magnitude of a measure, but to group the magnitudes within ranges formed by another measure. Therefore, Polar charts take a single dimension and two measure objects. In the graphic, we are looking at monthly transactions and grouping them within pie slices formed by the Revenue measure. This allows us to see that we had three months with about 200 transactions that generated between 0 and 1,000,000 in revenue. We can also see that we had one month with around 240 transactions that generated about -1,200,000 in revenue. In some businesses, such as broadcasting, we may desire that we have less than 1,000 outages with durations less than 60 seconds. This type of chart would be great for finding months that exceeded these expectations.

Scatter: Is similar to a polar chart, but it is linear. The Polar and Scatter charts in the graphic both graph the same data. Notice that it is more difficult to see that there are three data points between 0 and 1,000,000? However, since it is linear, we can now see that there are several points in the 240 Number of Transactions range - One near -1,000,000, one near 3,000,000, and maybe near 0 and 1,000,000. This was not as obvious in the Polar chart. So with Polar charts, we may be more interested in grouping and in Scatter charts, we are usually looking for patterns in the data.

Notes

Chart Properties (Display)

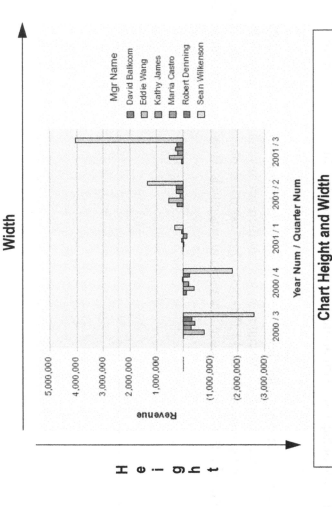

Chart Display Properties

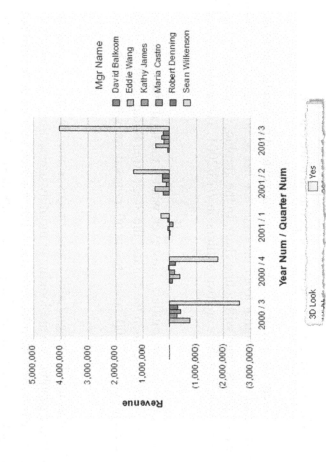

Chart Height and Width

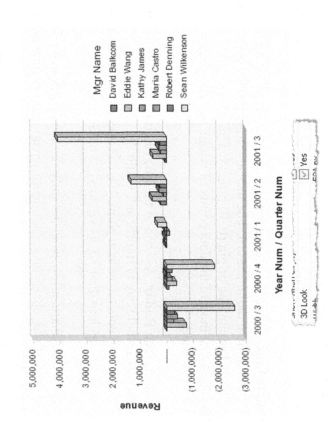

Chart Properties (Display)

Chart Display properties define how a chart will be displayed.

Avoid Duplicate Row Aggregation: If a dimension column is deleted from a table, then the remaining dimensions will roll-up (aggregate) to form unique rows of dimension combinations. The measure will re-aggregate to the new combinations of dimensions. Charts are created by rolling-up dimension values to create unique dimension values or combinations of multiple dimensions' values, and then the magnitudes of aggregated measures are graphed. Since charts behave this way, the Avoid Duplicate Row Aggregat on property usually has no affect on a chart.

Show Rows with Empty Dimension Values: Sometimes when we merge data providers, there are dimensions that do not appear in both sets of data, then when these sets are merged, the row with the NULL dimension value will also contain NULLs for the other columns in that data set. This option forces Web Intelligence to display the data, even when the values are NULL.

Show When Empty: We create charts in many contexts on a report. Sometimes a chart may have nothing to chart in the context where it is placed, such as in a section on a report. If this property is checked, then the chart will not be shown, if there are no values to graph.

Width/Height: These options allow us to define the width and height of a chart. We may want to do this to make sure that it fits in a section with a defined height, or to make sure that all charts on a report are the same height and width.

Notes

Chart Properties (Appearance)

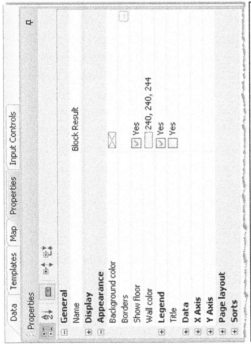

Chart Appearance Properties

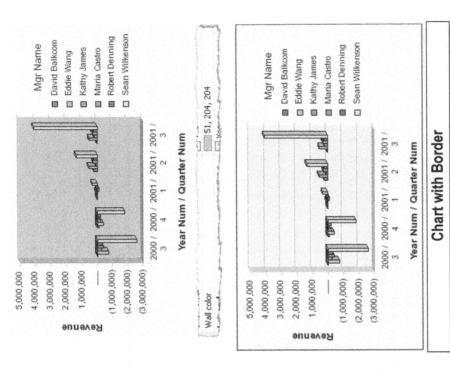

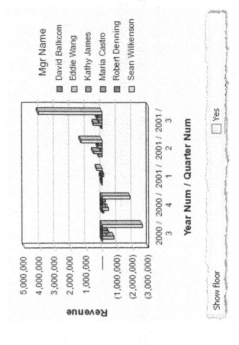

Chart with Border

Chart Properties (Appearance)

Chart Appearance properties allow us to modify the appearance of a chart.

Background Color: The background color of a chart is the area outside of the wall. The wall of a chart is generally behind the series. We can change the background color by selecting a color from the drop-down list.

Borders: We can place a border around the chart with this property.

Show Floor/Wall: The area that encloses the series in a chart is the Floor and Wall. In the chart above, the floor is the three faces that enclose the series, which is behind, under, and to the left of the series. We can hide these areas with this property.

Wall Color: We can change the wall/floor color with this property.

Notes

Chart Properties (Legend and Title)

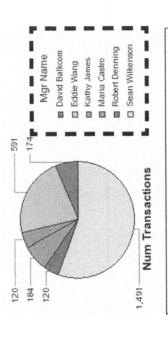

Chart Legend

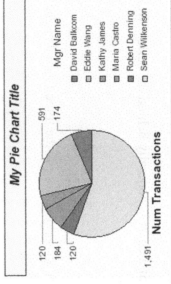

Chart Title Properties

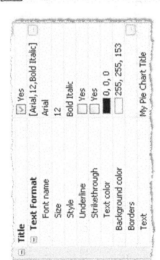

Chart Title Properties

Chart Properties (Legend and Title Properties)

Chart Properties panel:

Appearance	
Background color	☒
Borders	
Show floor	☑ Yes
Wall color	240, 240, 244
	☑ Yes
Legend	
Position	Right
Title	[Arial,10,Regular]
Text Format	
Background color	☒
Borders	
Values	
Text Format	[Arial,8,Regular]
Font name	Arial
Size	8
Style	Regular
Underline	☐ Yes
Strikethrough	☐ Yes
Text color	■ 0, 0, 0
Background color	☒
Borders	
Title	☑ Yes
Text Format	[Arial,10,Regular]
Font name	Arial
Size	10
Style	Regular
Underline	☐ Yes
Strikethrough	☐ Yes
Text color	■ 0, 0, 0
Background color	☒
Borders	
Text	

Chart Title Properties panel:

Title	
Text Format	☑ Yes
	[Arial,12,Bold Italic]
Font name	Arial
Size	12
Style	Bold Italic
Underline	☐ Yes
Strikethrough	☐ Yes
Text color	■ 0, 0, 0
Background color	☐ 255, 255, 153
Borders	
Text	My Pie Chart Title

Chart Properties (Legend and Title)

Many charts need a legend to let people know what each color in a series represents. In the chart in the graphic, the colors (pie pieces) represent Manager Names. Charts don't always need a title, since the chart can just graphically represent a table that it accompanies in a report. However, if there are several different charts, then you probably should use a title to inform viewers of the purpose of the chart.

Legend Position: Can be Left, Right, or Bottom. The chart in the graphic has the legend on the right.

Legend Title: The legend title is the name of the measure object used to create the series. Many times the object name is too abstract and people want to change the title text. To do this, create a variable with the name equal to the desired text in the title, then point the variable to the measure object using a formula similar to =[Measure Obj]. We will cover variables later. We can use the properties to format the text, background color and borders of the legend title.

Legend Values: These are the values of the Dimension used to define axis or group in a chart. In a pie chart they are the X-Axis values, in a bar chart they are the grouping dimension's values. We can use the properties to format the text, background color and borders of the legend values.

Title: This is the title of the chart, and it is located at the top-center of a chart. We can set the text to the desired title, by entering the title into the Text field. However, the title will not wrap, so avoid title that will be wider than the width of your chart. We can use the properties to format the text, background color and borders of the legend values.

Notes

Chart Properties (Data)

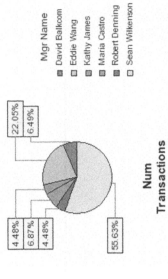

Num
Transactions

Pie Chart Data Labels

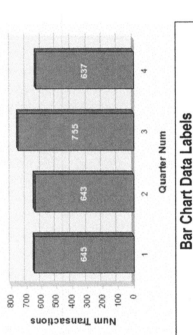

Quarter Num

Bar Chart Data Labels

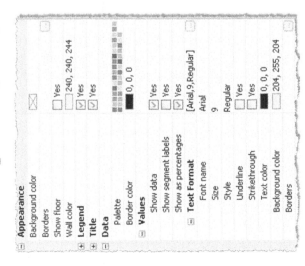

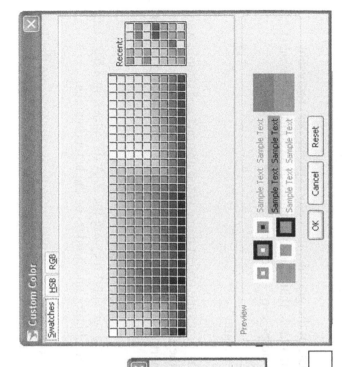

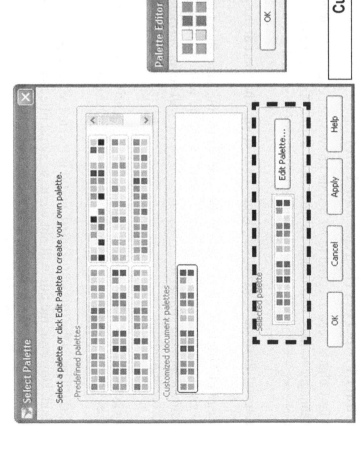

Customizing a Palette

Chart Properties (Data)

The data of a chart can also be called the series. We want to format the data so that viewers of the report will be able to discern the values in the chart.

Palette: The palette of a chart supplies the data elements with colors. The first element gets the first color in the Palette, then each element is assigned a color in the order that they appear in the chart. Usually the defined palettes will work, but sometimes we need more contrast or we need to use standard colors defined for our company. We can create a custom palette, by clicking on the *Edit Palette...* button in the Select Palette dialog. We can edit one color at a time by clicking on it, or we can edit all colors by clicking on the *Set All Colors...* button in the Palette Editor.

Values: The values are the text representation of the magnitude of the data element. We do not always have to show these values, as charts are used to visually compare the data elements. However, many times we are not only interested in the relative magnitude comparisons, but we are also interested in the actual magnitude or percentage of the data element. To show the values, we check the *Show Data* option.

Text Format: Sometimes when we show the data, we cannot read the values because of where they are placed on the chart, or some other intrinsic characteristic of the value. To help make the values more readable, we can use the Text Format properties. In the Bar chart, in the graphic, I set the text color to white and bolded the font.

Background Color / Borders: We can also set the background color and/or place a border around the value to help it be more visible.

Notes

Chart Properties (Axis)

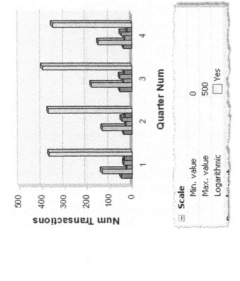

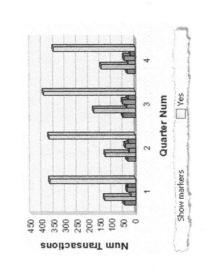

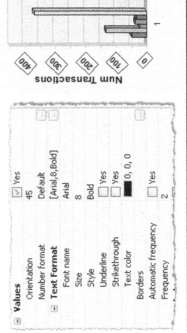

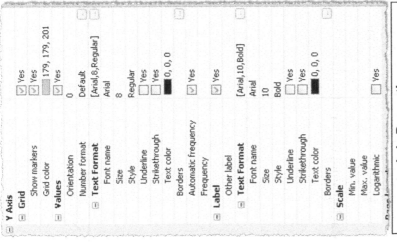

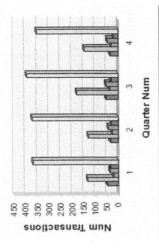

Axis Properties

Y Axis	
Grid	☑ Yes
Show markers	☑ Yes
Grid color	179, 179, 201
Values	☑ Yes
Orientation	Default
Number format	0
Text Format	[Arial,8,Regular]
Font name	Arial
Size	8
Style	Regular
Underline	☐ Yes
Strikethrough	☐ Yes
Text color	0, 0, 0
Borders	☑ Yes
Automatic frequency	☑ Yes
Frequency	
Label	
Other label	
Text Format	[Arial,10,Bold]
Font name	Arial
Size	10
Style	Bold
Underline	☐ Yes
Strikethrough	☐ Yes
Text color	0, 0, 0
Borders	
Scale	
Min. value	
Max. value	
Logarithmic	☐ Yes

Using Defuaults Above

Grid — ☐ Yes

Show markers — ☐ Yes

Axis Values Format

Values	☑ Yes
Orientation	45
Number format	Default
Text Format	[Arial,8,Bold]
Font name	Arial
Size	8
Style	Bold
Underline	☐ Yes
Strikethrough	☐ Yes
Text color	0, 0, 0
Borders	☐ Yes
Automatic frequency	
Frequency	2

Scale

Min. value	0
Max. value	500
Logarithmic	☐ Yes

Chart Properties (Axis)

Charts generally have two axes - X and Y. The X-axis is for dimension values and the Y-axis is to measure the measure magnitudes. Some charts have a third axis, which is the Z-axis. This axis allows a second dimension that is horizontally perpendicular to the X-axis. All the axes have Grid, Values, and Label properties. The Y-axis also has the Scale property.

Grid: The grid of an axis is the lines that are perpendicular to the axis, and they are used to help show the axis values position in the chart. We can choose to hide the grid, hide the markers, or change the color of the grid for an axis.

Values: The values on a grid are the Dimension values for dimensions and incremental magnitude values for the Y-axis. We can choose to hide the values, change their orientation, and format the numbers. We can also use the *Text Format* properties to format the text of the values. We can put borders around them, and we can also define the frequency that they will appear. In the graphic (Axis Values Format), we set the frequency to two, and this made the values appear on every other grid line.

Label: The default label of an axis is the name of the object used to define the axis. We can change this default value with the *Other Label* property. We can also use the *Text Format* properties to format the text of the label, or put a border around it with the *Borders* property.

Scale: The Y-axis is defined with a measure, and the grid is defined with increments from the minimum to the maximum value of the measure. These values are evenly distributed along the axis to help us measure the magnitudes of the measure's values. Sometimes, we may want to modify the scale to better show the differences in the magnitudes of the values. For example, suppose you had a chart where all data elements were at least 50,000 and the largest was 150,000. If we made the minimum value on the scale 40,000 or 50,000, the differences in the magnitudes will be more easily discerned.

Notes

Free-Standing Cells

Data | Templates | Map | Properties | Input Contr.

Templates

- Report Elements
  - Report
  - Tables
  - Charts
  - Free-Standing Cells
    - Formula and Text Cells
      - Blank Cell
      - Drill Filters
      - Last Refresh Date
      - Document Name
      - Query Summary
      - Prompt Summary
      - Report Filter Summary
    - Page Number Cells
      - Page Number
      - Page Number/Total Pages
      - Total Number of Pages

Query Summary

```
*** Query Name:Query 1 ***

   ** Query Properties:
      Universe:SI Data V3 (SQL Server US)
      Last Refresh Date:6/4/10 7:43 PM
      Last Execution Duration: 1
      Number of rows: 76
      Retrieve Duplicate Row: ON

   ** Query Definition:
      Result Objects: Mgr Name, Year Num, Quarter Num,
Company, Revenue
      Filters (    Year-To-Date
               AND  Manager
            )
```

Prompt Summary

```
*** Query Name:Query 1 ***

   Enter Date 5/31/2001
   Enter Manager Name(s) David Balkcom; Sean Wilkenson
```

Report Filter Summary

```
*** Filter on Report Manager Revenue   ***

      Filter on Block Block1:
         Year Num In List { 2001 }

*** Filter on Report Quarterly Revenue ***

      Global Report Filters:

         (
            Year Num In List { 2001 }
         )
            AND
         (
            Quarter Num In List { 2, 3 }
         )
```

Page Number Cells

Page Number
1

Page Number/Total Pages
1/27

Total Number of Pages
27

Formula Cells

Drill Filters
2,001 - 1

Last Refresh Date
5/20/10 12:10 PM

Document Name
CH02 - Report Structures

Blank Cell

Type Text
Press Ctrl+Enter to show Formula Editor

Free-Standing Cells

Free-Standing cells are used to hold singular information, such as titles, page numbers, refresh dates, document constraints (prompt input), report summaries, and so forth. To insert a free-standing cell, simply drag a free-standing cell template onto a report. We can populate a blank cell with text, by just double-clicking on it and then typing. We can also populate blank cells with formulas that return singular information, as mentioned above. There are several predefine free-standing cells that will contain a formula when inserted, these are as follows.

Page Number Cells: These cells will return page number information.

    Page Number: Returns the current page number
    Total Number of Pages: Returns the total number of pages in a report, as currently formatted.
    Page Number/Total Pages: This returns # / ##. Where # = Current Page, ## = Number of Pages)

Formula and Text Cells: These return various report and document information

    Drill Filters: We will learn about drilling later. This template returns the path use to drill down to deeper details in a report.
    Last Refresh Date: Returns the date of the last time a data provider was refreshed, which is important to display in most reports.
    Document Name: The file name of a document. A document is a report or a collection of reports in a single file.
    Query Summary: Returns information about a query in a document. See the graphic for details.
    Prompt Summary: Returns the prompts and the input values of the prompts. Can be replaced with the UserResponse function. If a document contains prompts, then the prompt input values should always be displayed on a report.
    Report Filter Summary: We have already seen filters used in some examples. Filters limit the data displayed in a report or report structure. Since filters can be placed on reports, sections, or report blocks, it can be difficult to determine what filters exist on the report. This summary lists all of the filters on a report and what objects they are applied to.

These free-standing cells are a great help, as they provide information about a report or document without us having to know the functions that Business Objects provides to return such information. You can double-click on any of the cells, after they have been inserted into a report, to see the function used. Later in this book, we will learn what functions are available and how to use them.

Notes

Formatting Cells

General		
Text	=LastExecutionDate()	
Display		
Autofit width	Yes	
Width	222 px	
Autofit height	Yes	
Height	18 px	
Read cell content as	Text	
Show when empty	Yes	
Appearance		
Text Format	[Arial,10,Bold]	
Font name	Arial	
Size	10	
Style	Bold	
Underline	Yes	
Strikethrough	Yes	
Text color	0, 0, 0	
Wrap text	Yes	
Vertical text alignment	Bottom	
Horizontal text alignment	Center	
Background color		
Background image		
Borders		
Number format	Date/Time	
Page layout		
Relative Position		
Left edge	201 px;30 px	
Top edge	201 px	
	30 px	
Repeat on every new page	Yes	
Avoid page break in free-standing cell	Yes	

Properties Tab for Free-Standing Cells

Formatting Cells

Free-standing cells have many of the same properties that the cells in tables have. However, there a few special properties that only apply to free-standing cells, such as:

Relative Position: We can place free-standing cells relative to other structures in a report. This allows us to create labels or title cells that will stay associated with a report structure, even if the structures are moved or resize when data is refreshed. This also allows us to have a consistent distance between labels and the report structures that they represent.

Repeat on Every New Page: Soon, we will learn that a report has a page header that allows report structures to repeat at the top of each page in a report. However, if we want a cell that is not in the header to repeat on each page, such as a section header cell, then we can repeat the cell on every new page with this property.

Avoid Page Break in Free-Standing Cell: Sometimes we have a free-standing cell in a section of a report or relative to the end of a table. In this cell, we may have variable length text that may span several rows. Since we do not know if this cell will fit in its entirety, and we may want to display the entire contents on a single page, then we may use this property to avoid a page break in the free-standing cell.

Show When Empty: This is an option to hide a free-standing cell if it's empty.

Background Image: Many report designers use this property to insert a company logo, or some other graphic, into a report.

Notes
_____

Aligning Report Structures

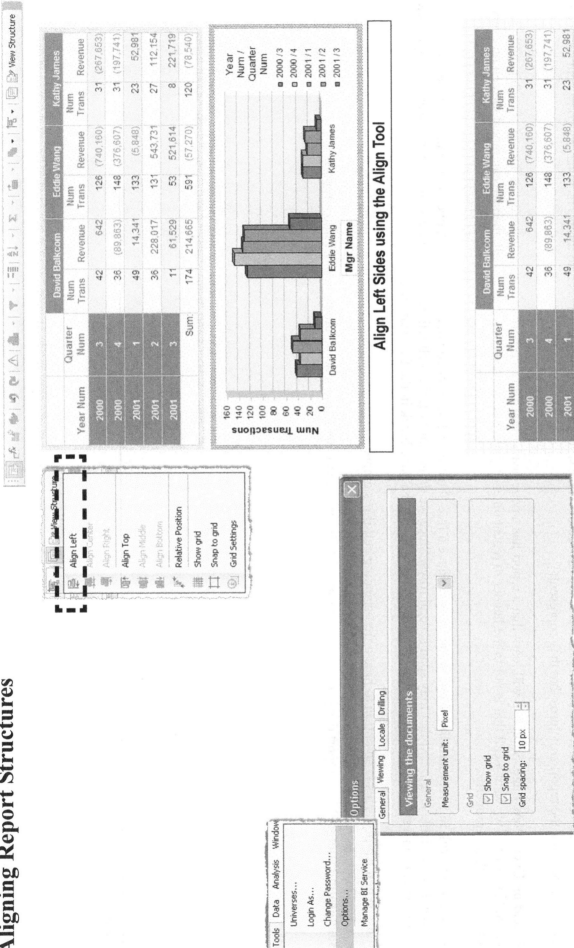

Align Left Sides using the Align Tool

Aligning Report Structures to a Grid

Aligning Report Structures

We can position report structures relative to other report structures or to a grid.

Alignment Control: With this control, we first select two or more report structures. We do this by first clicking on one structure to select it, and then by holding down the [Ctrl] key and clicking on the other report structures to also select them. Then to align them, we click the *Alignment* toolbar button and select the alignment that we are interested in. Web Intelligence will always align to the structure that is more in the desired direction, regardless of the order that the structures were selected. For example, when aligning left, the structures will be aligned to the left-most structure.

Snap to Grid: Another method of aligning is to use the grid. The grid is a matrix of lines that the upper-left of the structures will align to. This is also helpful when evenly distributing report structures. We define the Grid Spacing in the *Tools>Options...* dialog, on the *Viewing* tab.

Relative Position: Earlier, when discussing table properties, we learned about relative positioning. We can also align report structures using this feature, by setting the horizontal position to zero for left alignment or the vertical position to zero for top alignment. The advantage to aligning this way is that if one report structure is moved, then the other will also move to stay in alignment.

Notes

Report Page Structure

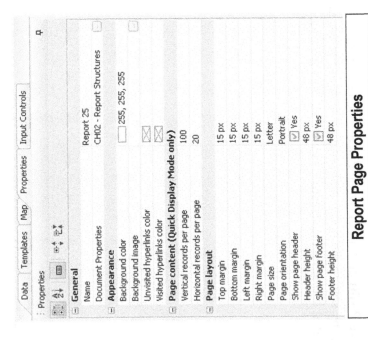

Data | Templates | Map | Properties | Input Controls

Properties

General
Name — Report 25
Document Properties — CH02 - Report Structures

Appearance
Background color — 255, 255, 255
Background image
Unvisited hyperlinks color
Visited hyperlinks color

Page content (Quick Display Mode only)
Vertical records per page — 100
Horizontal records per page — 20

Page layout
Top margin — 15 px
Bottom margin — 15 px
Left margin — 15 px
Right margin — 15 px
Page size — Letter
Page orientation — Portrait
Show page header — Yes
Header height — 48 px
Show page footer — Yes
Footer height — 48 px

Report Page Properties

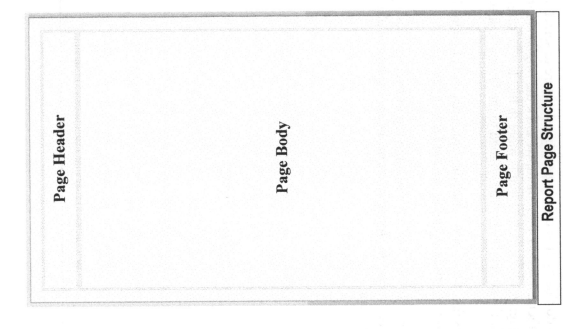

View Structure

Page Header

Page Body

Page Footer

Report Page Structure

Report Page Structure

Each page of a report consists of a page header, a page body, and a page footer.

Page Header: The header usually contains report level information, such as the Title, the Refresh Date, Prompt Information, and so forth.

Page Body: Contains report structures that may span several pages. It also can contain free-standing cells, such as Titles or Section Headers.

Page Footer: Contains report level information, such as Page Numbers, Document Names, Version Numbers, and so forth.

The areas of a report can be sized by placing the mouse cursor over the edge of the border and then dragging the border to size the area. The Page Layout properties can also be used to define the size of the areas. The properties are *Header Height* and *Footer Height*. The height of the Page Body is defined by the (Height of the paper) - (Header Height + Footer Height) - (Top Margin + Bottom Margin). The width of all of the areas is (Width of the paper) - (Left Margin + Right Margin). The margins can also be defined by dragging the borders, or by using the Top, Bottom, Left, and/or Right Margin properties.

When any of the areas are selected, then we can also set the Page Size and the Page Orientation properties. Many times the default page size is A4 and many printers in America cannot print this paper size, so if you are in America, then always check to see if the paper is compatible with your printer. Usually, we use Letter or Legal.

Notes

Chapter Exercise

Manager Report

May 20, 2010

Total Transactions: 2,680
Total Revenue: 1,577,196

Year Num	Quarter Num	David Balkcom		Eddie Wang		Kathy James	
		Num Trans	Revenue	Num Trans	Revenue	Num Trans	Revenue
2000	3	42	642	126	(740,160)	31	(267,653)
2000	4	36	(89,863)	148	(376,607)	31	(197,741)
2001	1	49	14,341	133	(5,848)	23	52,981
2001	2	36	228,017	131	543,731	27	112,154
2001	3	11	61,529	53	521,614	8	221,719
Sum:		174	214,665	591	(57,270)	120	(78,540)

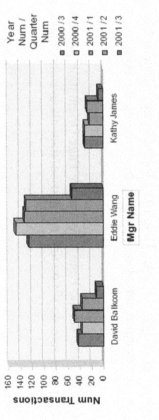

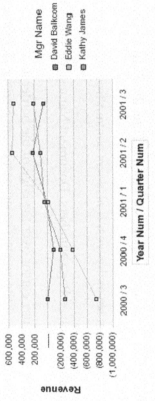

Chapter Exercise

Now let's see if you can put a report together. In this exercise, we will build the report in the graphic.

1. Create data source with Mgr Name, Year Num, Quarter Num, Num Transactions, and Revenue.
2. Create the Header
   a. Drag the Blank Cell template into the Header. Double-click on the blank cell and type Manager Report. Font Size: 16, Bold, remove the border.
   b. Drag the Last Refresh Date template into the header. Format the cell to only show the date. Font Size: 10, Bold, remove the border
   c. Center the text of both header cells, and then use the Align tool to align cell centers.
   d. Create the Measure Summary table by selecting Revenue and Num Transactions on the Data tab, and then dragging them to the lower-right of the header. Drop the Horizontal Table template onto the Measure Summary table. Double-click on each of the header cells and change the text to *Total Transactions:* and *Total Revenue:*. All Cells - Font Size: 8, No Borders, Text Color: Black, Background Color: White. Format the table by setting Alternate Row Color: White. Size rows and columns appropriately.
3. Create the Crosstab
   a. Make sure that the columns in the default table are ordered: Mgr Name, Year Num, Quarter Num, Num Transactions, and Revenue.
   b. Drag Mgr Name up to create the crosstab.
   c. Add the object headers: Click on the edge of the crosstab to select it and check the Display>Show Object Name property. Double-click on the Num Transactions header and change the text to Num Trans. Select all of the object name header values and format the text to Wrap Text, Horizontal Align: Center, Vertical Align: Bottom. Double-click on the Mgr Name object name and press [Delete] to remove the text, and then press [Enter].
   d. Merge the Mgr Name cells over the measure columns by clicking on the Mgr Name header cell over the Num Trans column, and then while holding down the [Ctrl] key, clicking on the empty header cell over the Revenue column. Lastly, click on the Merge Cells button. Center the Mgr Names across the merged cells.
   e. Size the columns and rows in the cross tabs to accommodate the cell contents.
   f. Add the summary information to the crosstab. Click on any of the Num Trans values, and then click the Insert Sum button. Do the same for Revenue. Remove the Num Trans summary column, located on the right side of the crosstab, by right-clicking on the column and removing it. Do the same for Revenue..

Notes

Chapter Exercise (Continued)

Manager Report

May 20, 2010

Total Transactions: 2,680
Total Revenue: 1,577,196

Year Num	Quarter Num	David Balkcom		Eddie Wang		Kathy James	
		Num Trans	Revenue	Num Trans	Revenue	Num Trans	Revenue
2000	3	42	642	126	(740,160)	31	(267,653)
2000	4	36	(89,863)	148	(376,607)	31	(197,741)
2001	1	49	14,341	133	(5,848)	23	52,981
2001	2	36	228,017	131	543,731	27	112,154
2001	3	11	61,529	53	521,614	8	221,719
Sum:		174	214,665	591	(57,270)	120	(78,540)

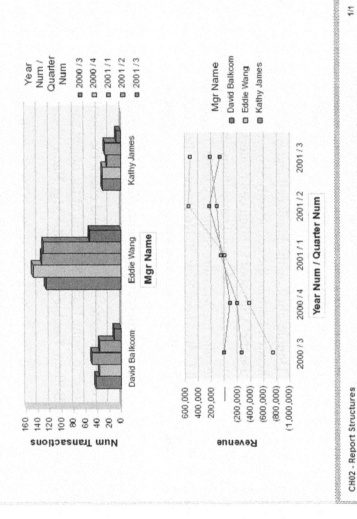

Chapter Exercise (Continued)

4. Create the Bar Chart

   a. Drag Mgr Name, Year Num, Quarter Num, and Num Transactions from the Data tab to the report.

   b. Drag Mgr Name up to create the crosstab.

3. Drag the Vertical Bar Chart template onto the crosstab. Size the chart by dragging the right side of the chart container.

4. Add the legend by checking the *Appearance>Legend* chart property.

5. Create the Line Chart

   a. Drag Mgr Name, Year Num, Quarter Num, and Revenue from the Data tab to the report.

   b. Drag Year Num and Quarter Num up to create the crosstab.

   c. Drag the Vertical Mixed Line Chart template onto the crosstab. Size the chart by dragging the right side of the chart container.

   d. Add the legend by checking the *Appearance>Legend* chart property.

   e. Remove the 3D look by unchecking the *Display>3D Look* property.

6. Align all Three Report Structures

   a. First select any of the three, and then while holding down the [Ctrl] key, select the other two.

   b. Use the Align Left button on the toolbar.

7. Create the Report Footer

   a. Drag the Page Number / Total Pages free-standing cell template the right side of the report footer. Align the cell contents to horizontal right. Remove the borders.

   b. Drag the Document Name free-standing cell template to the left side of the report footer. Align the cell contents to left align. Size the cell to display the entire document name. When sizing the cell, you should make it big enough to accommodate any document name that one may use in the future. Remove the borders.

   c. Align the tops of the cells by using the Align Top toolbar button.

Notes

Summary

Table Displaying Percentages

Mgr Name	Num Transactions	Percentage
David Balkcom	174	6.49%
Eddie Wang	591	22.05%
Kathy James	120	4.48%
Maria Castro	184	6.87%
Robert Denning	120	4.48%
Sean Wilkenson	1,491	55.63%
Percentage:		100.00%

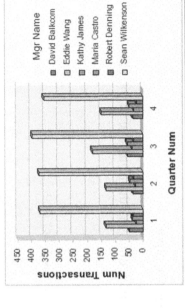

Pie Chart Illustrating Percentages

591
174
120
184
120
1,491

Num Transactions

Mgr Name
- David Balkcom
- Eddie Wang
- Kathy James
- Maria Castro
- Robert Denning
- Sean Wilkenson

Crosstab Displaying Magnitudes

	1	2	3	4
David Balkcom	49	36	53	36
Eddie Wang	133	131	179	148
Kathy James	23	27	39	31
Maria Castro	37	45	54	48
Robert Denning	34	32	33	21
Sean Wilkenson	369	372	397	353

Vertical Grouped Bar Illustrating Magnitudes

Num Transactions

450
400
350
300
250
200
150
100
50
0

Quarter Num

Mgr Name
- David Balkcom
- Eddie Wang
- Kathy James
- Maria Castro
- Robert Denning
- Sean Wilkenson

Summary

In this chapter, we learned about the report structures that are available in Web Intelligence. We learned about Tables, Charts, Crosstabs, and Free-standing Cells. We saw that tables report on list information, crosstabs report on summary information, and charts display magnitude summary information. We learned that crosstabs and charts are very similar, in that they both display summary information. Crosstabs display the exact magnitude of numbers, where charts display the relative magnitudes of numbers. We use crosstabs to observe numbers and percentages, and we use charts to compare numbers and percentages.

We saw that free-standing cells can be used to display report information, such as titles, page numbers, and summaries. Almost every report will contain a free-standing cell, as we need such information on most reports.

Notes

Creating Documents with Business Objects Web Intelligence XI V3

Chapter 3: Sorts, Filters, Ranks and Alerters

In this chapter, we are going to learn how to apply Sorts, Filters, Ranks, and Alerters. These functions help us to create reports the emphasize data of importance.

Introduction

Alerter Placed on Column

Portfolio Name	Year Num	Quarter Num	Revenue
DOW 30	2000	3	(2,578,025)
	2000	4	(1,807,388)
	2001	1	330,350
	2001	2	1,340,450
	2001	3	4,066,066
DOW 30			1,351,453

Portfolio Name	Year Num	Quarter Num	Revenue
Technology	2000	3	(740,160)
	2000	4	(376,607)
	2001	1	(5,848)
	2001	2	543,731
	2001	3	521,614
Technology			(57,270)

Alerter Placed on Row

Portfolio Name	Year Num	Quarter Num	Revenue
DOW 30	2000	3	(2,578,025)
	2000	4	(1,807,388)
	2001	1	330,350
	2001	2	1,340,450
	2001	3	4,066,066
DOW 30			1,351,453

Portfolio Name	Year Num	Quarter Num	Revenue
Technology	2000	3	(740,160)
	2000	4	(376,607)
	2001	1	(5,848)
	2001	2	543,731
	2001	3	521,614
Technology			(57,270)

Text Alerter on Year Half

Portfolio Name	Year Num	Year Half	Revenue
DOW 30	2000	Second Half	(2,578,025)
	2000	Second Half	(1,807,388)
	2001	First Half	330,350
	2001	First Half	1,340,450
	2001	Second Half	4,066,066
DOW 30			1,351,453

Portfolio Name	Year Num	Year Half	Revenue
Technology	2000	Second Half	(740,160)
	2000	Second Half	(376,607)
	2001	First Half	(5,848)
	2001	First Half	543,731
	2001	Second Half	521,614
Technology			(57,270)

Introduction

In all reports we are trying to deliver information from a collection of data. Sometimes, the information is obvious and other times, we need to help people see the information that we want them to see. We emphasize this information with various techniques. In the previous chapter, we learned about report structures. We chose a report structure to help emphasize information. For example, we may use a chart to compare the magnitudes of a measure across a dimension's values. With this chart we can easily see which of the dimension's values were the most productive, or the least productive. We can use other techniques as well, for example Sorting, Filtering, Ranking, and Applying Alerters.

We use sorts to help place the significant information near the top of a report. For example, we may sort a report so that the most productive dimension values are at the top of a report. Sometimes, we know which dimension values are the most productive, and instead of showing all values, we may choose to just show the productive values by using a filter. Other times, we may not know which values are the most productive, and we want to see the top most productive values. We can use the ranking feature to show only the top most productive values. Maybe, we have a threshold that we want to use to define if a value is productive or not. We can use Alerters to highlight the most productive and the least productive values in a report. With alerters, there is no need to place filters or sorts to emphasize the information, and we can choose the sort the data in some other convenient order.

Notes

_____

Applying Sorts

None ✓
Ascending
Descending
Custom sort....

View Structure

Table Default Sort

Portfolio Name	Year Num	Quarter Num	Revenue
Alternative Energy	2001	2	228,017
Alternative Energy	2001	3	61,529
Biotech	2001	2	273,348
Biotech	2001	3	295,519
DOW 30	2001	2	1,340,450
DOW 30	2001	2	4,066,066
Finance	2001	2	253,014
Finance	2001	3	244,383
Media	2001	2	112,154
Media	2001	3	221,719
Technology	2001	2	543,731
Technology	2001	3	521,614

Table Sorted on Revenue

Portfolio Name	Year Num	Quarter Num	Revenue
DOW 30	2001	3	4,066,066
DOW 30	2001	2	1,340,450
Technology	2001	2	543,731
Technology	2001	3	521,614
Biotech	2001	3	295,519
Biotech	2001	2	273,348
Finance	2001	2	253,014
Finance	2001	3	244,383
Alternative Energy	2001	2	228,017
Media	2001	3	221,719
Media	2001	2	112,154
Alternative Energy	2001	3	61,529

Crosstab Default Sort

	2000	2001	Sum:
Alternative Energy	(89,221)	303,886	214,665
Biotech	(369,888)	449,314	79,426
DOW 30	(4,385,413)	5,736,866	1,351,453
Finance	(507,101)	574,563	67,462
Media	(465,394)	386,854	(78,540)
Technology	(1,116,767)	1,059,497	(57,270)
Sum:	(6,933,784)	8,510,980	1,577,196

Crosstab Sorted on Portfolio Revenue

	2000	2001	Sum:
DOW 30	(4,385,413)	5,736,866	1,351,453
Alternative Energy	(89,221)	303,886	214,665
Biotech	(369,888)	449,314	79,426
Finance	(507,101)	574,563	67,462
Technology	(1,116,767)	1,059,497	(57,270)
Media	(465,394)	386,854	(78,540)
Sum:	(6,933,784)	8,510,980	1,577,196

Crosstab Sorted on Yearly Revenue

	2000	2001	Sum:
Sum:	(6,933,784)	8,510,980	
Alternative Energy	(89,221)	303,886	214,665
Biotech	(369,888)	449,314	79,426
DOW 30	(4,385,413)	5,736,866	1,351,453
Finance	(507,101)	574,563	67,462
Media	(465,394)	386,854	(78,540)
Technology	(1,116,767)	1,059,497	(57,270)

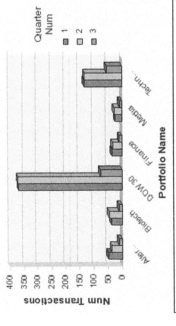

Chart Default Sort

Chart Sorted on Num Transactions Measure

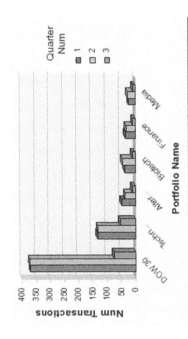

Chart Structure View

Applying Sorts

We sort data in a report structure to help others understand the purpose of a structure. For example, if the structure is sorted by department, then we may assume that the structure is a report on departments. If the structure is sorted by descending revenue, then we may assume the purpose is to show us the top performing departments. We can sort columns Ascending, Descending, or by Applying a Custom Sort.

Tables: The default sort for a table is leftmost column first, then the next, and so forth. If we want to change this sort, we just click on any cell in the column, and then click the *Apply/Remove Sort* toolbar button.

Crosstabs: Crosstabs are a little different than tables, because they can sort vertically and horizontally. The default is ascending dimension values in the leftmost header column and the topmost header row. To change the default, select any value in either header and click the *Apply/Remove Sort* button. If you click on one of the measures and sort it, then the total value of a row's measures will sort vertically, as seen in the *Crosstab Sorted on Portfolio Revenue* graphic. Once in a while, we want to sort the columns based on the total value of the measures in the column. To do this, we move the measure up into the header and sort it, as seen in the *Crosstab Sorted on Yearly Revenue* graphic.

Charts: Charts can be sorted by the dimension values along an axis or by the magnitudes of the data values. If a sort is applied to a table or crosstab when a chart template is applied it, then the sort will remain in the chart. To set or modify a sort in a chart, we enter structure mode by clicking the *View Structure* button, and then apply a sort to one of the objects in the chart control, as seen in the *Chart Structure View* graphic. To apply the sort, we just click on one of the objects, and then click the *Apply/Remove Sort* toolbar button.

Exercise: Applying Sorts

1. Create a query with Portfolio Name, Year Num, Quarter Num, and Revenue.
2. Select Revenue by clicking on any revenue in the Revenue column.
3. Click the little arrow by the Apply/Remove Sorts button, and select *Descending* from the drop down menu.
4. Drag Portfolio Name, Year Num, and Revenue from the data tab to create another table.
5. Drag the Year Num object from the table to just above the table to create a crosstab.
6. Click on Revenue and sort it Descending.
7. Drag Portfolio Name, Year Num, and Revenue from the data tab to create another table.
8. Drag the Year Num object from the table to just above the table to create a crosstab.
9. Drag the Vertical Grouped template from the Charts templates onto the crosstab.
10. Switch to structure mode, click on Revenue in the chart structure, and sort it descending.

Notes

Managing Sorts

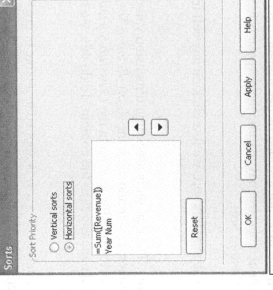

Sorts Dialog for a Table

Horizontal Sorts Dialog for a Crosstab

Vertical Sorts Dialog for a Crosstab

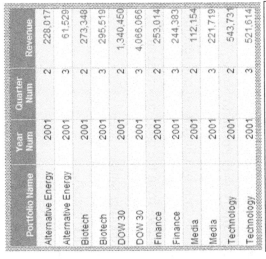

Portfolio Name	Year Num	Quarter Num	Revenue
Alternative Energy	2001	2	228,017
Alternative Energy	2001	3	61,529
Biotech	2001	2	273,348
Biotech	2001	3	295,519
DOW 30	2001	2	1,340,450
DOW 30	2001	3	4,066,066
Finance	2001	2	253,014
Finance	2001	3	244,383
Media	2001	2	112,154
Media	2001	3	221,719
Technology	2001	2	543,73
Technology	2001	3	521,614

Sorted Table

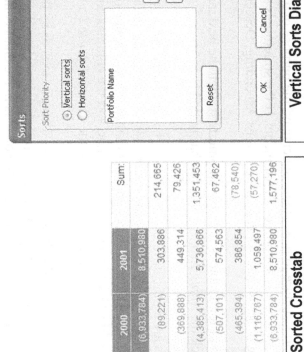

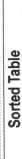

	2000	2001	Sum:
	(6,933,784)	8,510,980	
Alternative Energy	(89,221)	303,886	214,665
Biotech	(369,888)	449,314	79,426
DOW 30	(4,385,413)	5,736,866	1,351,453
Finance	(507,101)	574,563	67,462
Media	(465,394)	386,854	(78,540)
Technology	(1,116,767)	1,059,497	(57,270)
Sum:	(6,933,784)	8,510,980	1,577,196

Sorted Crosstab

Managing Sorts

Once in a while, we will place a sort on an object and nothing will seem to happen. Nothing happens, because the report structure is already sorted on some other objects that have priority over the newly added sort. For our new sort to have affect, we will need to modify the sort order or delete some of the existing sorts.

Deleting a Sort: If we know a sort exists, then we can simply select the sorted object, and then click the *Apply/Remove Sort* toolbar button. If we are not sure if a sort exists on an object, then we can select the object and observe the *Apply/Remove Sort* toolbar button. If it is depressed, then a sort exists. This means that we can determine the objects that have a sort placed on them by selecting each of the objects in turn, and observing the *Apply/Remove Sort* toolbar button.

Modifying Existing Sort Priority: Alright, it seems a little unreasonable to have to click every object in a report structure to determine if there is a sort on the object, and when we do determine that there is a sort, we still are not sure of the sort priority. This is why Web intelligence has the *Sorts* property in the Properties section for report structures. When we click the little (...) button on the Sorts property, the Sorts dialog is displayed. This dialog displays all of the sorts placed on a report structure. We can change the priority by rearranging the objects in the list. Notice that crosstabs (and most charts) have two tabs in the Sorts dialog - Vertical and Horizontal. These report structures can be sorted both horizontally and vertically.

We can also use the Sorts dialog to remove an existing sort from an object. To do this, click on the object in the list to select it, and then press the [Delete] key.

Exercise: Manage Sorts

1. Create a query with Portfolio Name, Year Num, Quarter Num, and Revenue.
2. Place a sort on Portfolio Name, Year Num and Quarter Num in the default table.
3. Select the table by clicking on the edge of the table.
4. Click on the Properties tab to select it.
5. Click on the plus (+) in front of the Sorts section, and then click on the little button in the Sorts Priority section.
6. Check out the Sorts dialog and the objects in the list. The sort priorities can be altered by rearranging the objects in the list. You can also delete an existing sort, by first selecting it, and then pressing the [Delete] key.

Notes

Custom Sorts

Trans Date	Num Transactions	Revenue
Sunday	1	62,160
Monday	440	(780,229)
Tuesday	561	(715,408)
Wednesday	545	(949,281)
Thursday	521	1,207,614
Friday	612	2,752,339

Custom Sort for Days

Trans Date	Num Transactions	Revenue
Friday	612	2,752,339
Monday	440	(780,229)
Sunday	1	62,160
Thursday	521	1,207,614
Tuesday	561	(715,408)
Wednesday	545	(949,281)

Default Sort for Days

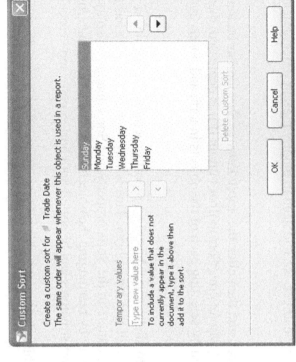

Custom Sort Dialog (Custom Sort)

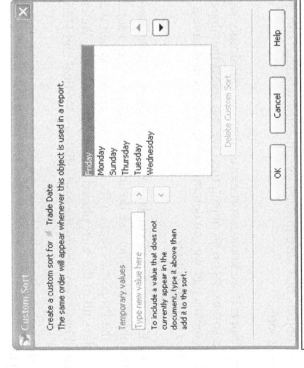

Custom Sort Dialog (Default Sort)

Custom Sorts

Dimension values don't always sort as we would like them to. For example, day and month names sort alphabetically, not chronologically. Also, numbers and dates that have been converted to text sort alphabetically, not numerically or chronologically. In addition, we may want to sort information, such as business departments in a non-alphabetical way. To override the default sorts of objects, we use *Custom Sorts*.

We apply custom sorts to objects, by selecting them in a report structure and then clicking the *Custom Sort...* menu item. You can also right-click on a selected object in a report structure, and then select *Sorts>Custom Sort...* from the pop-up menu. The Custom Sort dialog will be displayed and populated with the values of the selected object. We simply arranged the values in the list to the desired sort order. If there are values missing, such as Wednesday from the days of the week, then we can add the values to the list using the *Temporary Values* control. To use this control, type a value into the edit field, and then either press [Enter] or the Greater Than [>] key to move the value into the list. If missing values are not added to the list, then any new values added during future query refreshes will appear at the bottom of the sort.

The custom sort will apply to the object in all report structures in a document. This means that the sort order is applied to the object and not the table in which it is placed. Also, once the sort is defined, ascending and descending sorts can be applied to the object within report structures. To apply differing custom sorts to an object, a variable can be created that encapsulates the query variable. (We will discuss how to create variables in a future chapter.) Then, a different custom sort can be defined for each variable created from the query variable.

Exercise: Custom Sorts

8. Create a query with Day Name, Num Transactions, and Revenue.
9. Click on any day in the Day Name column, to select it.
10. Click the down arrow button, next to the *Apply/Remove Sort* button, and select *Custom Sort...*
11. Arrange the Days in the list Sunday, Monday, Tuesday, Wednesday, Thursday, Friday, Saturday.
12. Add Saturday to the Sort List.
    a. Type Saturday into the *Temporary Values* edit field.
    b. Click the *Move Right* (>) button to add Saturday to the list.
    c. Make sure that it appears after Friday in the list.

Notes

Sorting Sections and Breaks

Default Sort on Section

Biotech   449,314

Year Num	Quarter Num	Num Transactions	Revenue
2001	1	37	(119,552)
2001	2	45	273,348
2001	3	11	295,519

DOW 30   5,736,866

Year Num	Quarter Num	Num Transactions	Revenue
2001	1	369	330,350
2001	2	372	1,340,450
2001	3	75	4,066,066

Finance   574,563

Year Num	Quarter Num	Num Transactions	Revenue
2001	1	34	77,166
2001	2	32	253,014
2001	3	9	244,383

Sorted Dscending Revenue

Biotech   449,314

Year Num	Quarter Num	Num Transactions	Revenue
2001	1	37	(119,552)
2001	2	45	273,348
2001	3	11	295,519

Default Sort on Break

Portfolio Name	Year Num	Quarter Num	Revenue
Biotech	2001	1	(119,552)
	2001	2	273,348
	2001	3	295,519
Biotech			449,314
DOW 30	2001	1	330,350
	2001	2	1,340,450
	2001	3	4,066,066
DOW 30			5,736,866
Finance	2001	1	77,166
	2001	2	253,014
	2001	3	244,383
Finance			574,563

Sorted Descending on Revenue

Portfolio Name	Year Num	Quarter Num	Revenue
DOW 30	2001	1	330,350
	2001	2	1,340,450
	2001	3	4,066,066
DOW 30			5,736,866
Finance	2001	1	77,166
	2001	2	253,014
	2001	3	244,383
Finance			574,563
Biotech	2001	1	(119,552)
	2001	2	273,348
	2001	3	295,519
Biotech			449,314

Portfolio Totals

Portfolio Name	Revenue
Biotech	449,314
DOW 30	5,736,866
Finance	574,563

Formula used in Break

= [Revenue] In ([Portfolio Name])

Sorting Sections and Breaks

When a Section or a break is created from an object, the objects will be sorted and the sort will apply to the section or break. This works great in most cases, but what if we wanted to break on an object, but sort the report structure by the total of a measure in the report?

Sorting Sections: We create sections by dragging a dimension value onto a report. This creates sections that are filtered and sorted by the values of the dimension. Then, we can place any report structures into the sections. For example, we can insert charts, crosstabs, and/or free-standing cells. Free-standing calls are similar to the section master cell, as they are both free-standing cells. The sections are originally sorted by the dimension contained in the section's master cell. To override this default sort, we simply insert a data object into a free-standing cell in the section, and then apply a sort to this free-standing cell. We apply the sort by clicking on the cell to select it, and then clicking the *Apply/Remove* Sort toolbar button.

Sorting Breaks: When we place a break on an object in a report structure, then the breaks will be sorted by the object that was used to define the break. This is different from sections, where can override the default sort. This means that if we want to sort the breaks by a measure and not the dimension, then we have to create a new column in the table with a formula similar to: = *[Measure Obj] In [Dimension Obj]*. We have not yet studied this type of formula yet, but we will in a later chapter. This formula simply creates totals for the dimension values in a table. Then, we apply the break to the column with the totals formula. Finally, we must also apply a break on the column with the Dimension object from the formula, as this will prevent from grouping dimensions with identical totals. You can hide the formula column by removing borders and formats, and then sizing it as narrow as possible.

Exercise: Create a Table

1. Create a query with Portfolio Name, Year Num, Quarter Num, Num Transactions, and Revenue.
2. Drag Portfolio Name above the table to create Portfolio Name sections.
3. Drag the *Blank Cell* template from the *Free-Standing Cells>Formula and Text Cells* section on the Templates tab, and drop it to the right of the Portfolio Name master cell in the section.
4. Drag Revenue from the Data tab into the newly added blank free-standing cell.
5. Click on the newly added Revenue cell and click the small down arrow to the right of the *Apply/Remove Sort* button, and select Descending from the pop-up menu.

Notes

Applying Quick Filters

Portfolio Name	Year Num	Revenue
Alternative Energy	2000	(89,221)
Alternative Energy	2001	303,886
Biotech	2000	(369,888)
Biotech	2001	449,314
DOW 30	2000	(4,385,413)
DOW 30	2001	5,736,866
Finance	2000	(507,101)
Finance	2001	574,563
Media	2000	(465,394)
Media	2001	386,854
Technology	2000	(1,116,767)
Technology	2001	1,059,497
		1,577,196

Unfiltered Table

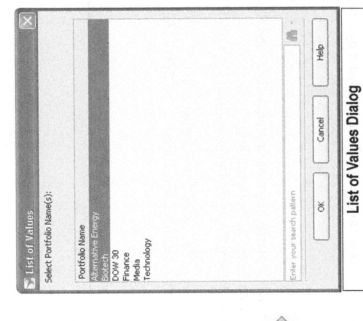

List of Values Dialog

Portfolio Name	Year Num	Revenue
Alternative Energy	2000	(89,221)
Alternative Energy	2001	303,886
Biotech	2000	(369,888)
Biotech	2001	449,314

Filtered Table

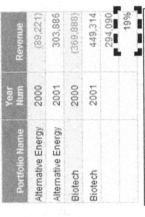

Portfolio Name	Year Num	Revenue
Alternative Energy	2000	(89,221)
Alternative Energy	2001	303,886
Biotech	2000	(369,888)
Biotech	2001	449,314
		294,090
		19%

Filtered Table with Percent

=[Revenue] / NoFilter([Revenue])

Percent Formula

Remove a Filter

Applying Quick Filters

Report structures can have many dimension values in a column. We are sometimes interested in only one or a few of these values. To only examine a few values in a report structure, we can place a *Quick Filter* on the dimension object in the column.

To apply a quick filter, we first select any value in the column by clicking on a cell in the column. We then click on the *Add Filter* toolbar button, which will display the List of Values dialog populated with all of the values (in the data provider) of the selected dimension. We select a value by clicking on any value in the list. To select multiple values, we can hold down the [Ctrl] key as we click on additional values. Click the *OK* button to dismiss the dialog and apply the filter.

Many times, when we place a filter on a structure to see values of interest, and in addition we want to see how these values compare to the values that we are not showing. We can do this by dividing the total of the values that we are displaying by the total of all values, even the ones that we are not displaying. To do this, we can use the following formula: = *[Revenue] / NoFilter([Revenue])*. We will learn more about the *NoFilter* function in a later chapter, but it is good to look at it here in a context that we can use it in. So, in the above example, the total of the visible values is 294,090. The total of all values is 1,577,196. Therefore, the percentage of the values we are interested in is 19% (294,090 / 1,577,196).

To remove a filter, select the column and then, click the *Remove Filter* toolbar button.

Exercise: Apply a Quick Filter

1. Create a report with Portfolio Name, Year Num, and Revenue.
2. Click on any Portfolio Name in the table, to select the data column.
3. Click the *Add Filter* toolbar button, to display the List of Values dialog.
4. Select a few portfolio names. To select multiple values, hold down the [CTRL] key while selecting.
5. Click OK to apply the filter.

Notes

_____

The Report Filter Pane

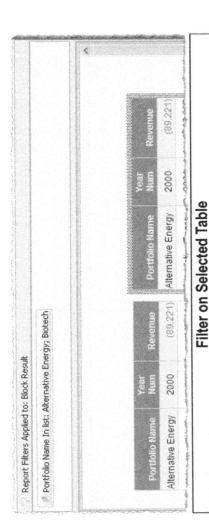

Filter on Selected Table

Available Filter Operators

Equal To	Between
Not Equal To	Not Between
Greater Than	In List
Greater Than or Equal To	Not In List
Less Than	Is Null
Less Than or Equal To	Is Not Null

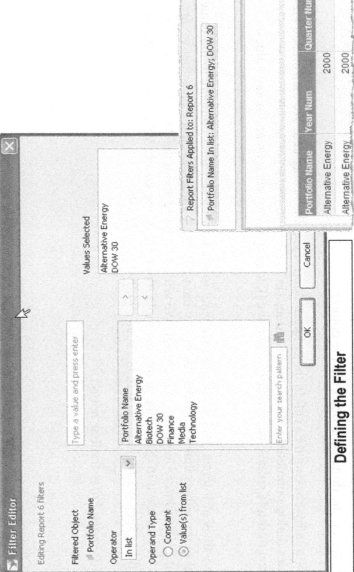

Defining the Filter

Filter on Report

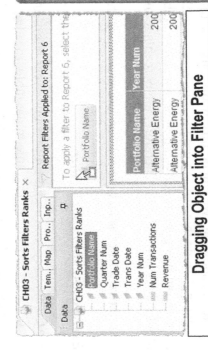

Dragging Object into Filter Pane

The Report Filter Pane

Quick filters work well, but sometimes we need to manage our filters more closely. The Filter Pane allows us to do this by showing us what filters are placed on report structures in a report. To open the Filter Pane, we click the *Show/Hide Filter Pane* toolbar button. Then, the filters applied to a selected report structure will be displayed in the pane, as seen in the *Filter on Selected Table* graphic.

We can also create filters using the pane, we do this by first selecting a report structure, and then by dragging an object into the pane from the Data tab. This will display the *Filter Editor* dialog. With this dialog, we first select an operator from the *Operator* drop list, and then we either type in a constant value or we select *Value(s) from List*, as seen in the *Defining the Filter* graphic. The available operators are also displayed in the Available Filter Operators dialog.

We can place filters on the report by first selecting the report (any white-space on the report), on sections by selecting a section (master cell or white space), or any report structure by first selecting it. To delete a filter, select it in the pane and press the [Delete] key.

Exercise: Report Filter Pane

1. Create a report with Portfolio Name, Year Num, and Revenue.
2. Click the *Show/Hide Filter Pane* toolbar button to show the Filter Pane.
3. Set Table Filter
   a. Click on the table to select it.
   b. Drag Portfolio Name from the Data tab into the Filter pane.
   c. Click the Value(s) from List option, to display the list of Portfolio Names.
   d. Double-click on at least four of the portfolio names to add them to the Values Selected list. Click OK to apply the filter.
4. Set Report Level filter
   a. Drag Portfolio Name, Year Num, and Revenue from the Data tab unto the report, to create another table. Notice that the previous filter has no effect on the newly inserted table.
   b. Click anywhere on the report, where there is no table or free-standing cell, to select the report.
   c. Drag Year Num from the Data tab into the Filter pane.
   d. Click the Value(s) from List option, to display the list of Year Nums.
   e. Double-click on the year 2001 to add it to the Values Selected list. Click OK to apply the filter. (This filter should apply to both tables)

Notes

Filters on Measures

Default Table (Which Includes all of the Data from the Query)

Portfolio Name	Trans Date	Year Num	Quarter Num	Revenue
DOW 30	7/13/01	2001	3	2,657,890
DOW 30	7/12/01	2001	3	526,604
Technology	7/13/01	2001	3	499,836
DOW 30	7/5/01	2001	3	298,503
DOW 30	7/10/01	2001	3	297,489
Finance	7/13/01	2001	3	260,523
DOW 30	5/8/01	2001	2	219,213
DOW 30	1/25/01	2001	1	215,100
Biotech	7/13/01	2001	3	211,317
Technology	8/31/00	2000	3	208,197
DOW 30	4/30/01	2001	2	207,675
DOW 30	6/5/01	2001	2	195,688
DOW 30	11/1/00	2000	4	180,125
DOW 30	5/22/01	2001	2	173,025
DOW 30	2/7/01	2001	1	158,375
DOW 30	5/21/01	2001	2	158,125
DOW 30	12/7/00	2000	4	156,425
Media	7/13/01	2001	3	155,906
DOW 30	7/9/01	2001	3	153,858
DOW 30	9/12/00	2000	3	152,000
DOW 30	10/31/00	2000	4	150,175
DOW 30	3/30/01	2001	1	150,050
DOW 30	5/23/01	2001	2	149,950
DOW 30	3/8/01	2001	1	149,450
Finance	2/1/01	2001	1	147,548
DOW 30	4/19/01	2001	2	145,925
Technology	9/5/00	2000	3	143,782
DOW 30	5/1/01	2001	2	143,050
DOW 30	5/9/01	2001	2	135,700
DOW 30	4/24/01	2001	2	133,888
DOW 30	9/7/00	2000	3	127,262

Detail Rows Sorted Descending

Report Level Revenue > 500,000

Portfolio Name	Trans Date	Year Num	Quarter Num	Revenue
DOW 30	7/13/01	2001	3	2,657,890
DOW 30	7/12/01	2001	3	526,604

Table Level Revenue > 500,000

Portfolio Name	Trans Date	Year Num	Quarter Num	Revenue
DOW 30	7/13/01	2001	3	2,657,890
DOW 30	7/12/01	2001	3	526,604

Reaggregated Table (Trans Date Column Removed)

Portfolio Name	Year Num	Quarter Num	Revenue
Alternative Energy	2000	3	642
Alternative Energy	2000	4	(89,863)
Alternative Energy	2001	1	14,341
Alternative Energy	2001	2	228,017
Alternative Energy	2001	3	61,529
DOW 30	2000	3	(2,578,025)
DOW 30	2000	4	(1,807,388)
DOW 30	2001	1	330,350
DOW 30	2001	2	1,340,450
DOW 30	2001	3	4,066,066
Technology	2000	3	(740,160)
Technology	2000	4	(376,607)
Technology	2001	1	(5,848)
Technology	2001	2	543,731
Technology	2001	3	521,614

Report Level Revenue > 500,000

Portfolio Name	Year Num	Quarter Num	Revenue
DOW 30	2001	3	3,184,494

Table Level Revenue > 500,000

Portfolio Name	Year Num	Quarter Num	Revenue
DOW 30	2001	2	1,340,450
DOW 30	2001	3	4,066,066
Technology	2001	2	543,731
Technology	2001	3	521,614

Filters on Measures

Measures are objects that usually have a default function associated with them that cause them to re-aggregate whenever its context on a report changes. For example, if someone deletes a column, the measure will re-aggregate to the new context. This makes it difficult to define a filter for the measure values, as they are not constant. This is why the Quick Filter toolbar button is not enabled for measures.

Web Intelligence does allow filters to be defined for measures via the Filter Pane. However, the filter will apply to the context in which the measure object is placed. This means that if the filter is applied to the report, then it will apply directly to the data on a report level, which is independent of the structures in the report. If it is placed on a report structure, such as a table, then it will apply to the aggregate at the table level. This can be seen in the two groups of tables in the graphic. The default table on the left is aggregated exactly the same as the data provider for the document. Therefore, the filter on Revenue, on both the report and table levels, yields identical results.

The table on the right has re-aggregated, because the Trans Date column has been removed. Now, the Revenues in the table are different than the ones in the data provider, because they have re-aggregated to their new context. The report level filter yields the total of all revenues that are greater than 500,000, which is 3,184,494 (2,657,890 + 526,604). The table level filter yields all rows in the table where Revenue is greater than 500,000. Therefore, care must be taken when applying filters to measures in a report, because they may not yield the desired results.

Notes

Input Controls

Report from Previous Page Using Input Control

Portfolio Name	Year Num	Quarter Num	Revenue
DOW 30	2001	3	4,066,066
DOW 30	2001	2	1,340,450
Technology	2001	2	543,731
Technology	2001	3	521,614

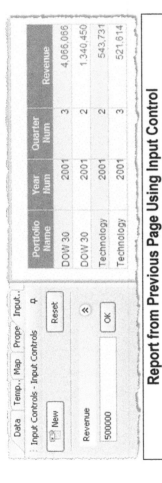

1) Click New on the Input Controls Tab

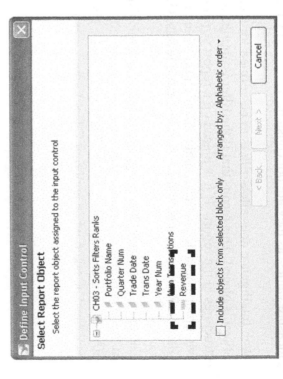

2) Select an Object to Place Filter On

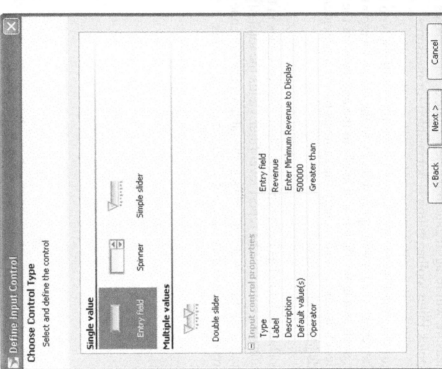

3) Define Control Parameters

4) Select Filter Level

Input Controls

Input controls allow people to adjust filter values through a graphical interface, and without modifying the existing filter. On the previous page, we placed a filter on a table where Revenue is Greater Than 500,000. In this example, we have created an Entry Field control that allows viewers of the report to change the value of the filter operand. In the graphic, the value is 500,000, but this value can be changed through the control.

We create input controls by first clicking on the *Input Controls* tab, and then by clicking *New* to start the Input Control Wizard. In the first step of the wizard, we select an object for the control to work on. The next step allows you to select from the controls that may be compatible with the type of object that you selected. This means that the available controls will vary depending on what object you have selected. Finally, we select which report elements the control should apply to. Remember, since we are using a measure, we need to be careful not to select objects that are not compatible with the level of aggregation that we are focusing on. In this, case, I just applied it to the table level aggregate.

More than one input control can be defined for an object. If more than one is defined, than the control logic will be And'ed together. For example, if one control was Revenue Greater Than 500,000 and another control was Revenue Less Than 1,000,000, then the resulting logic would be: *Revenue Greater Than 500,000 AND Revenue Less Than 1,000,000.*

Exercise: Input Controls

1. Create a report with Portfolio Name, Year Num, Quarter Num, and Revenue.
2. Activate the Input Controls tab, and then click the *New* button.
3. Select Revenue on the first step of the *Define Input Control* wizard, and then click *Next.*
4. Select the Single Value *Entry Field* control.
5. Change the Operator to *Greater Than or Equal to,* and then click *Next.*
6. Select *Report Body* in the Assign Report Elements step of the wizard, and then click *Finish.*
7. Enter values into the control and see how it affects the data in the table.

Notes

Modifying Input Controls

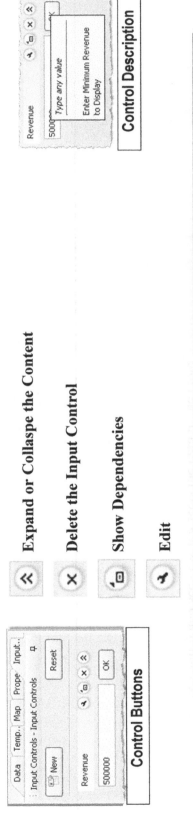

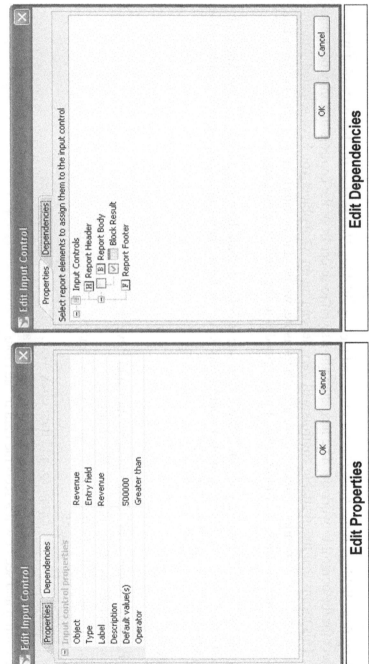

Expand or Collaspe the Content

Delete the Input Control

Show Dependencies

Edit

Control Buttons

Control Description

Edit Dependencies

Edit Properties

Modifying Input Controls

Input controls apply filter through a graphical control. This means that we may not always know how the filter is being applied. Therefore, Web Intelligence has given us a way to modify the input controls through four buttons that are associated with the control. By default, the buttons are not displayed. To see the buttons, place the mouse cursor over the control.

Expand or Collapse the Content: This button will show or hide the input associated with the control. This is most useful when there are many controls on a report, because we can show only the inputs that we are currently working with.

Delete the Input Control: This button will delete the filter and the control from the report.

Show Dependencies: Input controls can be applied to different report elements, including tables, crosstabs, charts, sections, and reports. It is very important to know which report elements that an input control is operating on. To find out which elements are assigned to a control, click the Show Dependencies button.

Edit: The Edit button allows you to examine and modify the Properties and Dependencies of an input control.

   Properties: We can see the Object that the control applies to and the type of the control. However, we cannot change these two properties. We can modify the Label, Description, Default Value(s), and the Operator.

   Dependencies: We select/modify the report elements that the control will apply to.

Notes

Numeric Input Controls

Edit Control and Properties

Spinner Control and Properties

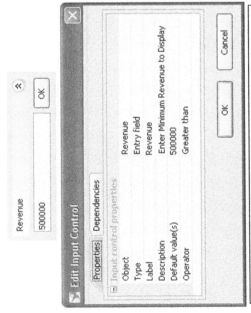

Slider Control and Properties

Double Slider Control and Properties

Numeric Input Controls

There are four types of numeric input controls, at the time of this writing - Edit, Spinner, Slider and Double Slider. All expect one number for input, except the Double Slider, which expects two: a minimum and a maximum value.

Edit: The Edit control expects a single number to be typed into the input field. Its operators are Equal to, Not Equal to, Greater Than, Greater Than or Equal to, Less Than, and Less Than or Equal to.

Spinner: The input to the Spinner is defined by clicking on the up/down arrows located on the right-side of the edit field associated with the control. The input number will increment by the value in the Increment property field of the Properties tab when creating or modifying the control. If the increment value is 100,000, then the control will increment as follows: 100,000, 200,000, and so forth. A value can also be typed into the edit field. Its operators are Equal to, Not Equal to, Greater Than, Greater Than or Equal to, Less Than, and Less Than or Equal to.

Slider: The input to the Slider is defined by sliding the slider left and right on the control. The input number will increment by the value in the Increment property field of the Properties tab, which is assigned when creating or modifying the control. If the increment value is 100,000, then the control will increment as follows: 100,000, 200,000, and so forth. Its operators are Equal to, Not Equal to, Greater Than, Greater Than or Equal to, Less Than, and Less Than or Equal to.

Double Slider: The input to the Double Slider is defined by sliding the sliders left and right on the control to define the minimum and maximum values. The input number will increment by the value in the Increment property field of the Properties tab, which is assigned when creating or modifying the control. If the increment value is 100,000, then the control will increment as follows: 100,000, 200,000, and so forth. Its operators are Between and Not Between.

Notes

Character Input Controls

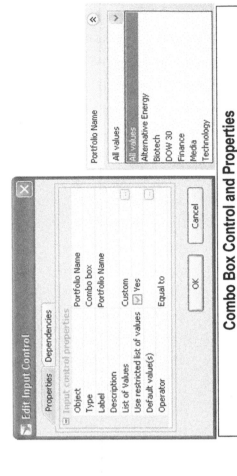

Edit Control and Properties

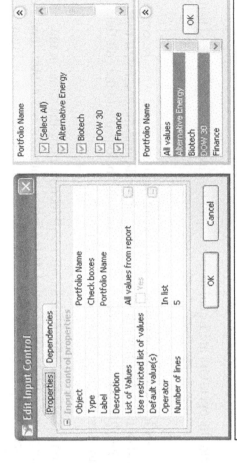

Combo Box Control and Properties

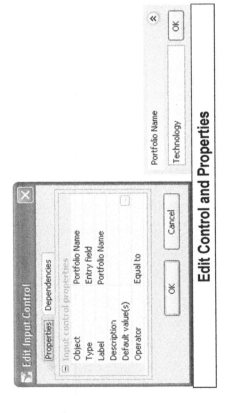

Single Input Controls: Radio Buttons / List Box and Properties

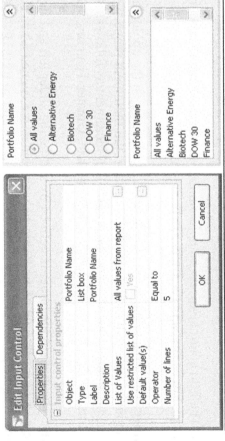

Multiple Input Controls: Check Boxes / List Box and Properties

Character Input Controls

At the time of this writing there are six input controls. Four single input controls, Edit, Combo Box, Radio Buttons and List Box, and two multiple input controls, Check Boxes and Multiple List Box.

Edit: The Edit control expects a character entry that exactly matches one of the object's values, including its case. To have the Edit control show all values, there should be no value entered in the edit field. Available operators are Equal to, Not Equal to, Greater Than, Greater Than or Equal to, Less Than, and Less Than or Equal to.

(With the following controls you can limit the values in the list with the *List of Values* property, by creating a Custom list.)

Combo Box: Not sure why this is called a combo box, as it is really a drop list. Combo boxes infer that you can type an entry into the edit field, but with this control, we can only pick from the list. Available operators are Equal to, Not Equal to, Greater Than, Greater Than or Equal to, Less Than, and Less Than or Equal to.

Radio Buttons / List Box: These two controls are basically the same, as they both display the available values in a list and only one value can be selected. Available operators are Equal to and Not Equal to.

Check Boxes / Multiple List Box: These two controls are also basically the same, as they both display the available values in a list and multiple values can be selected. Available operators are In List and Not In List.

Notes

Displaying Filter Values

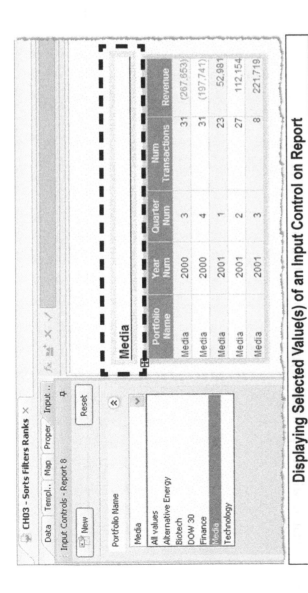

Displaying Filter Values

Displaying Selected Value(s) of an Input Control on Report

Displaying Filtered Value(s)

=ReportFilter([Portfolio Name])

Formula For Filter Value(s)

=ReportFilterSummary("Report Filter Summary")

Formula For Filter Summary

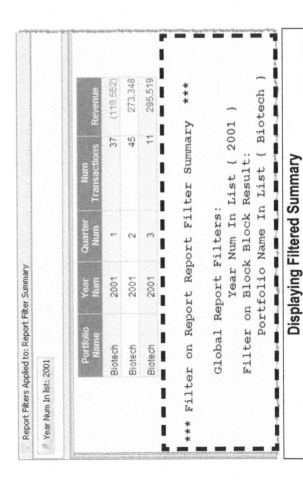

Displaying Filtered Summary

Displaying Filter Values

Filters can be placed on report elements or on the entire report. They can also be applied through the Filter Pane or Input Controls. In addition, when a report is printed, there is no indication if any filters are placed on a report, or if there is a filter, then the filter values are not known. This can make it very difficult for viewers of a report to determine exactly what filters are placed on a report.

Web Intelligence offers two functions that allow the filtered values to be echoed on a report. These functions are ReportFilter and ReportFilterSummary. To use these functions, place a blank free-standing cell on a report and type in the formula. Later, we will learn how to use the formula editor to create such formulas.

Report Filter: This function will only display the values of report level filters and not the values of filters place on report elements, such as tables, crosstabs, and charts. The argument for the function is the name of the object with the filter applied to it.

Report Filter Summary: ReportFilterSummary displays all of the filters on all of the elements in a report. Global filters are filters that are placed on the entire report, as seen in the graphic. This function takes one argument, which is the name of the report in a document. This means that you can display the filters on report other than the report where the values are displayed. If no argument is provided, then all the filter values on all of the reports in a document will be displayed. This is the default, if the ReportFilterSummary free-standing cell from the templates list is used.

Notes

Ranking Dimensions

Table to Rank

Portfolio Name	Year Num	Num Transactions
Alternative Energy	2000	78
Alternative Energy	2001	96
Biotech	2000	91
Biotech	2001	93
DOW 30	2000	675
DOW 30	2001	816
Finance	2000	45
Finance	2001	75
Media	2000	62
Media	2001	58
Technology	2000	274
Technology	2001	317

Context of Rank

Portfolio Name	Num Transactions
DOW 30	1,491
Technology	591
Biotech	184
Alternative Energy	174
Finance	120
Media	120

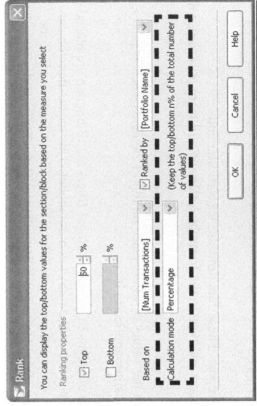

Rank

You can display the top/bottom values for the section/block based on the measure you select

Ranking properties

☑ Top 2

☐ Bottom

Based on [Num Transactions]

Calculation mode Count

☑ Ranked by [Portfolio Name]

(Keep the top/bottom n values)

OK   Cancel   Help

Top Two Portfolios Definition

Top Two Portfolios

Portfolio Name	Year Num	Num Transactions
DOW 30	2000	675
DOW 30	2001	816
Technology	2000	274
Technology	2001	317

Rank

You can display the top/bottom values for the section/block based on the measure you select

Ranking properties

☑ Top 50 %

☐ Bottom %

Based on [Num Transactions]

Calculation mode Percentage

☑ Ranked by [Portfolio Name]

(Keep the top/bottom n% of the total number of values)

OK   Cancel   Help

Top 50% of Portfolios Definition

Top 50% of Portfolios

Portfolio Name	Year Num	Num Transactions
DOW 30	2000	675
DOW 30	2001	816
Technology	2000	274
Technology	2001	317
Biotech	2000	91
Biotech	2001	93

Ranking Dimensions

Previously, we learned that filters placed on report elements will allow us to display only data of interest from a document's data provider. We set these filters by selecting text values or using simple logic, such as equal to, greater than, and so forth. Rankings are similar to filters, but we define them to show the top or bottom ranked dimensions in a data provider. We rank the dimensions on a measure associated with the dimensions.

To apply a rank to a report structure, we select the structure, and then click on the *Apply/Remove Ranking* button on the Reporting toolbar. Clicking this button will display the Rank dialog, where we define the parameters for a rank. We can select either *Top* or *Bottom*, or both *Top* and *Bottom*. We then select a measure object, in the *Based on* drop list, to base the rank on. If we want to rank the measure in the context of the report structure, then we do not check the *Ranked by* control. This will simply rank the values according to the measure's value in each row. However, if we want to rank a particular dimension in the report, then we check the *Ranked by* control, and then select the dimension in the drop list. The next step is to select the calculation mode, of which there are four to select from – Count, Percentage, Cumulative Sum, and Cumulative Percentage.

Count: Will simply rank the top n dimensions. In the graphic, we are ranking the top two Portfolio Names based on Num Transactions. Therefore, the result in the ranked table has two portfolio names.

Percentage: Will rank the percentage of dimension values available. For example, Portfolio Names has six values, and in the example, we are ranking 50% of the Portfolio Names. Therefore, the resulting ranked table has three Portfolio Names (50% of six is Three).

Exercise: Ranking Dimensions

1. Create a report with Portfolio Name, Year Num, and Num Transactions.
2. Click on any Portfolio Name in the Portfolio Name column.
3. Click the *Apply/Remove Ranking* toolbar button.
4. Make sure the *Top* option is checked, and then enter '2' into the *Top* control.
5. Select Revenue in the *Based on* control.
6. Check the *Rank by* option, and then select Portfolio Name in the drop list.
7. The Calculation Mode is Count.
8. Click OK to apply the Ranking.

Notes

Cumulative Ranks

Portfolio Name	Year Num	Num Transactions
DOW 30	2000	675
DOW 30	2001	816
Technology	2000	274
Technology	2001	317
Biotech	2000	91
Biotech	2001	93

Top Cumulative Sum (2400)

Portfolio Name	Num Transactions	Cumulative Sum
DOW 30	1,491	1,491
Technology	591	2,082
Biotech	184	2,266
Alternative Energy	174	2,440
Finance	120	2,560
Media	120	2,680

Cumulative Sum

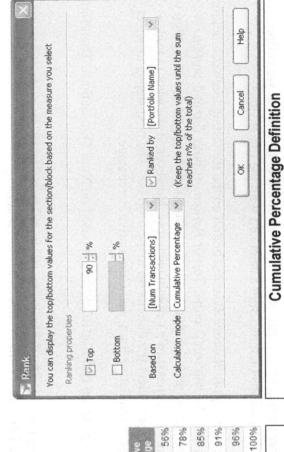

Cumulative Sum Definition

Portfolio Name	Year Num	Num Transactions
DOW 30	2000	675
DOW 30	2001	816
Technology	2000	274
Technology	2001	317
Biotech	2000	91
Biotech	2001	93

Top Cumulative 90%

Portfolio Name	Num Transactions	Cumulative Percentage
DOW 30	1,491	56%
Technology	591	78%
Biotech	184	85%
Alternative Energy	174	91%
Finance	120	96%
Media	120	100%

Cumulative Percentages

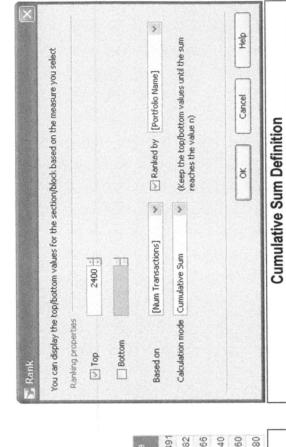

Cumulative Percentage Definition

Cumulative Ranks

Cumulative ranks use a running total to determine the dimension values to rank. Cumulative Sum uses a running sum, and Cumulative Percentage uses a running percentage.

Cumulative Sum: This will rank dimensions until the total of the measure values associated with the ranked dimension values is equal to, but not greater than the number entered into the Top or Bottom edit controls. In the example, in the graphic, the number entered into the Top edit field is 2,400. Therefore, the dimensions included in the ranked table will have a total measure value equal to or less than 2,400. The Cumulative Sum table, in the graphic, shows the running sum of the Num Transactions with the Num Transactions sorted in descending order. You can see that the dimensions included in the ranked table are the dimensions before the running sum exceeds 2,400.

Cumulative Percentage: This will rank dimensions until the percentage of the total of the measure values associated with the rank dimension values is up to, but not exceeding the percentage in the Top or Bottom edit fields. In the example, the number entered into the Top edit field is 90. Therefore, the sum of the Num Transactions in the ranked table will be 90%, or less than the total of all Num Transaction in the report. The Cumulative Percentages table shows the running percentage of Num Transaction listed in descending order of Num Transactions. You can see that the Top Cumulative 90% table only includes the dimensions up to when the running percentage exceeds 90%.

Notes

___

Ranks and the NoFilter Function

Portfolio Name	Year Num	Num Transactions
DOW 30	2000	675
DOW 30	2001	816
Technology	2000	274
Technology	2001	317
	Top 2:	2,082
	Others:	598
	Percentage:	78%

Top Two Rank

Portfolio Name	Year Num	Num Transactions
DOW 30	2000	675
DOW 30	2001	816
Technology	2000	274
Technology	2001	317
Biotech	2000	91
Biotech	2001	93
	Top 90%	2,266
	Others:	414
	Percentage:	85%

Cumulative 90% Rank

= NoFilter([Num Transactions]) - [Num Transactions]

Others Formula

= [Num Transactions] / NoFilter([Num Transactions])

Percentage Formula

Ranks and the NoFilter Function

Usually, if I create a ranking report, then the next questions are "What is the total of the others?" and "What percentage is that of the total?" This is why I am showing these formulas before we formally cover formulas.

In the Top Two report from the previous exercise, we can see that the top two portfolios generated 78% of the total transactions, and that the other portfolios only had 598 transactions. This information makes the ranking much more useful. For example, what if I told you that oranges were the best selling fruit in the local supermarket? Wouldn't you be interested in what percentage of the total fruit sold were oranges? If there were five different fruits and oranges represented 21% of the total sells, then that would not be too interesting. However, if oranges represented 50% of the total fruit sold, then that would mean something!

Notice in the Cumulative 90% Rank table that the total of the top 90% is 85% of the total. Well that's weird. I thought that we wanted the top 90%. We did, and that's what we got. If Web Intelligence added another dimension, then the total percentage would exceed 90%. Remember that it's up to 90%, but not exceeding.

Exercise: NoFilter Function

8. Sum the Revenues in the table, from the *Ranking Dimensions* exercise, by selecting any Revenue in the column, and then clicking the *Insert Sum* button. (Notice that the sum is the total revenue of only the ranked dimensions.)

9. Insert two rows after the table footer with the sum of Revenue
   a. Click on the Sum in the footer to select a cell in the footer row.
   b. Click the *Insert Row Below* toolbar button three times.

3. In the cell below the sum, type the following: = *NoFilter([Num Transactions]) - [Num Transactions]*

4. In the next cell down, type the following: = *[Num Transactions] / NoFilter([Num Transactions])*

The NoFilter function ignores the ranking filter, and allows the total number of transactions to be summed. We are not using the Sum function, because Sum is the default aggregate function for Num Transactions. So, in these formulas, *[Num Transactions]* represents the ranked total, and *NoFilter ([Num Transactions])* represents the total Num Transactions returned by the data provider.

Notes

Ranks and Report Breaks

Portfolio Name	Year Num	Quarter Num	Year - Quarter	Num Transactions
Alternative Energy	2001	1	2001 - 01	49
	2000	3	2000 - 03	42
Alternative Energy				

Portfolio Name	Year Num	Quarter Num	Year - Quarter	Num Transactions
Biotech	2001	2	2001 - 02	45
	2000	4	2000 - 04	48
Biotech				

Portfolio Name	Year Num	Quarter Num	Year - Quarter	Num Transactions
DOW 30	2001	1	2001 - 01	369
	2001	2	2001 - 02	372
DOW 30				

Top Two Rank In Each Break

Alternative Energy

Year Num	Quarter Num	Num Transactions
2001	1	49
2000	3	42

Biotech

Year Num	Quarter Num	Num Transactions
2001	2	45
2000	4	48

DOW 30

Year Num	Quarter Num	Num Transactions
2001	1	369
2001	2	372

Top Two Rank In Each Section

Variable Editor

Variable Definition

Name: Year - Quarter

Qualification: Dimension

Type: String

Formula:
= FormatNumber([Year Num]; "0000") + " - " + FormatNumber([Quarter Num]; "00")

Data
- CH03 - Sorts Filters F
  - Portfolio Name
  - Quarter Num
  - Trade Date

Functions
- All
  - Abs
  - Asc
  - Average

Operators

Description

Variable Editor

OK   Cancel   Help

Formula for Year Quarter

= FormatNumber([Year Num]; "0000") + " - " + FormatNumber([Quarter Num];"00")

Ranks and Report Breaks

When we apply Ranks to objects within breaks or sections, the rank will apply to the values in the context of the break or section. Previously, we applied ranks to the entire table, and the result was a rank for all of the values in the context of the table. Therefore, a rank of top two applied to a table with no breaks or sections will result in the top two values being displayed. However, a top two rank applied to a table with breaks, or within a section, will result with the top two values in each break or section being displayed, as seen in the graphic.

In this example, we wanted to get the top two quarters for each portfolio. We do not have a quarter object in the report that includes the year information, so if we ranked by Quarter Num, then we would merge the quarters in each year, which is incorrect. For example, there is a third quarter in both the year 2000 and 2001. If we simply look at quarter and ignored year, then the Num Transactions for the two quarters would sum. We need to compare them at a quarter level. For example, 2000-03, 2000-04, 2001-01, 2001-02, and 2001-03.

We could do this with two methods. We could add First of Quarter in the data provider and rank by this object. This method will work, because it includes the year information (7/1/2000 for the third quarter of 2000). We could also, concatenate Year Num to Quarter Num to create identifiers, such as 2000-03. The latter approach is the one we took in the example. I chose this method, because many people think that formulas are too complicated and not worth learning. This kind of attitude can severely limit your career in the data field, as most data needs some type of formulas applied to it to help viewers of reports understand the data that the reports contain.

Exercise: Ranks and Breaks

8. Create a query with Portfolio Name, Year Num, Quarter Num, First of Quarter, and Num Transactions.
9. Click on any Portfolio Name in the Portfolio Name column, and then click the *Apply/Remove Break* toolbar button.
10. Click on any First of Quarter value in the column, and then click the Apply Ranking toolbar button.
11. Check the Top option, and then enter '2' into the edit field.
12. Based on Revenue, Ranked by First of Quarter.
13. Calculation Mode is Count.
14. Click OK.
15. Right-click on the First of Quarter column, and then select *Remove>Remove Column* from the pop-up menu. (Notice that we can rank by objects that are not shown in the report structure.)

Notes

Grouping Dimesion Values

Year Num	Quarter Num	Revenue
2000	3	(4,278,686)
	4	(2,655,098)
2000	Sum:	(6,933,784)

Year Num	Quarter Num	Revenue
2001	1	349,438
	2	2,750,713
	3	5,410,828
2001	Sum:	8,510,980
	Sum:	1,577,196

Default Table by Quarter

Year Num	Year Half	Revenue
2000	Second Half	(6,933,784)
2001	First Half	3,100,152
2001	Second Half	5,410,828
	Sum:	1,577,196

Custom Table by Year Halves

= If [Quarter Num] InList (1;2) Then "First Half" Else "Second Half"

Formula in Year Half Column

Grouping Dimension Values

This is a bit advanced, and it could be in the chapter on formulas, but Business Objects used to offer grouping functionality. Therefore, I am including the topic here.

Our data has Year Num and Quarter Num, which means that we can create reports on the yearly or quarterly resolution. But, what if we wanted to have a semi-annual report? We can do this by grouping the quarter values into First Half and Second Half. To accomplish this, we use the If logical function. The If function is a Boolean operation, which means there is a true action and a false action. The following is the pseudo code:

If (Some Comparison) Is True Then (Some Action) Else if it is False Then (Some Other Action).

The formula used in the Year Half column is as follows:

= If [Quarter Num] InList (1;2) Then "First Half" Else "Second Half"

Where *[Quarter Num] InList (1;2)* is the comparison. If Quarter Num is in the list of (1;2), then put *First Half* in the cell. Else, if it not in the list, then put *Second Half* in the cell.

Notes

Alerters

Alerter Placed on Column

Portfolio Name	Year Num	Quarter Num	Revenue
DOW 30	2000	3	(2,578,025)
	2000	4	(1,807,388)
	2001	1	330,350
	2001	2	1,340,450
	2001	3	4,066,066
DOW 30			1,351,453

Portfolio Name	Year Num	Quarter Num	Revenue
Technology	2000	3	(740,160)
	2000	4	(376,607)
	2001	1	(5,848)
	2001	2	543,731
	2001	3	521,614
Technology			(57,270)

Alerter Placed on Row

Portfolio Name	Year Num	Quarter Num	Revenue
DOW 30	2000	3	(2,578,025)
	2000	4	(1,807,388)
	2001	1	330,350
	2001	2	1,340,450
	2001	3	4,066,066
DOW 30			1,351,453

Portfolio Name	Year Num	Quarter Num	Revenue
Technology	2000	3	(740,160)
	2000	4	(376,607)
	2001	1	(5,848)
	2001	2	543,731
	2001	3	521,614
Technology			(57,270)

Text Alerter on Year Half

Portfolio Name	Year Num	Year Half	Revenue
DOW 30	2000	Second Half	(2,578,025)
	2000	Second Half	(1,807,388)
	2001	First Half	330,350
	2001	First Half	1,340,450
	2001	Second Half	4,066,066
DOW 30			1,351,453

Portfolio Name	Year Num	Year Half	Revenue
Technology	2000	Second Half	(740,160)
	2000	Second Half	(376,607)
	2001	First Half	(5,848)
	2001	First Half	543,731
	2001	Second Half	521,614
Technology			(57,270)

Alerters

So far, we have used sorts, filters, ranks and groups to help viewers of our report to understand the data that we are presenting. Each one of these methods actually ordered, limited or altered the data presentation. Alerters, don't alter the data. Alerters format the data to make data stand out.

In the *Alerter Placed on Column* graphic, there is an alerter that shades the background of column cells where revenue is greater than 500,000. This helps viewers of the report to quickly spot revenues that we may consider high.

In the *Alerter Placed on Row* graphic, the alerter is placed on the entire row. If we are using only one column in a structure to define the alerter, then applying the alerter to the entire row makes it easier for viewers to observe the alerter. In this graphic, there is also an additional alerter applied to the table, which formats a row with red shading when the revenue is less than -500,000.

In the *Text Alerter on Year Half* graphic, we used an Alerter to format the quarters to First Half or Second Half. We did something very similar in a previous exercise where we grouped the quarters into first and second halves. In the grouping exercise, the values were actually grouped and there were fewer rows in the Year Half table than there were in the Quarter table. However, when using an alerter, we are not actually replacing the values, as we did with the If function. We are simply formatting the output in the column, and the original quarter values are still in the column. Therefore, the column will still behave as if it is still populated with the quarter values.

Notes

Creating Alerters

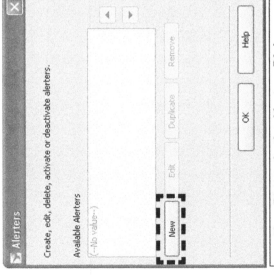

New Button in the Alerters Dialog

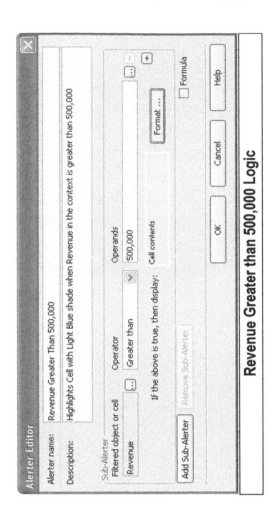

Revenue Greater than 500,000 Logic

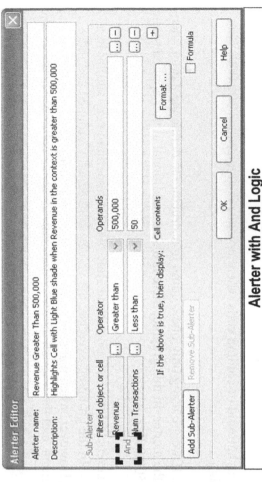

Alerter with And Logic

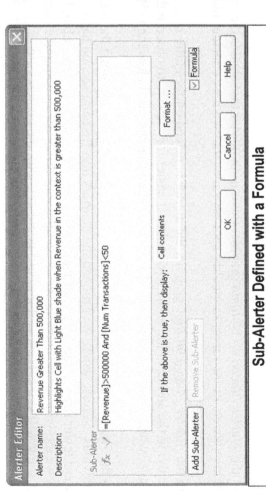

Sub-Alerter Defined with a Formula

Creating Alerters

To manage Alerters in a document (Alerters are available to all reports in a document), click on the Alerters button in the Reporting toolbar. This will display the Alerter dialog, where we can create, edit, delete, and apply alerters.

To create a new alerter, click the *New* button in the Alerters dialog, which will display the Alerter Editor dialog. In this dialog we can define,

Alerter Name and Description: The identifiers of an alerter. It is important to name and describe alerters well, especially if there are to be several in a document.

Sub-Alerter Section: This section defines the alerter. There can be up to eight sub-alerters. If there are more than one sub-alerters with intersecting logic, then the first alerter defined will have priority. For example, if there were two alerters defined in the following order: **1)** Revenue > 0, **2)** Revenue > 25, then the action defined in the Revenue > 0 sub-alerter will have priority.

Filtered Object or Cell: The object that we want to use in the alerter logic. To display a list of available objects, click the small button (...) associated with the field. Choose an object from the list and click OK to set the field's contents.

Operator: The operator for the alerter logic. Can be Equal to, Not Equal to, Greater than, and so forth.

Operand: The value in this field can be a typed in constant or another data object in the report. For example, we can have *Revenue Greater Than 500,000*, as in our example, or we can have *Revenue Greater than Average Revenue*.

Plus (+)/Minus(-) Buttons: Creates another row in the sub-alerter where the logic will be And'ed with the existing row(s). This can be seen in the *Alerter with And Logic* graphic, where the logic is *Revenue Greater than 500,000* **AND** *Num Transactions Less than 50*.

Formula Checkbox: Allows a formula to be used to define the sub-alerter. Later, we will use the Formula editor to create powerful formulas. We can use this same editor to bypass the Object, Operator, and Operand controls, and define a formula for the alerter, as in the *Sub-Alerter Defined with a Formula* graphic.

Notes

Alerter Formats

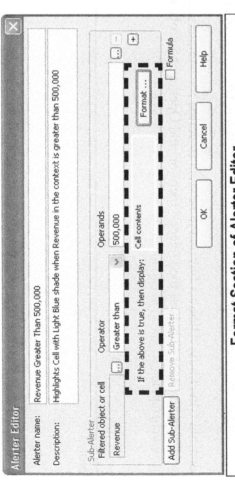

Format Section of Alerter Editor

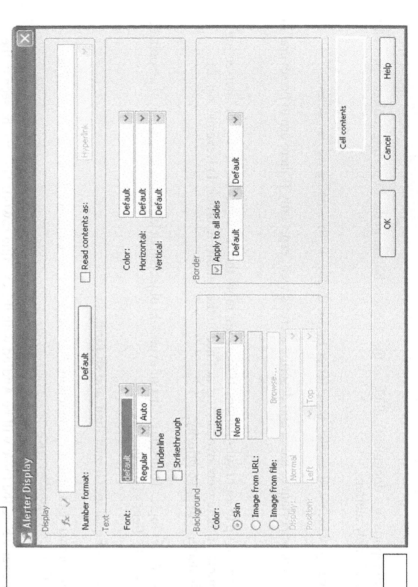

Alerter Display Dialog

Alerter Formats

After defining the alerter logic, we need to define what the alerter will do. We use the Alerter Display dialog to define the alerter actions. This dialog consists of four areas: Display, Text, Background, and Border.

Display: This section allows the content of the cell to be defined. If none of the fields in this section are defined, then the cell contents will not be altered.

Edit Field: The edit field accepts any valid formula or text, and the contents of this field will replace the contents of the cell when the alerter is true. The *fx* button will display a formula editor to help create a formula.

Number Format: This button will display the number format dialog.

Read Contents As: This control will format the contents of the cell as a hyperlink, HTML, or an image URL. This means that you can associate a web site or graphic with a row, when an alerter is true.

Text: This section will override any existing formats currently placed on a cell. You can simply format the text in a cell to italic when an alerter is true. You can also change the font and the alignment of the cell contents.

Background: The Background section will change the background of cells when an alerter is true. For example, you can change the shading of a cell or you can set an image as a cell's background.

Border: Will alter the borders of a cell when an alerter is true.

Notes

Alerter Example (Revenue)

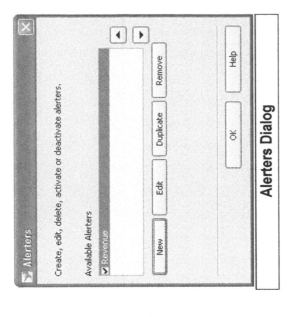

Default Table

Portfolio Name	Year Num	Quarter Num	Revenue
DOW 30	2000	3	(2,578,025)
	2000	4	(1,807,388)
	2001	1	330,350
	2001	2	1,340,450
	2001	3	4,066,066
DOW 30			1,351,453

Portfolio Name	Year Num	Quarter Num	Revenue
Technology	2000	3	(740,160)
	2000	4	(376,607)
	2001	1	(5,848)
	2001	2	543,731
	2001	3	521,614
Technology			(57,270)

Table with Revenue Alerter

Portfolio Name	Year Num	Quarter Num	Revenue
DOW 30	2000	3	(2,578,025)
	2000	4	(1,807,388)
	2001	1	330,350
	2001	2	1,340,450
	2001	3	4,066,066
DOW 30			1,351,453

Portfolio Name	Year Num	Quarter Num	Revenue
Technology	2000	3	(740,160)
	2000	4	(376,607)
	2001	1	(5,848)
	2001	2	543,731
	2001	3	521,614
Technology			(57,270)

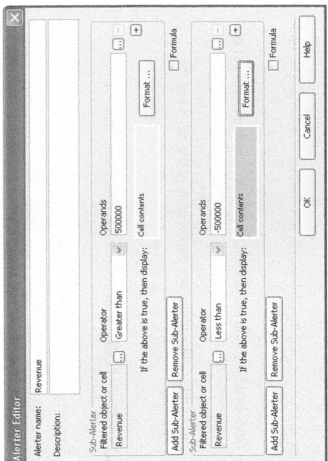

Alerters Dialog

Alerters

Create, edit, delete, activate or deactivate alerters.

Available Alerters

☑ Revenue

New   Edit   Duplicate   Remove

◀ ▶

OK   Help

Alerter Editor for Revenue Alerter

Alerter Editor

Alerter name: Revenue

Description:

Sub-Alerter
Filtered object or cell: Revenue   Operator: Greater than   Operands: 500000

If the above is true, then display: Cell contents   Format ...   ☐ Formula

Add Sub-Alerter   Remove Sub-Alerter

Sub-Alerter
Filtered object or cell: Revenue   Operator: Less than   Operands: -500000

If the above is true, then display: Cell contents   Format ...   ☐ Formula

Add Sub-Alerter   Remove Sub-Alerter

OK   Cancel   Help

Alerter Example (Revenue)

In this example, we are going to create an alerter that does the following:

Logic	Action
Revenue > 500,000	Set background color to light blue
Revenue < -500,000	Set background color to light red

Exercise: Create a Revenue Alerter

1. Create a query with Portfolio Name, Year Num, Quarter Num, and Revenue.
2. Set a break on Portfolio Name and Sum the Revenues, as in the Default table in the graphic.
3. Click on any row value in the Revenue column. Do not click on the header or footer, just click on one of the revenues in the data rows.
4. Click the *Alerters* toolbar button to display the Alerters dialog.
5. Click on the *New* button in the Alerters dialog.
6. Create Alerter logic
   a. Name the Alerter: *Revenue*.
   b. Notice that Revenue is in the *Filtered Object or Cell* field.
   c. Select *Greater than* in the operator drop list.
   d. Type 500000 in the Operands field. Do not put the comma in the number (500,000), as this will cause it to err.
7. Format the Output
   a. Click the *Format...* button.
   b. Change the Text Color to Default (We don't want to format text).
   c. Select Custom in the Background Color drop list, and then click on the light cyan color.
   d. Click OK to dismiss the Alerter Display dialog.

8. Click the *Add Sub-Alerter* button to add the logic for < -500,000.
9. Create Sub-Alerter Logic
   a. Change the operator to *Less than*.
   b. Type -500,000 in the Operands field.
10. Format the Output
    a. Click the *Format...* button.
    b. Change the Text Color to Default.
    c. Select light red in the Background Color drop list.
    d. Click *OK* to dismiss the Alerter Display dialog.
11. Click *OK* in the Alerter Editor to dismiss the dialog.
12. Notice our Alerter listed in the Alerters dialog. Also, notice that the checkbox in front of the Alerter is checked. This means that it will apply to the selected column in the report. Click *OK* to dismiss the Alerters dialog.
13. The revenue column now has the Alerter applied to it. If you want to apply the Alerter to the row, then select one column at a time, click the *Alerters* button, and check the check control in front of our Revenue Alerter. This will apply our Alerter to each column, and therefore the entire row.

Notes

Alerter Example (Revenue and Transactions)

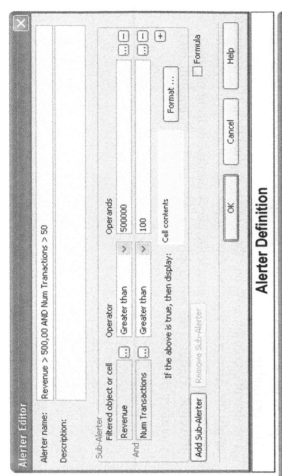

Alerter Applied to Table

Applied Alerter with Check

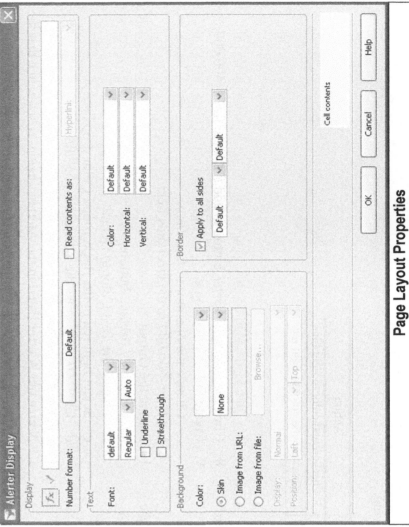

Alerter Definition

Page Layout Properties

Alerter Example (Revenue and Transactions)

In the previous example, each Sub-Alerter was independent of the other, with the first one having precedence over the later. In this example, we are going to create an Alerter that AND's the logic, as in Revenue > 500,000 AND Num Transactions > 100.:

Logic	Action
Revenue > 500,000 AND Num Transactions > 100	Set background color to light yellow.

Exercise: Create a Revenue And Num Transactions Alerter

1. Create a query with Portfolio Name, Year Num, Quarter Num, Num Transactions, and Revenue.
2. Set a break on Portfolio Name. (Not necessary for the Alerter, but it looks better.)
3. Click on any value in the Revenue column, to select it.
4. Click the Alerters button on the Reporting toolbar.
5. Click the New button in the Alerters dialog, to display the Alerter Editor.
6. Define the Alerter
   a. Name the Alerter Revenue>500,00 AND Num Transactions>50
   b. Place Revenue in the *Filtered Object or Cell* field.
   c. Select Greater than in the *Operator* drop list.
   d. Type 500000 in the *Operands* field.
   e. Click the plus (+) button to add another logic line.
   f. Click the little button (...) next to the *Filtered Object or Cell* field. and select *Select an Object of Variable* from the menu. Select Num Transaction from the Objects and Variables dialog.
   g. Select Greater than from the *Operators* drop list.
   h. Type 100 in the *Operands* field.

7. Define the Format
   a. Click the *Format...* button.
   b. Set the *Font Color* to Default. (Changing the font color with Alerters does not work well, if the report is printed. I've found that it is better to shade the background or even change the font type.)
   c. Set the *Background Color* to light yellow.
   d. Click OK to return to the Alerter Editor.
8. Click OK to return to the Alerters dialog.
9. Click OK to apply the Alerter and return to the report.
10. Apply Alerter to all columns in table
    a. For each column do the following: Select any value in the column, click the *Alerters* toolbar button, check the Alerter to Apply, and then click OK to apply the Alerter and dismiss the Alerters dialog.

Notes

Alerter Example (Hyperlink)

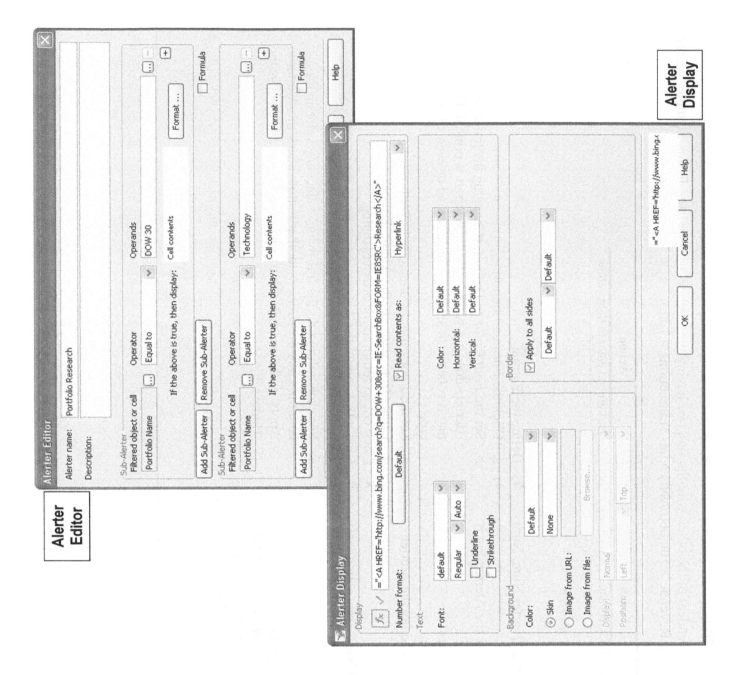

Alerter Example (Hyperlink)

In this example, we are going to insert hyperlinks into our report for more research on a portfolio.

Logic	Action
Portfolio Equals DOW 30	="<A HREF="http://www.bing.com/search?q=DOW+30&src=IE-Search-Box&FORM=IE8SRC">Research</A>"
Portfolio Equals Technology	="<A HREF="http://www.bing.com/search?q=Technology&src=IE-Search-Box&FORM=IE8SRC">Research</A>"

Exercise: Create a Hyperlink Alerter

1. Create a query with Portfolio Name, Year Num, Quarter Num, Num Transactions, and Revenue.
2. Set a break on Portfolio Name.
3. Click on an empty cell in the break footer, to select it.
4. Click the Alerters button on the Reporting toolbar.
5. Click the New button in the Alerters dialog, to display the Alerter Editor.
6. Define the Alerter
   a. Name the Alerter Portfolio Research.
   b. Place Portfolio Name in the *Filtered Object or Cell* field.
   c. Select *Equal to* in the *Operator* drop list.
   d. Type DOW 30 in the *Operands* field.
7. Format the Output
   a. Click the *Format...* button.
   b. Type the text from the first row of the Action column in the above table, into the *Display* edit field. (Note, instead of typing the entire text, you can Bing the portfolio name and copy the URL text from the address bar.)

   c. Check the *Read Contents as:* check box, and select Hyperlink in the drop down list of values.
   d. Click *OK* to dismiss the Alerter Display dialog.
8. Click the *Add Sub-Alerter* button to add another sub-Alerter.
9. Define the Alerter
   j. Place Portfolio Name in the *Filtered Object or Cell* field.
   k. Select *Equal to* in the *Operator* drop list.
   l. Type Technology in the *Operands* field.
10. Format the Output
    a. Click the *Format...* button.
    b. Type the text from the second row of the Action column in the above table, into the *Display* edit field.
    c. Check the *Read Contents as:* check box, and select Hyperlink in the drop down list of values.
    d. Click *OK* to dismiss the Alerter Display dialog.
11. Click *OK* to dismiss the Alerter Editor.
12. Click *Ok* to dismiss the Alerters dialog and apply the Alerter.

Notes

Summary

Alerter Placed on Column

Portfolio Name	Year Num	Quarter Num	Revenue
DOW 30	2000	3	(2,578,025)
	2000	4	(1,807,388)
	2001	1	330,350
	2001	2	1,340,450
	2001	3	4,066,066
DOW 30			1,351,453

Portfolio Name	Year Num	Quarter Num	Revenue
Technology	2000	3	(740,160)
	2000	4	(376,607)
	2001	1	(5,848)
	2001	2	543,731
	2001	3	521,614
Technology			(57,270)

Alerter Placed on Row

Portfolio Name	Year Num	Quarter Num	Revenue
DOW 30	2000	3	(2,578,025)
	2000	4	(1,807,388)
	2001	1	330,350
	2001	2	1,340,450
	2001	3	4,066,066
DOW 30			1,351,453

Portfolio Name	Year Num	Quarter Num	Revenue
Technology	2000	3	(740,160)
	2000	4	(376,607)
	2001	1	(5,848)
	2001	2	543,731
	2001	3	521,614
Technology			(57,270)

Text Alerter on Year Half

Portfolio Name	Year Num	Year Half	Revenue
DOW 30	2000	Second Half	(2,578,025)
	2000	Second Half	(1,807,388)
	2001	First Half	330,350
	2001	First Half	1,340,450
	2001	Second Half	4,066,066
DOW 30			1,351,453

Portfolio Name	Year Num	Year Half	Revenue
Technology	2000	Second Half	(740,160)
	2000	Second Half	(376,607)
	2001	First Half	(5,848)
	2001	First Half	543,731
	2001	Second Half	521,614
Technology			(57,270)

Summary

After studying this chapter, you should see how important it is to present information so that we emphasize the point we are trying to make. For example, if we are creating a sales report, we may want to put the sales people with the highest sales at the top of a table, by sorting the total sales for each sales person in descending order. Then, we can see our best sales people at the top of the list and the worst at the bottom. This way, we do not have to search the list for these stand-outs.

In addition, if we are manager of a very large store with many departments, then maybe we will only be interested in the top sales people in each department. We can do this by breaking on department, and then placing a rank on sales person. We can also compare our top sales people to total sales of a department, by using the *NoFilter* function (= [Sales] / NoFilter([Sales] In Report). If there are 40 sales people in a department and one sales person had 40% of the total sales, then something is probably going on.

Suppose that we are a manager of a certain department, and we receive a report for all departments. Maybe, we would want to filter to see only our department. We could then use the *NoFilter* function to compare our department to the others (= [Sales] / NoFilter([Sales] In Report).

In addition, maybe we are the district manager and we get a report with all stores in a district. We may not want to have to study the report to see what stores loss money or made money. We could set Alerters with thresholds, such as shade light blue if more than 20% gain over last quarter and light red if more than 20% loss over the previous quarter.

Notes

Chapter 4: Creating Queries

Introduction

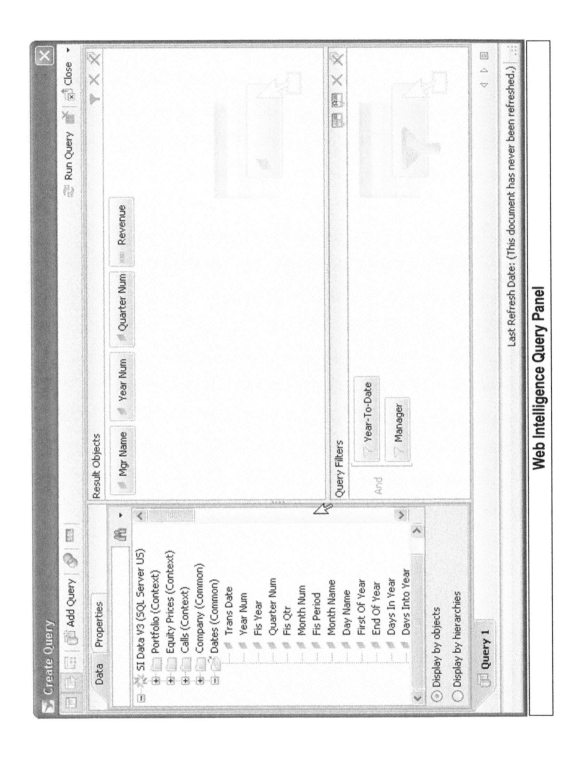

Web Intelligence Query Panel

Introduction

In this chapter, we are going to learn how to retrieve data from the objects in a universe. We will learn that we can retrieve data from a data base through a universe, and we can also retrieve data from other data sources, such as MS Excel.

Notes

Business Objects Universes

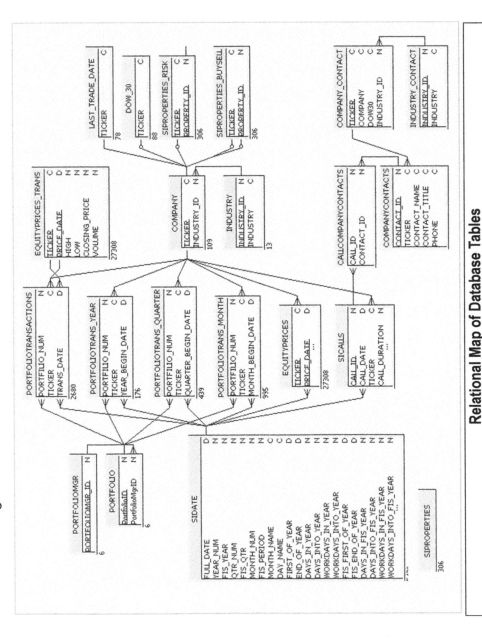

Relational Map of Database Tables

Universe Folders and Objects

- Portfolio (Context)
  - Portfolioid
  - Portfoliomgr Id
  - Mgr Name
  - Portfolio Name
  - Initial Cash
  - Num Portfolios
  - Num Managers
  - Portfolio Transactions
    - Trans Id
    - Price
    - Num Shares
    - Revenue
    - Num Transactions
  - Portfolio Transactions - LOW
    - Tickers
  - Daily Price and Volume
  - *Portfolio Transactions - Advanced*
- Equity Prices (Context)
- Calls (Context)
- Company (Common)
  - Industry Id
  - Industry
  - Ticker
  - DOW 30
  - Risk
  - Buy Sell Rec
  - Last Trade Date
  - Company
  - Num Companies
  - Num Industries
  - Company - Advanced
- Dates (Common)
  - Trans Date
  - Year Num
  - Fis Year
  - Quarter Num
  - Fis Qtr
  - Month Num
  - Fis Period
  - Month Name

Business Objects Universes

In the early days of relational databases, we had to create SQL to return data sets to our reports. SQL is a query language that instructs the database on which data should be returned. Using SQL was okay, and it worked well, but people had to be trained to develop SQL. Also, not everybody wrote the same quality of code, which meant that some queries were much more efficient than others. A business unit could have hundreds of reports and hundreds of queries to supply the data to the reports. Usually, only one or two people wrote all of the queries. When one of these people left the company, there was chaos for a period of time, because no one knew which queries worked with their respective reports.

Business Objects offered a better solution to this craziness, which was a consistent mapping of the tables and their relationships in a database. They called this mapping a Universe. The universe map of the database that this book uses is shown in the graphic. Now, that all of the relationships between the tables are solidified in a map, reports became much more consistent. However, they didn't want everybody to directly access the fields of the tables, as this could lead to inconsistent use of the tables. Therefore, they developed objects that would allow the tables to be accessed. Objects can directly access a field in a table, or they can access the field through a formula.

These objects are Dimensions, Measures, and Details. When a person wants to access the data in a database, they simply open Web intelligence and create a query by selecting the objects in the universe. The person needs not be concerned on how the objects are accessing the data. They just need to know that the objects will return the data of interest. This does not mean that any combination of objects will always return the correct data, as this is the responsibility of the Universe Designer, who created the universe. It does mean that the results returned will be consistent, no matter who is creating the query. If a person realizes that the data is not correct, then they should notify the Universe Designer. Then, the designer will hopefully fix the problem.

Notes

_____

Dimension Objects (From Chapter 1)

Portfolio Name	Ticker	Year Num
Finance	C	2000
Finance	C	2001
Finance	GS	2000
Finance	GS	2001
Media	DIS	2000
Media	DIS	2001
Media	FOX	2000
Media	FOX	2001

Table of Dimension Objects

Portfolio Name
Finance
Media

Portfolio Name Context

Portfolio Name	Ticker
Finance	C
Finance	GS
Media	DIS
Media	FOX

Portfolio Name - Ticker Context

Portfolio Name	Ticker	Year Num
Finance	C	2000
Finance	C	2001
Finance	GS	2000
Finance	GS	2001
Media	DIS	2000
Media	DIS	2001
Media	FOX	2000
Media	FOX	2001

Portfolio Name - Ticker - Year Num Context

Dimension Objects (From Chapter 1)

Dimensions create the context for a report, in much the same way that the frame of your house provides support for your walls and roof. Without the frame of your house, your home would just be a pile of wood, glass, and a few sinks thrown about. Without dimensions in a data set, our reports would just be a collection of meaningless numbers. Dimensions create the rows in a data set by providing unique combinations of values.

In the table of dimension objects, shown in the graphic, there are no two rows containing the same combination of dimension values. Some of the values repeat, such as Finance, but the other dimension values on the row make each row unique. Therefore, the context of this table is created by the Portfolio Name, Year Num, and Ticker dimensions.

Each dimension in a table will add to the context of the table and will usually create more rows within a table. For example, a table containing only the Portfolio Name will contain two rows - one for Finance and one for media. If we add Ticker to the table, then the rows will have to increase to display all of the possible Portfolio Name – Ticker combinations. Now, if we add Year Num to the table, then the context will change and the rows will once again have to increase to accommodate the new combinations of values.

Notes

Measure Objects (From Chapter 1)

Portfolio Name	Ticker	Year Num	Num Transactions
Finance	C	2000	9
Finance	C	2001	11
Finance	GS	2000	5
Finance	GS	2001	15
Media	DIS	2000	11
Media	DIS	2001	7
Media	FOX	2000	14
Media	FOX	2001	19

Num Transactions Measure Object

Portfolio Name	Ticker	Num Transactions
Finance	C	20
Finance	GS	20
Media	DIS	18
Media	FOX	33

Measure Adjusts when Year Num is Removed

Select PorfolioName, Ticker, YearNum, Sum(NumTransactions)

From PortfolioTransactions

Group By PorfolioName, Ticker, YearNum

Measures Usually Create Summary Queries

Measure Objects (From Chapter 1)

Measure objects do not create contexts, as do Dimensions. They usually conform to contexts through a preassigned aggregate function. In this example, Num Transactions is the measure and Sum is its predefined function. Notice the measure in the Num Transactions Measure Object graphic does not add any rows to the table.

Business Objects populates tables in a report using a dataset defined from selected objects. Tables in the report can display the entire dataset, or a subset of the data. The context of a table will change when a dimension object is removed from a table. For example, when Year Num is removed, the remaining values of Portfolio Name and Ticker will consolidate to form unique rows, as shown in the graphic. The measures in the table must conform to the new context. Num Transactions conforms, by summing the yearly values in the dataset for each ticker.

Measure objects usually cause a query to return summarized data, which basically means that only unique combinations of dimension values will be returned, and the measure will contribute an aggregated value to each row in the dataset. This can be seen in the following SQL:

Select PorfolioName, Ticker, YearNum, Sum (NumTransactions)
From PortfolioTransactions
Group By PorfolioName, Ticker, YearNum

The Group By clause instructs the database to only return distinct rows based on the values of the columns stated in the clause. Notice that the Group By clause is also the context of the dataset.

Notes

Detail Objects (From Chapter 1)

Dimension | Measure

Mgr Name	Revenue
David Balkcom	214,665
Eddie Wang	(57,270)
Kathy James	(78,540)
Maria Castro	79,426
Robert Denning	67,462
Sean Wilkenson	1,351,453

Data Set 1

Dimension | Detail

Mgr Name	Mgr Phone
David Balkcom	5555551900
Eddie Wang	5555552003
Kathy James	5555552000
Maria Castro	5555551278
Robert Denning	5555552002
Sean Wilkenson	5555551276

Data Set 2

Dimension | Detail | Measure

Mgr Name	Mgr Phone	Revenue
David Balkcom	5555551900	214,665
Eddie Wang	5555552003	(57,270)
Kathy James	5555552000	(78,540)
Maria Castro	5555551278	79,426
Robert Denning	5555552002	67,462
Sean Wilkenson	5555551276	1,351,453

Combined Data Set 1 & 2

Dimension | Measure

Mgr Name	Revenue
David Balkcom	214,665
Eddie Wang	(57,270)
Kathy James	(78,540)
Maria Castro	79,426
Robert Denning	67,462
Sean Wilkenson	1,351,453
Sum:	1,577,196

Data Set 1

Dimension | Dimension

Mgr Name	Ticker
David Balkcom	CPST
David Balkcom	FCEL
Eddie Wang	CIEN
Eddie Wang	PSFT
Kathy James	AOL
Kathy James	VIA
Maria Castro	DGX
Maria Castro	GENZ
Robert Denning	JPM
Robert Denning	LEH
Sean Wilkenson	AA
Sean Wilkenson	JPM
Sean Wilkenson	MMM

Data Set 3

Dimension | Dimension | Measure

Mgr Name	Ticker	Revenue
David Balkcom	CPST	214,665
David Balkcom	FCEL	214,665
Eddie Wang	CIEN	(57,270)
Eddie Wang	PSFT	(57,270)
Kathy James	AOL	(78,540)
Kathy James	VIA	(78,540)
Maria Castro	DGX	79,426
Maria Castro	GENZ	79,426
Robert Denning	JPM	67,462
Robert Denning	LEH	67,462
Sean Wilkenson	AA	1,351,453
Sean Wilkenson	JPM	1,351,453
Sean Wilkenson	MMM	1,351,453

Combined Data Set 1 & 3

Detail Objects (From Chapter 1)

A Detail object is an attribute of a Dimension object. It has only one value for each of its dimension's values. For example, an employee ID dimension should only have one employee name detail value.

In the graphic, we have data set 1 and data set 2. Data set 1 consists of a dimension (Mgr Name) and a measure (Revenue). The context of data set 1 is Mgr Name. Data set 2 consists of a dimension (Mgr Name) and a detail (Mgr Phone). The context of data set 2 is also Mgr Name. Data set 1 has a measure that should not be multiplied by duplicating the rows in the table. For example, if we were to repeat each row of the table, then the total of the table would be two times larger than it should be. Therefore, it is very important to not change the context of the table by adding objects that would cause the rows to repeat. If we were to combine data sets 1 & 2, then the number of rows would not increase, because there is only one Mgr Phone detail value for each Mgr Name value. This is why Mgr Phone can be defined as a detail.

The context of data set 1 is Mgr Name, because Mgr Name is the dimension. The context of data set 3 is Mgr Name and Ticker, because they are both dimensions. Notice that the Ticker object causes the Mgr Name to repeat, and thus creates more rows, than if Mgr Name were the only dimension in the table. If we were to combine data set 1 & 3, than the context of data set 1 would change to accommodate for the new Ticker dimension. This change in context would cause the Revenue values to repeat for each ticker owned by the manager, as can be seen in the graphic (Combined Data Set 1 & 3), and thus fan (repeat) the revenues across the repeated Mgr Name values, which may make it appear that the total revenue were much higher than the actual total.

Therefore, it is safe to bring a detail object into any context, as long as its related dimension is also present in the context. Dimensions that will change the context of a data set should not be allowed into the set, because it may cause the revenues to fan (repeat) across the new dimension's values.

Notes

Universe Contexts

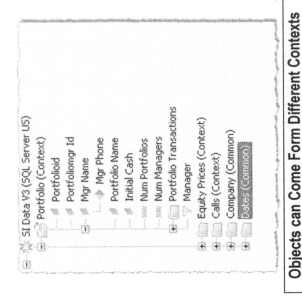

Objects can Come Form Different Contexts

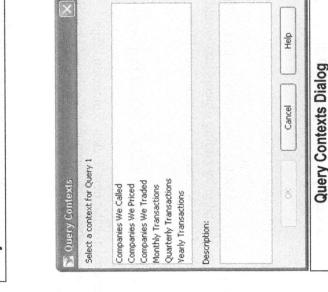

Query Contexts Dialog

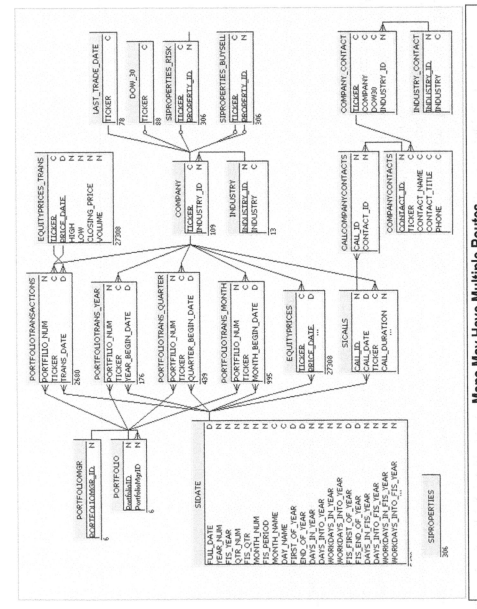

Maps May Have Multiple Routes

Incompatible Objects Dialog

Universe Contexts

As we can see from the *Maps May Have Multiple Routes* diagram, the table mappings in universes can be a little complicated. We can see that there can be several different paths from one table to another. For example, we can go through any of the center column of tables to go from Company to SIDate, and each of the paths could yield different results. For example, if the path went through PortfolioTransactions, then we would get dates that companies were traded. If we went from Company through SICalls to get to SIDate, then we would get dates that companies that were called. If Web Intelligence selected any path that it wanted, then the query results would not be consistent.

Web Intelligence will pick a path based on the objects in a query. For example, if a person selected Full Date from SIDate, Company from Company, and Revenue from PortfolioTransactions, then the path would go through Portfolio Transactions. Therefore, if an object is selected from a table that will determine the path, then that path will be taken. So then, there are two other situations - No object selected that can determine the path, and objects selected from two different paths.

We'll start with the first case - no object selected that can determine the path. The object that determines the path is an object that comes from a deciding table. For example, if someone selected only from the Company and SIDate tables, then there is no deciding object. In this case, Web Intelligence needs to know which path to take. To find out, Web Intelligence will ask the report developer via a Query Contexts dialog, which can be seen in the graphic. Notice that this universe has six contexts to select from. Hopefully, the contexts are named to make the selection obvious. When presented with this dialog, a person simply selects a context, and then clicks OK.

If objects are selected from two different paths, then Web Intelligence has a choice. It can refuse to return the data, and display a dialog complaining about incompatible objects, as seen in the graphic. This is usually my preferred choice, when I am developing universes. Web Intelligence can also return multiple data sets - one for each set of objects that define an alternative path. When this happens, Web Intelligence will usually create multiple default tables on the report. The designer of the universe decides which choice Web Intelligence will make.

When I create universes, I will usually label the classes in the universe as either Context or Common. Context means that objects in this class will define which path to take. It also means that you cannot select from two different context classes, as you will get the Incompatible Objects dialog when the query is refreshed. The Common folders are common to all of the context folders, as they do not define paths. So, in my universes, a person can select objects from one Context folder and objects from any of the Common folders. This is just my solution, and your Universe Designer may present a different solution. Whatever the solution is, it should be obvious if there are multiple contexts in the universe and which objects belong to their respective contexts.

Notes

Query Panel

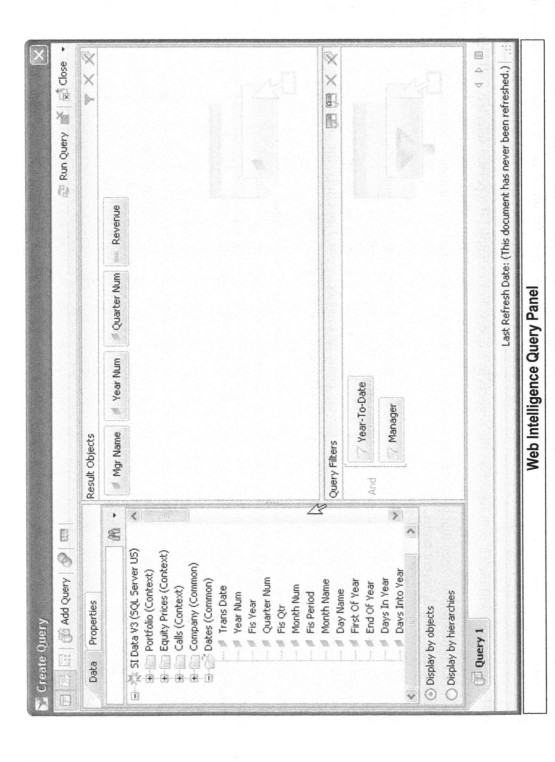

Web Intelligence Query Panel

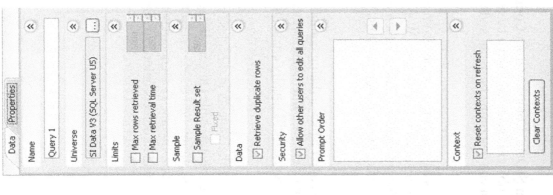

Properties Tab

Query Panel

The Query Panel is where we create queries for our documents. If you do not know how to access this dialog, then please refer to chapter one, where we discussed how to select universes for both the Web and Rich Client versions of Web Intelligence. There are basically four areas in the dialog, which are The Data and Properties tabs, the Result Objects, the Query Filters, and the Toolbar.

Data Tab: This is where the objects are presented to the report developer, who selects from these objects to create queries for a document.

Properties Tab: On this tab, we can set properties for our queries. We can name our universes. The default name is usually Query1, which is okay if there is only one query. If there are multiple queries in a document, then the queries should be given more descriptive names, so that people know what the query is for.

Result Objects: Objects placed here will define the data to be returned. In the graphic, there are four objects in the Result Objects section. This means that the default table will have four columns - one for each object. The column headers will be the names of the objects.

Query Filters: The objects in this section will constrain the data sets. In the graphic, we have two Query Filters, which are Year-To-Date and Manager. The Year-To-Date filter will limit the results to dates from the beginning of the year to some date in the year. The Manager filter will allow a list of managers to be defined through a prompted dialog, and then the data returned will only contain these managers. The filters in the graphic were created by the universe designer. As we will see, we can also create our own query filters.

Query Panel Toolbar: This toolbar hides and shows different areas in the panel, it also allows us to add queries, create combination queries, view the SQL created by the panel, and run the query (refresh). We will talk about these features as we work our way through this chapter.

Notes

Selecting Objects

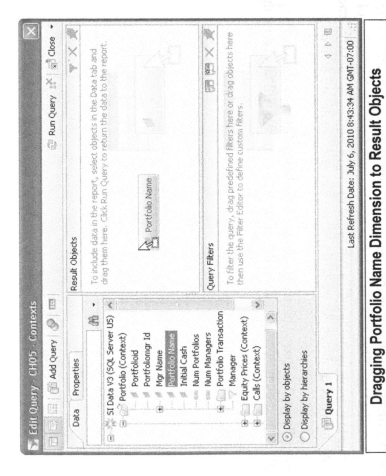

Dragging Portfolio Name Dimension to Result Objects

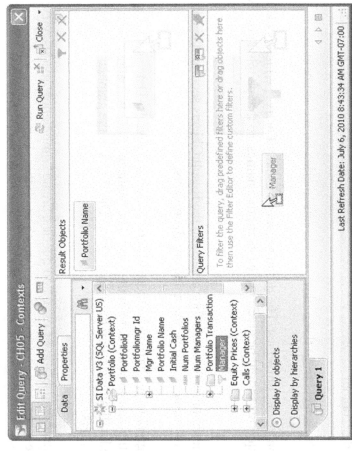

Dragging Manager Query Filter to Query Filters

Selecting Objects

With Web Intelligence, we drag objects to the Result Objects section of the panel to select the data that we want in our documents. We also drag Query Filters tot eh Query Filter section of the panel to limit the amount of data returned to our documents. Both Objects and Query Filters are created by the Universe Designers that designed the universe.

As we have seen, Dimensions, Details, and Measures all have certain intrinsic behavior. For example, Dimensions create contexts and measures aggregate to the contexts. Since every universe can have these objects, we should be able to create documents and reports from almost every well designed universe. I am also a consultant, and I have worked at 100's of companies throughout the years. In the beginning, I was always a little confused when I arrived on a jobsite, because I didn't know the company's data. However, as I became more confident in how Web Intelligence objects behave, I was able to create usable reports within hours of arriving. I could do this, because all I needed to do was to identify a few important dimensions, and every business has them. For example, a communications company may have hardware, routing centers, and service people. A finance company may have financial instruments, counterparties, and settlement dates. Once these important dimensions are identified, then we need to have a look at what measures are available. We then use the dimensions to *slice and dice* the measures.

For example, we can slice and dice the total downtime (measure) with each piece of communications equipment (dimension). We can divide revenue (measure) by each financial instrument (dimension) that is settling tomorrow (dimension). I am amazed at how fast a person can start making powerful reports with Web intelligence.

Notes

Query SQL

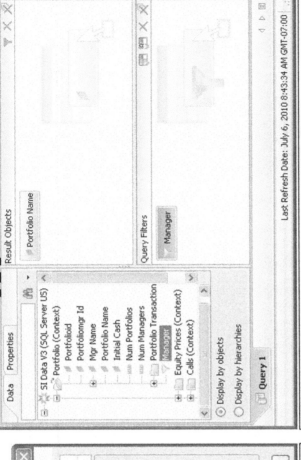

SQL Viewer Button in Query Panel

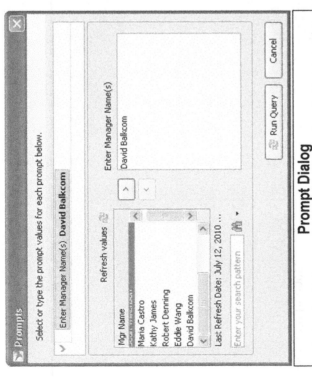

Prompt Dialog

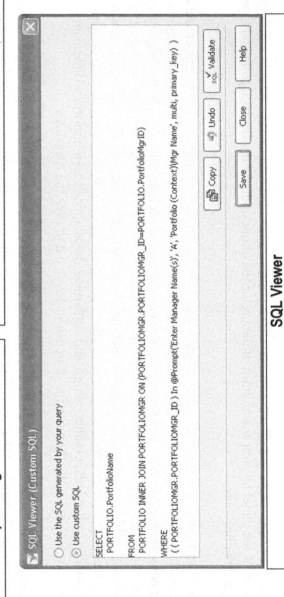

SQL Viewer

Query SQL

Universes can be based on different types of data sources. In this book the universe is based on a SQL Server relational database. Therefore, when we click the *SQL* button in the Query Panel, we will get to see the SQL that Web Intelligence will send to the database. We can see from the graphic that the SQL that is generated is usually quite simple and easy to understand.

In our case, we have placed Portfolio Name in the Result objects window. This is why in the SQL, we have PORTFOLIO.PortfolioName in the Select clause. So, whatever is placed in the Result Objects section of the Query Panel, will also be in the Select clause of the SQL. By the way, PORTFOLIO.PortfolioName represents the data in the PortfolioName field in the PORTFOLIO table.

We have a Dimension object and a Query Filter object in our panel. These objects may come from a single table, or they may come from tables that have any number of joins between them. In any case, all of the tables on the join path between the objects will be included in the From clause. Our From clause contains two tables, so we can assume that our objects represent data from two different tables that are separated by one join.

The Query Filter that we have placed in our Query Filters section is called Manager. It does not specify which manager, so we must assume that when we run our query, Web Intelligence will prompt for which manager we are interested in. If we look in the Where clause we will see the syntax for this prompted filter. It is simply:
((PORTFOLIOMGR.PORTFOLIOMGR_ID) In @Prompt('Enter Manager Name(s)', 'A', 'Portfolio (Context)\Mgr Name', multi, primary_key)).

If we run the query, select David Balkcom for our manager, and then revisit the SQL in the Query Panel, then we will be able to see that we sent David (primary key 6) to the database as a filter. The Where clause will look like: ((PORTFOLIOMGR.PORTFOLIOMGR_ID) In (6)).

Notes

Running a Query

Sending SQL to Database

Retrieving Data

Processing Request

Estimated wait: 5s
The estimated wait is based on the last refresh.

Cancel | Help

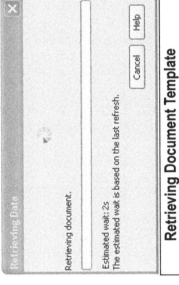

Retrieving Document Template

Retrieving Data

Retrieving document.

Estimated wait: 2s
The estimated wait is based on the last refresh.

Cancel | Help

Retrieving Data

Decoding Document

Estimated wait: 1s
The estimated wait is based on the last refresh.

Cancel | Help

Decoding the Template

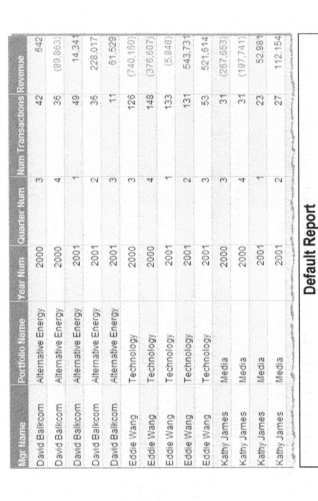

Mgr Name	Portfolio Name	Year Num	Quarter Num	Num Transactions	Revenue
David Balkcom	Alternative Energy	2000	3	42	642
David Balkcom	Alternative Energy	2000	4	36	(89,863)
David Balkcom	Alternative Energy	2001	1	49	14,341
David Balkcom	Alternative Energy	2001	2	36	228,017
David Balkcom	Alternative Energy	2001	3	11	61,529
Eddie Wang	Technology	2000	3	126	(740,160)
Eddie Wang	Technology	2000	4	148	(376,607)
Eddie Wang	Technology	2001	1	133	(5,848)
Eddie Wang	Technology	2001	2	131	543,731
Eddie Wang	Technology	2001	3	53	521,614
Kathy James	Media	2000	3	31	(267,653)
Kathy James	Media	2000	4	31	(197,741)
Kathy James	Media	2001	1	23	52,981
Kathy James	Media	2001	2	27	112,154

Default Report

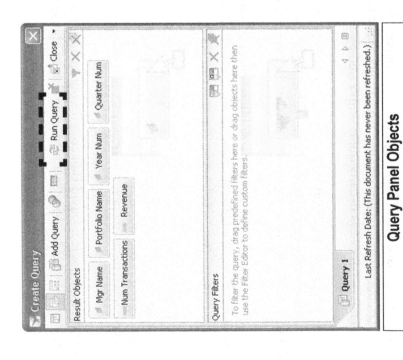

Create Query — Add Query — Run Query — Close

Result Objects

Mgr Name | Portfolio Name | Year Num | Quarter Num
Num Transactions | Revenue

Query Filters

To filter the query, drag predefined filters here or drag objects here then
use the Filter Editor to define custom filters.

Query 1

Last Refresh Date: (This document has never been refreshed.)

Query Panel Objects

Running a Query

When the Run Query button is pressed, Web Intelligence (WI) creates the SQL and sends it to the database for processing. After the database returns the data for the document, WI retrieves the document template, and decodes the template so that it can populate the template with the data from the query. WI keeps you informed on these steps by updating the Retrieving Data dialog during query execution. If it is not the first time that a query has been ran, then WI can give an estimated wait time based on the previous refresh.

The first time a query is executed, Web Intelligence will create a default report, which is usually a table. The table will contain a column for each object in the Result Objects section, and each column header will be the name of the object in the row. If the query is edited and objects are added to the Result Objects section, then those objects will not automatically become a column in the existing table when the query is ran. These new objects will have to be dragged into the report from the Data tab section of Web Intelligence or entered into the existing structures through a new formula. If an object is removed from the query, then the object will be removed from any report structure that was using the object.

Notes

Dimension Only Query

SELECT
PORTFOLIOMGR.MGRNAME,
PORTFOLIO.PortfolioName,
COMPANY.COMPANY

FROM

COMPANY INNER JOIN PORTFOLIOTRANSACTIONS ON (PORTFOLIOTRANSACTIONS.TICKER=COMPANY.TICKER)
INNER JOIN PORTFOLIO ON (PORTFOLIO.PortfolioID=PORTFOLIOTRANSACTIONS.PORTFILIO_NUM)
INNER JOIN PORTFOLIOMGR ON (PORTFOLIOMGR.PORTFOLIOMGR_ID=PORTFOLIO.PortfolioMgrID)

Dimension Only Query

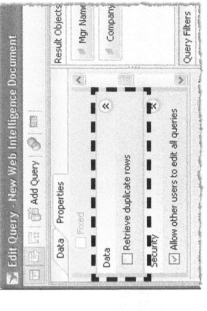

SELECT **DISTINCT**
PORTFOLIOMGR.MGRNAME,
PORTFOLIO.PortfolioName,
COMPANY.COMPANY

FROM

COMPANY INNER JOIN PORTFOLIOTRANSACTIONS ON (PORTFOLIOTRANSACTIONS.TICKER=COMPANY.TICKER)
INNER JOIN PORTFOLIO ON (PORTFOLIO.PortfolioID=PORTFOLIOTRANSACTIONS.PORTFILIO_NUM)
INNER JOIN PORTFOLIOMGR ON (PORTFOLIOMGR.PORTFOLIOMGR_ID=PORTFOLIO.PortfolioMgrID)

Retrieve Duplicate Rows Option Not Checked

Dimension Only Query

When we select objects for our queries, the objects can come any number of tables. Each of these tables may have a multiplying effect on the number of rows returned. For example, a company table will probably have each company listed only once, but a trade table may have companies involved with many different transactions, so if a dimension is selected from both the company and trade table, then the query probably will return many rows that are not unique. For example, Intel - 1/2/2010, Intel - 1/2/2010, Intel - 1/2/2010. It may do this, because Intel was traded three times on 1/2/2010.

On the Properties tab of the Query Panel, there is an option called *Retrieve Duplicate Rows*. If this option is checked, and only dimensions are in the Result Objects section, then there is a chance that the query will return many duplicate rows. The default for this option is checked. Therefore, if you are only selecting dimension objects in your query, then you should clear the check on this option. Notice, when the option is unchecked, then the DISTINCT keyword is added to the query.

We only clear the *Retrieve Duplicate Rows* option when we have only dimensions in the Result Objects section of the panel. If we have any measures, we do not clear the option, and we leave it checked. The reason for not clearing the check is that measures add a group by statement to the query. The group by statement groups all duplicate dimensions into a single row, and then the measure is aggregated to these unique rows. Therefore, it is unnecessary to clear the option. In fact, if the *Retrieve Duplicate Rows* option is not checked, and there is a measure in the Result Objects section of the Query Panel, then the query can return incorrect results, because the measures will only aggregate numerical values that are different. For example, if the option were cleared for the following set of data: A - 10, A - 10, A-20, then the result would be A - 30, which would be incorrect.

Therefore, if there are only dimension objects in the Result Objects section of the Query Panel, then clear the *Retrieve Duplicate Rows* option. If there are Measures in the Result Objects section, then do not clear the option.

Notes

_____

Measures in Queries

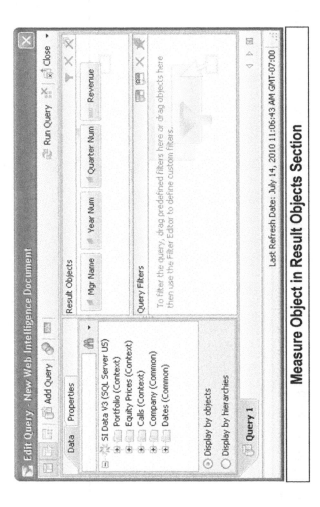

Measure Object in Result Objects Section

SELECT
max (PORTFOLIOMGR.MGRNAME),
SIDATE.YEAR_NUM,
SIDATE.QTR_NUM,
Sum(PORTFOLIOTRANS_QUARTER.REVENUE)

FROM

PORTFOLIOMGR INNER JOIN PORTFOLIO ON (PORTFOLIOMGR.PORTFOLIOMGR_ID=PORTFOLIO.PortfolioMgrID)
INNER JOIN PORTFOLIOTRANS_QUARTER ON (PORTFOLIO.PortfolioID=PORTFOLIOTRANS_QUARTER.PORTFOLIO_NUM)
INNER JOIN SIDATE ON (SIDATE.FULL_DATE=PORTFOLIOTRANS_QUARTER.QUARTER_BEGIN_DATE)

GROUP BY
PORTFOLIOMGR.PORTFOLIOMGR_ID,
SIDATE.YEAR_NUM,
SIDATE.QTR_NUM

Measures in Queries

On the previous page, we learned that clearing the Retrieve Duplicate Rows options will cause the query to only return unique combinations of dimension values. Measures will also cause a query to return unique combinations of dimension values, because the measure will cause a group by in the SQL.

The Group By statement tells the database to group all rows that have identical dimension values into single rows, and then any measure values that are on the rows should aggregate to the single row using their default aggregate functions. For example, Revenue's default is Sum. So when it is included in a query, the Revenue values for identical rows will sum, while the dimension values will roll-up to one row.

By the way, this is why we don't clear the Retrieve Duplicate Rows option when measures are included in the query, as only the unique measure values will sum, and any identical values on identical dimension rows will be ignored. Therefore, never clear the option when a measure is included in the query.

In many dimension only queries, without the *Retrieve Duplicate Rows* option cleared or a measure included, many duplicate rows could be returned. I have seen documents as big as 100 megabytes that contain reports that only show a few rows. The writers of these reports than say that Web Intelligence is not working efficiently, because the files are so large for so few rows. However, Web Intelligence is working fine. It is just that the duplicate rows are not displayed on the report, so the report developer is not aware of the large number of duplicate rows. Remember the *Avoid Duplicate Row Aggregation* option that hides the duplicate rows by default.

Notes

Limiting Dimension Values

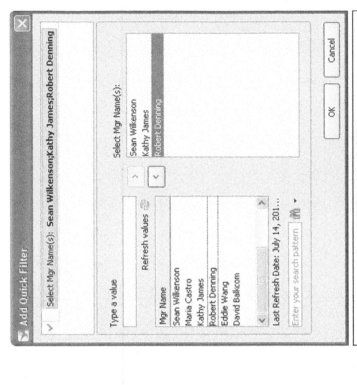

Quick Filter Button in Query Panel

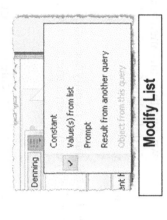

Quick Filter List of Values

Modify List

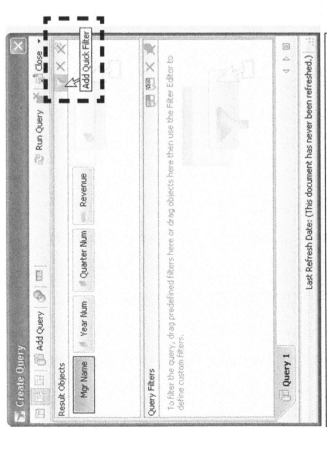

Filter in Query Filters Section

Limiting Dimension Values

Many dimensions have a List of Values (LOV) associated with them. This LOV is a list of all of a dimension's unique values. When creating a query, a person can use the LOV for an object to limit the values returned when the query is run. To use the Quick Filter, click the Quick Filter button in the Query Panel.

This action will display the Quick Filter dialog, which should be populated with a list of the dimension's unique values. Select the values and move them over to the *Select* list on the right side of the dialog. The values can be moved by double-clicking on them, or by first selecting the values, and then clicking the *move* button (>). Once the *Select* list is populated, then click the OK button to create the filter.

Once the filter is created, you can still modify the list, by clicking on the button on the right-side of the filter, and selecting *Value(s) from list*. This will display the *List of Values* dialog that is very similar to the Quick Filter dialog. Once the dialog is displayed, use the move buttons (>, <), to add and remove values from the *Select* list.

The LOV for both the Quick Filter and the List of Values dialog is usually a static list, which means that once the list is created, then it is not refreshed until the refresh request is made through the *Refresh Values* button in the dialogs. The reason the list is static is that many people do not want to wait for the list to populate with more current values each time the dialog is displayed. Refreshes can take less than a minute, to much more than a minute. If the list seems to not be current enough, simply click the *Refresh Values* button in the dialog.

Notice that there is a *Search* button and field located under the list of values. If a text string is entered into the field and the button is pressed, then all values containing the string will be displayed in the list. An asterisk ('*') is a wildcard that will display all values. Sometimes, when the dialog is opened, the list is empty. When this happens, many people will click the Refresh Values button, and then wait for the list to be re-populated. A better option is to enter an asterisk into the search field, and then click the search button. This will populate the list, without refreshing it through a query, which should be much faster.

_____

Notes

Adding Additional Queries

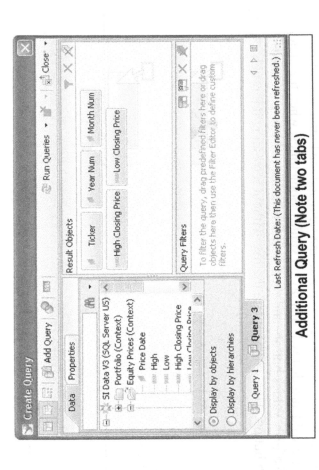

Add Query Button in Query Panel

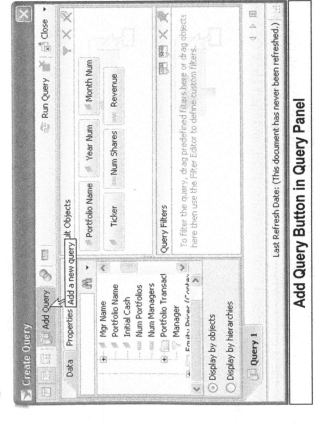

Additional Query (Note two tabs)

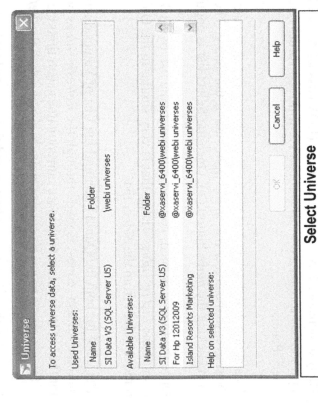

Select Universe

Table for Query 1

Portfolio Name	Year Num	Month Num	Ticker	Num Shares	Revenue
Alternative Energy	2001	1	ACPW	-700	26,063
Alternative Energy	2001	1	APWR	-300	11,963
Alternative Energy	2001	1	CPST	-800	24,725
Alternative Energy	2001	1	FCEL	600	(15,637)
Alternative Energy	2001	1	HPOW	1,000	(5,532)
Alternative Energy	2001	1	PLUG	300	(4,913)
Alternative Energy	2001	2	APWR	0	2,500
Alternative Energy	2001	2	BLDP	-100	11,363
Alternative Energy	2001	2	CPST	-200	10,575
Alternative Energy	2001	2	EFCX	-500	4,141
Alternative Energy	2001	2	FCEL	1,600	(45,944)
Alternative Energy	2001	2	HPOW	300	(1,963)
Alternative Energy	2001	2	PLUG	-2,400	59,538

Additional Query Table

Ticker	Year Num	Month Num	High Closing Price	Low Closing Price
ACPW	2001	1	29.06	19.81
ACPW	2001	2	23.75	19.44
APWR	2001	1	51.06	33.13
APWR	2001	2	43.13	33.38
CPST	2001	1	41.88	22.81
CPST	2001	2	42.25	24.19
FCEL	2001	1	38.59	23.5
FCEL	2001	2	34.38	23.47
HPOW	2001	1	9.81	5.75
HPOW	2001	2	8.44	5.69
PLUG	2001	1	31.38	15
PLUG	2001	2	26.44	15.75

Adding Additional Queries

A document can contain multiple queries. We may add additional queries to display data from different universes, different contexts within the same universe, or any other reason that allows us to get the data that we need in our documents. In this example, we included data from two different contexts in the same universe - The Transactions context and the Equity Prices context. We may do this to compare the stock (equity) prices to the trader's purchase prices to evaluate how the trader is performing.

To add an additional query, we click the Add Query button in the Query Panel. This will pop up several dialogs that allow us to choose the data source for our additional query. Notice that in the *Select Universe* graphic, the Universe that is currently in our document is listed in the Used Universes section. This makes it easier to discern the current universe from the other available universes. After we select a universe, there will be a new tab in the Query Panel that will allow us to create the addition query.

Notes

Additional Queries Tips

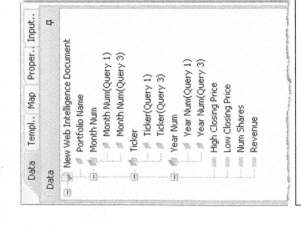

Naming Queries

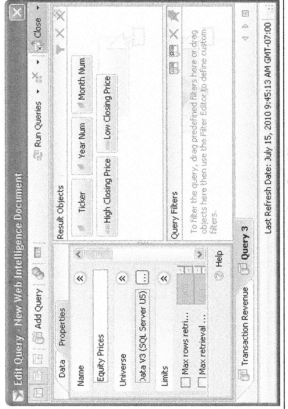

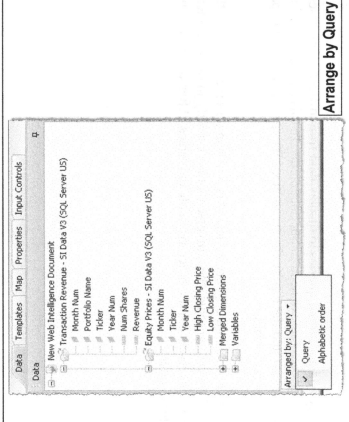

Arrange by Query

Additional Queries Tips

When there is more than one query in a document, it is best to name the queries. We should name the queries, because people need to know the purpose for the additional queries. It also makes it easier to identify where the objects come from, when viewing them in the Data tab.

One time I was hired to make a company's reports more efficient. I went to the jobsite and they told me that Web Intelligence was not efficient, because it was taking way too long to retrieve data. I opened and looked at several documents. I notice that all of their reports were multiple query reports, and many had as many as 10 or 12 queries. I asked them why they had these extra queries, and they were not sure. The queries names were Query 1, Query 2, Query n..., so there was no way to know what the queries were doing from their names. After some investigation, I found that many of the documents only used data from half of the queries that they contained. I deleted the unused queries, and the documents became much speedier. I bet that company now names all of their queries.

The data in the Data tab is usually organized in alphabetical order. This organization will make objects with the same name appear together in the list. Then, they are differentiated by suffixing the query name to the object name. There is also another view that groups the objects into folders represented by the query names in the document. This view is good when trying to select multiple objects from the same query.

Notes

Merged Dimensions

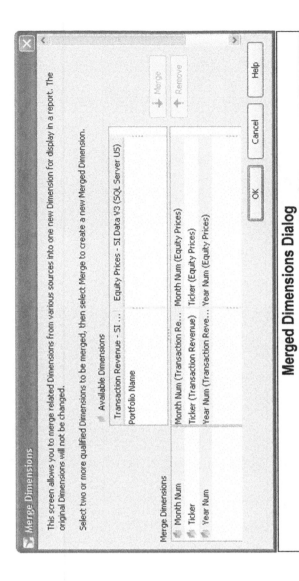

Merged Dimension in Data Tab

Merged Dimensions Dialog

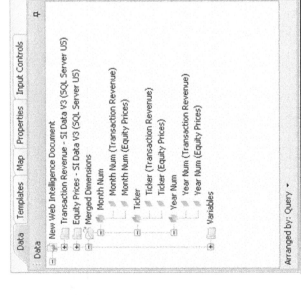

Portfolio Name	Year Num	Month Num	Ticker	Num Shares	Revenue	Avg Sell Price	Low Closing Price	% Over Low	Avg Buy Price	High Closing Price	% Below High
Alternative Energy	2001	1	ACPW	-700	26,063	37.23	19.81	88%			
Alternative Energy	2001	1	APWR	-300	11,963	39.88	33.13	20%			
Alternative Energy	2001	1	CPST	-800	24,725	30.91	22.81	35%			
Alternative Energy	2001	1	FCEL	600	(15,637)				26.06	38.59	32%
Alternative Energy	2001	1	HPOW	1,000	(5,532)				5.53	9.81	44%
Alternative Energy	2001	1	PLUG	300	(4,913)				16.38	31.38	48%
Alternative Energy	2001	2	APWR	0	2,500						
Alternative Energy	2001	2	BLDP	-100	11,363	113.63	46.88	142%			
Alternative Energy	2001	2	CPST	-200	10,575	52.88	24.19	119%			
Alternative Energy	2001	2	EFCX	-500	4,141	8.28	5.25	58%			
Alternative Energy	2001	2	FCEL	1,600	(45,944)				28.71	34.38	16%
Alternative Energy	2001	2	HPOW	300	(1,963)				6.54	8.44	22%
Alternative Energy	2001	2	PLUG	-2,400	59,538	24.81	15.75	58%			

Report with Merged Dimensions

Merged Dimensions

In the previous example, we created two queries for a document. On the report, we had two separate tables - one for each data set. Report structures using discrete data sets works with some types of reporting. For example, some sort of dashboard that displays the current status of several different areas of a business. However, we often create multiple queries to analyze the data has a whole.

Each set of data usually has one or more dimensions that define the context of the data set. These dimensions create the rows in a report, and on each row there is usually a measure. This measure displays an aggregate total for the dimensions on the row. The total of all of a measure values on the rows is the total for the data set. If any of the rows in the data set repeat, for any reason, then there could be a chance that the measure may contribute to the total more than once, which would skew the total of the measure. Therefore, it is important not to change the context of a data set by causing some of the rows to repeat.

In the previous example, we had two data sets:

4. **Portfolio Name, Ticker, Year Num, Month Num,** Num Transactions, and Revenue.
5. **Ticker, Year Num, Month Num,** High Closing Price, and Low Closing Price.

The dimensions in each set are in bold font. The dimensions in set two are a subset of the dimensions in set one. Therefore, if we were to link the dimensions in the two sets to their respective counterparts, then set two will not cause set one's rows to repeat. The rows in set two may repeat, but we do not aggregate prices, so there is no danger of erroneous totals in set two. If we were to link (merge) the dimensions in set two to set one, then the data sets would be synchronized and appear to be a single set of data. This means that any combination of Ticker, Year Num, and Month Num will reference a row that contains High Closing Price and Low Closing Price for the combination of values.

This merged behavior allowed me to create the report in the graphic that compares the average selling or buying price of a stock from the Transactions context, to the Low and High Closing Prices found in the Equity Prices context.

Notes

Merged Dimensions (Continued)

Data from Query Two

Ticker	Year Num	Month Num	High Closing Price	Low Closing Price
ACPW	2001	1	29.06	19.81
ACPW	2001	2	23.75	19.44
APWR	2001	1	51.06	33.13
APWR	2001	2	43.13	33.38
BLDP	2001	1	76.81	55.25
BLDP	2001	2	75	46.88
CPST	2001	1	41.88	22.81
CPST	2001	2	42.25	24.19
EFCX	2001	1	8	4.44
EFCX	2001	2	7.69	5.25
FCEL	2001	1	38.59	23.5
FCEL	2001	2	34.38	23.47
HPOW	2001	1	9.81	5.75
HPOW	2001	2	8.44	5.69
PLUG	2001	1	31.38	15
PLUG	2001	2	26.44	15.75

Unmerged Dimensions

Portfolio Name	Ticker	Year Num	Month Num	Num Shares	Revenue	High Closing Price	Low Closing Price
Alternative Energy	ACPW	2001	1	-700	26,063	76.81	4.44
Alternative Energy	APWR	2001	1	-300	11,963	76.81	4.44
Alternative Energy	APWR	2001	2	0	2,500	76.81	4.44
Alternative Energy	BLDP	2001	2	-100	11,363	76.81	4.44
Alternative Energy	CPST	2001	1	-800	24,725	76.81	4.44
Alternative Energy	CPST	2001	2	-200	10,575	76.81	4.44
Alternative Energy	EFCX	2001	2	-500	4,141	76.81	4.44
Alternative Energy	FCEL	2001	1	600	(15,637)	76.81	4.44
Alternative Energy	FCEL	2001	2	1,600	(45,944)	76.81	4.44
Alternative Energy	HPOW	2001	1	1,000	(5,532)	76.81	4.44
Alternative Energy	HPOW	2001	2	300	(1,963)	76.81	4.44
Alternative Energy	PLUG	2001	1	300	(4,913)	76.81	4.44
Alternative Energy	PLUG	2001	2	-2,400	59,538	76.81	4.44

Data from Query One

Portfolio Name	Ticker	Year Num	Month Num	Num Shares	Revenue
Alternative Energy	ACPW	2001	1	-700	26,063
Alternative Energy	APWR	2001	1	-300	11,963
Alternative Energy	APWR	2001	2	0	2,500
Alternative Energy	BLDP	2001	2	-100	11,363
Alternative Energy	CPST	2001	1	-800	24,725
Alternative Energy	CPST	2001	2	-200	10,575
Alternative Energy	EFCX	2001	2	-500	4,141
Alternative Energy	FCEL	2001	1	600	(15,637)
Alternative Energy	FCEL	2001	2	1,600	(45,944)
Alternative Energy	HPOW	2001	1	1,000	(5,532)
Alternative Energy	HPOW	2001	2	300	(1,963)
Alternative Energy	PLUG	2001	1	300	(4,913)
Alternative Energy	PLUG	2001	2	-2,400	59,538

Merged Dimensions

Portfolio Name	Ticker	Year Num	Month Num	Num Shares	Revenue	High Closing Price	Low Closing Price
Alternative Energy	ACPW	2001	1	-700	26,063	29.06	19.81
Alternative Energy	APWR	2001	1	-300	11,963	51.06	33.13
Alternative Energy	APWR	2001	2	0	2,500	43.13	33.38
Alternative Energy	BLDP	2001	2	-100	11,363	75	46.88
Alternative Energy	CPST	2001	1	-800	24,725	41.88	22.81
Alternative Energy	CPST	2001	2	-200	10,575	42.25	24.19
Alternative Energy	EFCX	2001	2	-500	4,141	7.69	5.25
Alternative Energy	FCEL	2001	1	600	(15,637)	38.59	23.5
Alternative Energy	FCEL	2001	2	1,600	(45,944)	34.38	23.47
Alternative Energy	HPOW	2001	1	1,000	(5,532)	9.81	5.75
Alternative Energy	HPOW	2001	2	300	(1,963)	8.44	5.69
Alternative Energy	PLUG	2001	1	300	(4,913)	31.38	15
Alternative Energy	PLUG	2001	2	-2,400	59,538	26.44	15.75

Merged Dimensions (Continued)

In the upper part of the graphic, we have the data sets from Query One and Query Two. In the lower part of the graphic, we have placed High Closing Price and Low Closing Price from Query Two in the same table as the data from Query One.

The lower-left table represents the data from the two data sets that have been merged. Notice how the high and low prices are correctly distributed throughout the table. For example, ACPW, 2001, 1 in the merged set has 29.06 and 19.81, for the High and Low prices, respectively. The same is true in the table for Query Two in the graphic. This is true, because the merge data set uses the values of Ticker, Year Num, and Month Num in the merged data set to look up the measure values in Query Two. Therefore, when we merge data sets, we should include enough dimensions to uniquely identify the values of interest in the merged data set.

The lower-right table also contains High Closing Price and Low Closing Price. However, the values are all the same. The value of 76.81 is the highest closing price in Query Two, and 4.44 is the lowest. The values repeat, because the data sets are not merged. Therefore, it cannot look up the correct values based on the dimensional key values, as in the merged set. So, it just lists the highest and the lowest for the entire data set for each combination of dimension values.

Notes

Merging Dimensions

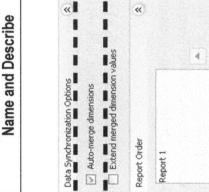

Merge Dimensions

This screen allows you to merge related Dimensions from various sources into one new Dimension for display in a report. The original Dimensions will not be changed.

Select two or more qualified Dimensions to be merged, then select Merge to create a new Merged Dimension.

Available Dimensions

Query 1 - SI Data V3 (SQ...	Query 2 - SI Data V3 (SQL Server US)
Portfolio Name	Ticker
Ticker	Year Num
Year Num	

Merge Dimensions

Month Num	Month Num

→ Merge
← Remove

≫ Values

OK   Cancel   Help

Select Available Dimensions

Edit Merged Dimension

Select a source dimension to provide default properties for the merged dimension:

Source Dimension

Ticker (Query 1 - SI Data V3 (SQL Server US))

Merged Dimension Name

Master Ticker

Description

Data type: string

Number Format:

OK   Cancel   Help

Name and Describe

Data Synchronization Options

☑ Auto-merge dimensions

☐ Extend merged dimension values

Report Order

Report 1

Auto-Merge Dimensions Property

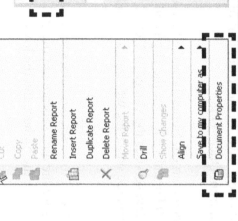

| Cut |
| Copy |
| Paste |
| Rename Report |
| Insert Report |
| Duplicate Report |
| Delete Report |
| Move Report |
| Drill |
| Show Changes |
| Align |
| Save to my computer as |
| Document Properties |

Data   Templates   Map   Properties   Input Con..

Data

- CH035 - Creating Merged Queries
  - Query 1 - SI Data V3 (SQL Server US)
  - Query 2 - SI Data V3 (SQL Server US)
  - Merged Dimensions
    - Master Ticker
      - Ticker (Query 1)
      - Ticker (Query 2)
    - Month Num
      - Month Num (Query 1)
      - Month Num (Query 2)
    - Year Num
      - Year Num (Query 1)
      - Year Num (Query 2)
  - Variables

Merged Dimensions

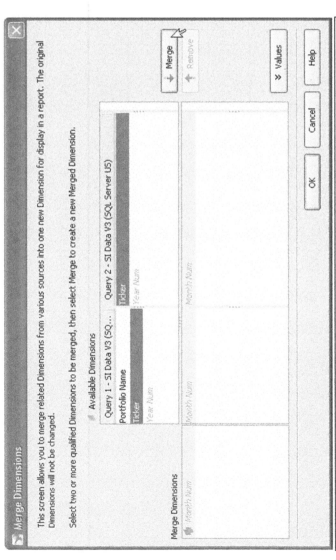
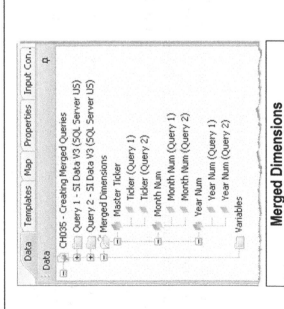

Merging Dimensions

Dimensions with the same name, from the same universe, but in different queries, in the same document will be automatically merged when the query is executed. Web Intelligence assumes that since the objects are so similar that the report developer will want to include the results from the queries in a single report structure. This is probably correct most of the time, but I have heard people complain that they not want the auto-merge feature, and they want to explicitly merge the dimensions. Therefore, Web Intelligence has included an option in the Document Properties for a document. This option is the *Auto-Merge Dimensions* option, and it can be unchecked, if the auto-merge behavior is undesired in the document.

Dimension objects with the same name, from the same universe will be automatically merged. However, if the names differ or they come from different universes, then they will not be merged. When this happens, and we still want to merge the dimensions, then we can use the Merge Dimensions dialog. To display this dialog, click the *Merge Dimensions* toolbar button. To merge two dimensions, select them from the available dimensions list, and then click the *Merge* button in the dialog. The Edit Merged Dimensions dialog will appear. With this dialog, we can name our newly merged dimension and also give it a description. Click OK, and the merged dimension will appear in the *Merged Dimensions* list of the Merge Dimensions dialog.

To un-merge dimensions, select the merge dimension in the Merged Dimensions list, and then click the *Remove* button.

Notes

Changing Universes

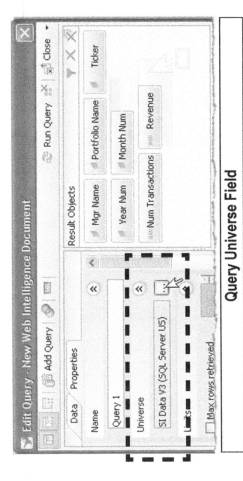

Query Universe Field

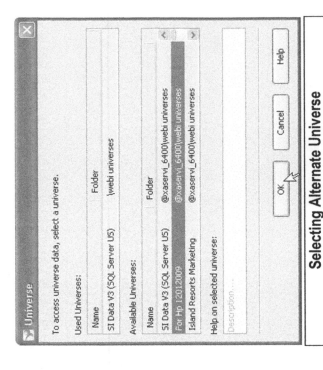

Selecting Alternate Universe

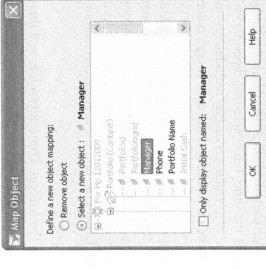

Remapping Mgr Name

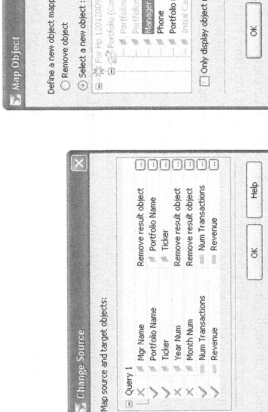

Change Source Dialog

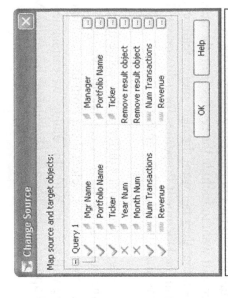

Mgr Name Mapped to Manager

Changing Universes

At times, we need to change the universe for a document's query. We may do this to switch from a development universe to a production universe. We may also want do this, because the universe designers have created a newer universe and they want the report developers to point existing documents to the newer universe.

To change the universe of a query:

4. Click the small button (...) in the Universe section, of the Properties tab for a query. This will display the Universe dialog that is populated with a list of all available universes. (This is the same dialog displayed when selecting a universe for multiple queries). Select the new universe and click *OK*.

5. The Change Source dialog will appear with a mapping of all objects in the query and their respective mappings into the new universe. In this dialog there are two states for the mappings. A green check means that the mapping found an object with the same name in the new universe. A blue 'X' means that it cannot find a match for the current object in the new universe.

   a. If an object has an 'X', then we can try to map it to an object in the new universe. To do this, we click the small button (...) associated with the mapping to display the Map Object dialog. In this dialog, we locate an object that can be mapped to the current object, and then click *OK*. We do this for each object mapping with an 'X'.

   b. If the object with an 'X' is not mapped, then the object will be removed form the Result Objects section in the Query Panel.

Notes

Other Data Source

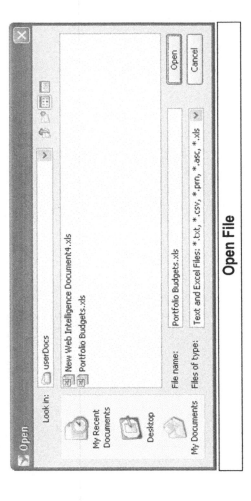

Other Data Source

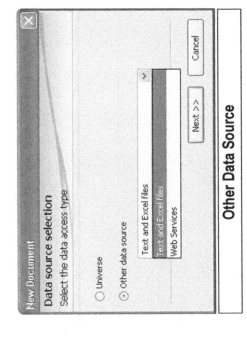

Open File

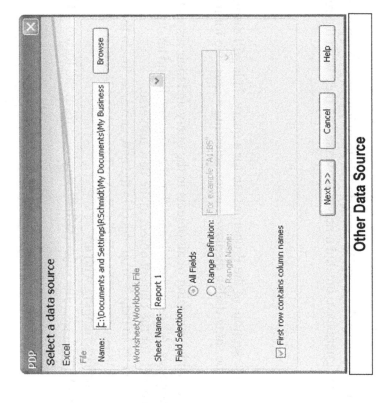

Other Data Source

Other Data Source

So far, we have only used universes for the data providers in our documents. With Web Intelligence Rich Client, we can also use Other Data Sources, which are Text and Excel files, or Web Services. In this example, we are going to look at using Excel as a data provider.

When we click *File>New...*, we are presented with a New Document dialog. In this dialog, we can select the type of data provider that we are interested in. In this example, we will select Text and Excel Files, and then click the *Next >>* button. The next step is to find and open the file that contains the data that we are interested in. We do this through the standard Open dialog.

When using an Excel file, we have to tell Web Intelligence where the data resides in the Excel file. We do this by first selecting the sheet name in the Excel file. In this example, the sheet name is just *Report 1*. Next, we define the field selection. If the Excel report simply contains data, and does not have a header or other data groups on the report, then we can just select *All Fields*. If you are only interested in a subset of data on the Excel sheet, then you enter the fields where the data is populated. The fields can be defined by a range, such as "A1:D15", which is 15 rows, in columns A through D. Many times the rows are a variable, and we are not sure how many rows we will need. If this is the case, then the data may reside in a named ranged, in which case, the name of the range can be entered into the *Range Name* field.

Notes

Other Data Source (Page 2)

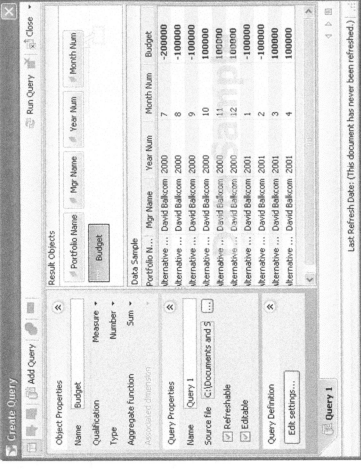

Change Erroneous Measures to Dimensions

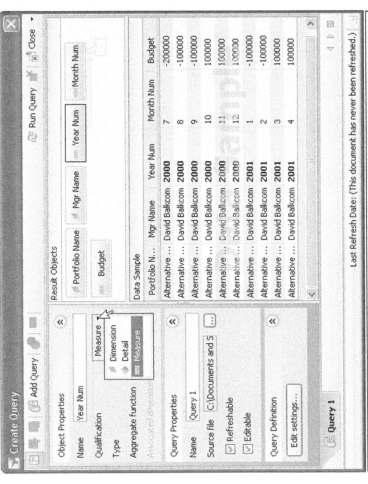

Make Sure Measures have Correct Aggregate Function

Portfolio Name	Mgr Name	Year Num	Month Num	Budget
Alternative Energy	David Balkcom	2,000	7	-200,000
Alternative Energy	David Balkcom	2,000	8	-100,000
Alternative Energy	David Balkcom	2,000	9	-100,000
Alternative Energy	David Balkcom	2,000	10	100,000
Alternative Energy	David Balkcom	2,000	11	100,000
Alternative Energy	David Balkcom	2,000	12	100,000
Alternative Energy	David Balkcom	2,001	1	-100,000
Alternative Energy	David Balkcom	2,001	2	-100,000
Alternative Energy	David Balkcom	2,001	3	100,000
Alternative Energy	David Balkcom	2,001	4	100,000

Query Results

Other Data Source (Page 2)

When Designers create universes, they qualify objects as Measures, Dimensions, and Details. They define them based on the object's behavior within a report. When we import data using other data sources, we must make sure the objects are correctly qualified. For example, many times numbers are qualified as measures, by default. In our example, the Year Num object is a number, but it is not to behave as a measure. As a measure, it will aggregate to existing contexts, and not define them. As a Dimension, the Year Num will add to the context definition, which is how we want the object to behave. The same goes for Month Num. Therefore, we will need to change the Qualification of both these objects to a dimension.

The Budget object should be a measure, and it is defined as one, which is the default behavior. However, we must make sure that its aggregate function is the one that we want. In this case we want Sum, and that is the default aggregate for most numbers.

Suppose that the header labels were included in the data set as a row of data, or one row of the data was defining the column headers for the data set. Both of these situations are not correct, and will occur if we checked *First Row Contains Column Names*, when there was no header row, during the PDP step of the data provider definition, or if we did not select *First Row Contains Column Names*, when there was a header row. To fix this, just click the *Edit Settings...* button and rectify the selection. Check the option if there is a header row, and clear it, if there is no header row in the data.

After any qualification adjustments, we click Run Query to bring the data into Web Intelligence.

Notes

Other Data Source (Page 3)

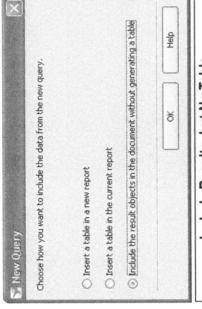

Add Query from Universe

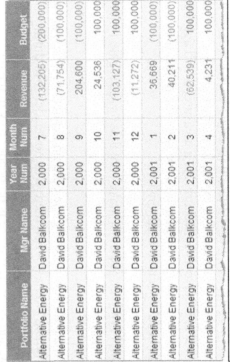

Include Results, but No Table

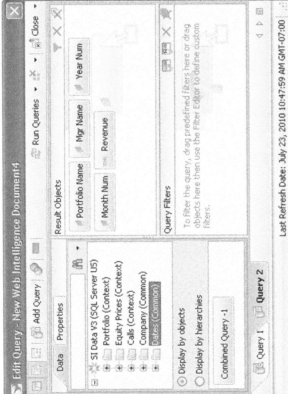

Merge Common Dimensions

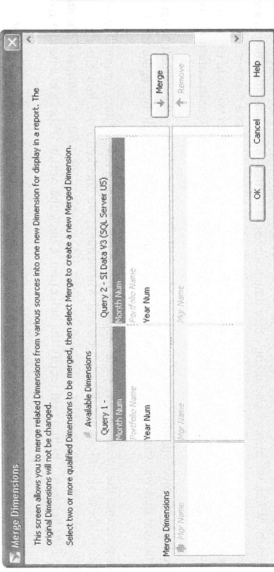

Merged Data in Table

Other Data Source (Page 3)

Now that we know how to use other data sources, let's see what happens when we combine it with a universe query. In this example, another query is added to the Excel query in the previous example. To add the query, we just clicked the *Edit Query* button, and then Added a Query in the Query Panel. We included all of the dimensions that were in the Excel query, and also the Revenue measure object. When the query was refreshed, Web Intelligence asked if we wanted to display the new data in the document. It asked this through the New Query dialog, as seen in the graphic.

Once the query returned the data to the document, the Universe data was independent of the Excel data. Therefore, we could not successfully include data from one in a table containing data from the other. To synchronize the data sets, we must merge the dimensions in the queries. This is one of the reasons for correctly qualifying the objects in the Excel query. In this example, we merged all of the dimensions to their counterparts in the other query.

To launch the Merge Dimensions dialog, click the *Merge Dimensions* toolbar button. In this dialog, we highlight pairs of dimensions in the *Available Dimensions* list, and then merge them by clicking the *Merge* button. In order to successfully include data from queries in the same report structure, all of the dimensions in the queries must be linked. Once they are all linked, then we can place the Revenue measure object in the default table from the Excel example. We can even add another column to compare the actual Revenues to the Budgeted Revenue.

Notes

Summary

Retrieving Data

Processing Request

Estimated wait: 5s
The estimated wait is based on the last refresh.

Cancel Help

Sending SQL to Database

Retrieving Data

Retrieving document.

Estimated wait: 2s
The estimated wait is based on the last refresh.

Cancel Help

Retrieving Document Template

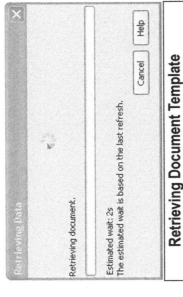

Retrieving Data

Decoding Document

Estimated wait: 1s
The estimated wait is based on the last refresh.

Cancel Help

Decoding the Template

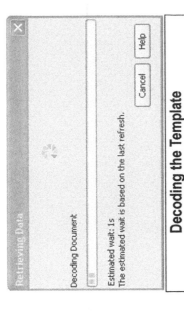

Mgr Name	Portfolio Name	Year Num	Quarter Num	Num Transactions	Revenue
David Balkcom	Alternative Energy	2000	3	42	642
David Balkcom	Alternative Energy	2000	4	36	(89,863)
David Balkcom	Alternative Energy	2001	1	49	14,341
David Balkcom	Alternative Energy	2001	2	36	228,017
David Balkcom	Alternative Energy	2001	3	11	61,529
Eddie Wang	Technology	2000	3	126	(740,160)
Eddie Wang	Technology	2000	4	148	(376,607)
Eddie Wang	Technology	2001	1	133	(5,848)
Eddie Wang	Technology	2001	2	131	543,731
Eddie Wang	Technology	2001	3	53	521,614
Kathy James	Media	2000	3	31	(267,653)
Kathy James	Media	2000	4	31	(197,741)
Kathy James	Media	2001	1	23	52,981
Kathy James	Media	2001	2	27	112,154

Default Report

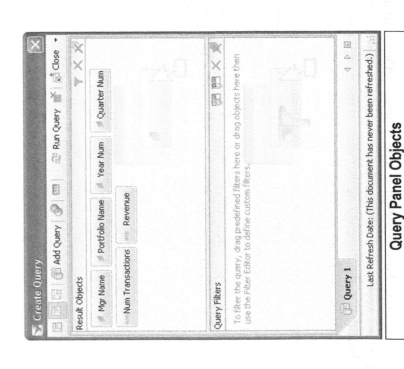

Create Query   Add Query   Run Query   Close

Result Objects

Mgr Name   Portfolio Name   Year Num   Quarter Num
Num Transactions   Revenue

Query Filters

To filter the query, drag predefined filters here or drag objects here and then use the Filter Editor to define custom filters.

Query 1

Last Refresh Date: (This document has never been refreshed.)

Query Panel Objects

Summary

In the chapter, we learned how to create queries that bring data into our documents. We saw that the objects in the Result Objects section of the Query Panel will create entries in the Select statement of the SQL generated by Web Intelligence. We also saw that selecting only dimensions could create a very large sized report, even though there are only a few rows on the report, because there may be many thousands of duplicates in the data set. We learned that including a measure in the result objects section should cause the SQL to return a summarized data set that could be much smaller than a query with no measures.

We learned that we could include more than one query in a document. We found that each query will return a separate data set, and that we could synchronize the data sets by merging the dimensions that are in common to both data sets. We also learned that we could create queries that accessed data in other data sources, such as MS Excel. We discovered that Web Intelligence will qualify numeric data as a measure, even when it is supposed to be a dimension. We saw that we could re-qualify the erroneous measures to make them dimensions.

In the next chapter, we are going to learn how to limit the data returned to documents, and we will also learn some more data techniques that will allow us to better control the data being returned to our documents.

Notes

Creating Documents with Business Objects Web Intelligence XI V3

Chapter 5: Query Filters

Introduction

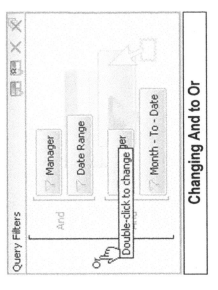

Four Query Filters

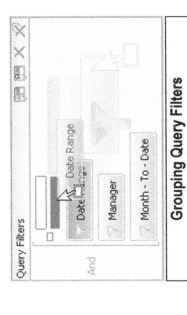

Grouping Query Filters

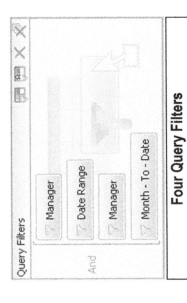

Changing And to Or

Introduction

In this chapter, we are going to continue with the Query Panel, by discussing how to create limited data sets. We know that the data that we want is in the database, because we have objects that point to and identify the data. If we just selected these data objects, and did not consider the context of the data returned, such as a date range, then we may get way too much data returned to our document. Some companies will limit the amount of data that can be returned by limiting the number of rows that the query can return, or by limiting the amount of time that a query can run. If we hit one of these limits, before our complete data set is returned, then we may only get a partial set of data to work with. Therefore, it is best to consider what limits we can place on the data to limit it to the scope of our documents.

We set these limits with the use of Query Filters and other data set techniques that we will learn in this chapter.

Notes

_____

Designer Query Filters

- Ticker
- Manager
- Date Range
- Month - To - Date
- Quarter - to - Date
- Week - to - Date
- Year-To-Date

Query Filters

@Select(Dates (Common)\Trans Date) BETWEEN
@Prompt('Enter Begin Date','D','Dates (Common)\Trans Date',,) AND
@Prompt('Enter End Date','D','Dates (Common)\Trans Date',,)

Definition for Date Range From Designer

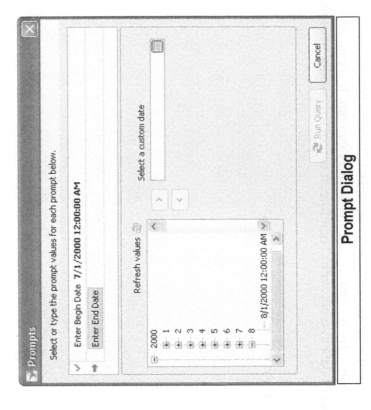

Prompt Dialog

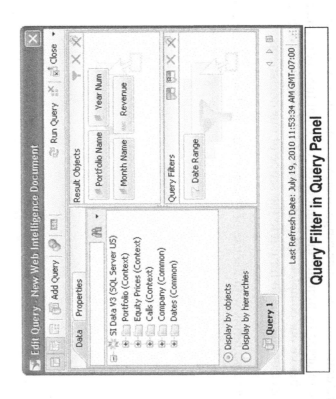

Query Filter in Query Panel

Designer Query Filters

When the Universe Designers create universes, they create Dimensions, Measures, and Details. In addition to these objects, designers also create Query Filters. Some designers create hundreds of filters and other designers create just a few. Query filters enable the report developers to limit the data returned to a document using desired parameter values. For example, possible filters could be Active Clients, Closed Accounts, or the Eastern Region. These types of filters usually require no input from the report refresher, because they are already defined. Other prompts could be Manager, Ticker, or Date Range. These types of filters usually require input from the report refresher, because the refresher will have to select the parameter values from a list of managers, a list of tickers, or enter the desired date range. This type of filter is known as a prompt.

If a query contains a prompted query filter in the Query Filters section of the Query Panel, then when the report is refreshed, a Prompts dialog will be displayed, as shown in the graphic. This dialog allows values to be entered for the prompt parameters. In the graphic, the prompt is asking for the begin and end dates of a date range. This type of date range filter is very common.

When presented with the prompt dialog, values can be typed in the edit field or selected from the list of values. Some prompts do not allow for values to be typed, and force the refresher to select from a list of values. Other prompts may not have a list of values, and the refresher will have to type the value in the edit field. Some prompts allow for multiple values to be entered, and others only allow for one value. The date prompt in the graphic, wants a single date for both the Begin and End Date. We know this, because there is only a single edit field. If multiple values were allowed, then there would be a larger box that allows for multiple entries.

Notes

Selecting Query Filters

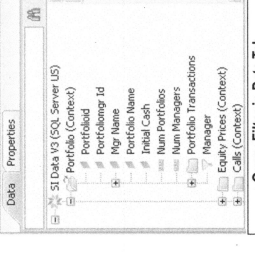

Query Filter in Data Tab

Data | Properties

SI Data V3 (SQL Server US)
Portfolio (Context)
Portfolioid
Portfoliomgr Id
Mgr Name
Portfolio Name
Initial Cash
Num Portfolios
Num Managers
Portfolio Transactions
Manager
Equity Prices (Context)
Calls (Context)

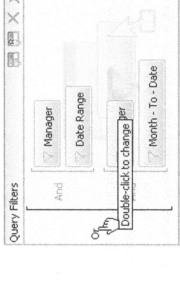

Changing And to Or

Query Filters

And

Manager
Date Range

Or

Double-click to change per

Month - To - Date

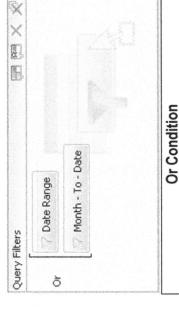

And Condition

Query Filters

And

Date Range
Manager

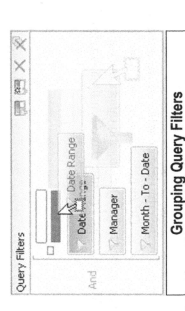

Or Condition

Query Filters

Or

Date Range
Month - To - Date

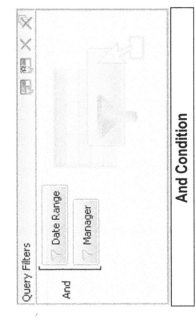

Four Query Filters

Query Filters

And

Manager
Date Range
Manager
Month - To - Date

Grouping Query Filters

Query Filters

And

Date Range
Date Range
Manager
Month - To - Date

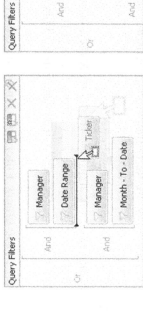

Adding Ticker to a Group

Query Filters

And

Or

And

Manager
Date Range
Ticker
Manager

Query Filters

Or

And

And

Manager
Date Range
Manager
Month - To - Date

Ticker

Selecting Query Filters

Designer Query Filters are found in the Data Tab, along with the other types of objects. When one is double-clicked on, Web Intelligence will place a copy of the object in the Query Filters section of the panel. Query filters can also be dragged into the Query Filters section.

When multiple query filters are placed in the Query Filters section, they must be logically related. Web Intelligence uses two logical operators: the *And* and the *Or* operators. To toggle between the two operators, double-click on the operator that relates the Query Filters.

And logic has the following: True And False = False, False And False = False, True And True = True. This means that both Query Filters must be true for a row to be returned to the data set. For example, the statement *Manager = David Balkcom And Year Num = 20001*, will only return a row from the database where both the manager is David Balkcom and the Year Num is 2001.

Or logic has the following: True Or False = True, False Or False = False, True Or True = True. This means that only one of the query filters needs to be true in order to return a row form the database. For example, the statement *Manager = David Balkcom Or Year Num = 20001*, will return a row from the database where either the manager is David Balkcom or the Year Num is 2001.

In algebra, we group operations with parentheses and we have the order of operation rules. For example, A*(B+C) = A*B + A*C, which is known as the distributive rule. Logic is very similar, where the times sign is analogous to the *And* operator, and the Plus sign is analogous to the *Or* operator. With Web Intelligence we can group query filters by dragging one filter near another, as seen in the graphic. This is analogous to parentheses. The operator to the left of the group is the logical operator that relates the objects in the group. To add another object to a group, do not drag the object next to another object, drag it to one of the grouping lines, as seen in the graphic.

We usually use *Or* logic when the Query Filters are on the same object. For example, Manager = David Balkcom Or Manager = Kathy James, which would return data when the Manager field in the database is either manager. If we tried to use And logic, then we would get no data back, because the Manager field cannot be both managers at one time. We usually use *And* logic when combining query filters that operate on different objects. For example, Year Num = 2001 and Manager = David Balkcom, which would return rows from the database where Manager is David Balkcom and the Year Num is 2001. If we used *Or* logic, the rows returned would have David Balkcom as the manager, but would return rows with any Year Num Value, and it would return all rows with Year Num = 2001, regardless of which manager is also on the row.

Notes

Custom Query Filter

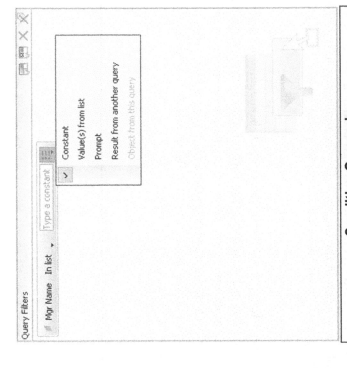

Condition Operators

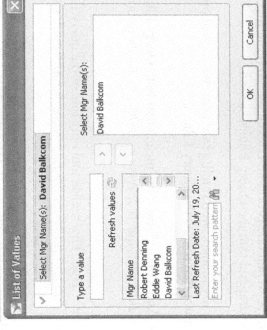

Condition Operands

Object Operator Operand

Most Filters Have Three Components

Constant Operand

List of Values (LOV)

Custom Query Filter

Earlier, I said that some universe designers create fewer query filters than others. This doesn't mean that their universes will be less usable than the universes with more filters, because these designers think that the report developers will create their own filters. These designers usually just create the filters that are not possible to create in Web Intelligence.

We create custom filters by dragging an object from the Data tab into the Query Filters section of the Query Panel. The query filter object differs from the objects in the Result Objects section, because there is also an Operator and an Operand associated with the object. To create the filter, we select an operator, and if necessary, also select an operand. For example, Mgr Name Equal to David Balkcom, where Mgr Name is the object, Equal to is the Operator, and David Balkcom is the Operand.

Some operators do not need an operand. For example, the Is Null Operator, which does not need an operand, because Is Null infers that we want rows where the field has not been assigned a value. You can see the list of operators available in the graphic.

The Matches Pattern allows for the use of Wildcard characters. For Example, Matches Pattern David B%, will return David Balkcom, and any other David whose last name starts with a 'B'. Therefore, the percent (%) sign is a wildcard for any number of characters. Other examples could be, %Balkcom (would return all with the last name of Balkcom) and %David% (Would return all with David anywhere in their name). These later two examples are not very efficient, because the database must check every row in the data set to see if the condition is true, which is known as a table scan. The first example had a first character defined, so the database could go directly to the 'D' section in the index, much like an index in a book. If the first character is a wildcard, then the database cannot use the index.

The available operands allow for a constant to be typed in the Operand field. We enter a constant by just typing in the Operand field, and there is no need to select Constant from the list, unless you are changing to Constant from a different operand type. Entering constants is fine for many conditions. For example, a date is easy to enter. However, some values are not easily typed in. For example, David Balkcom, which is difficult for many to spell, and may be case-sensitive in the database. In these difficult situations, it is better to select from a list of values. Usually, the list of values does not refresh upon use, but if the list looks out of date, then it can be refreshed by clicking the *Refresh Values* button in the dialog.

Notes

Prompted Filter

Mgr Name   In list   ▸   Enter value(s) for Mgr Name

Mgr Name   In list   ▸   Enter value(s) for Mgr Name:

- Constant
- Value(s) from list
- ✓ Prompt
- Result from another query
- Object from this query

Prompted Operand

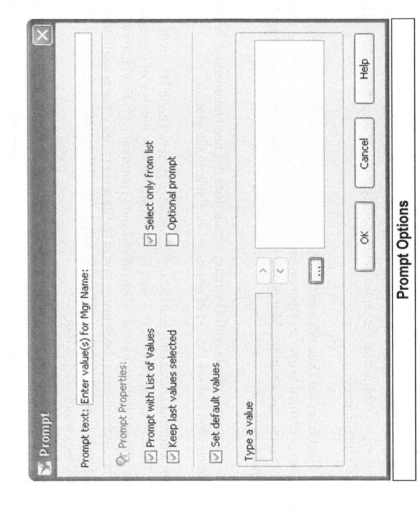

Prompt

Prompt text: Enter value(s) for Mgr Name:

Prompt Properties:

- ☑ Prompt with List of Values
- ☑ Keep last values selected

☑ Select only from list
☐ Optional prompt

☑ Set default values

Type a value

⌄ ⌃   ...

OK   Cancel   Help

Prompt Options

Prompted Filter

We have talked about Designer defined prompted query filters. Here, we see that report developers can also create prompted query filters. The report prompts created by developers are more flexible for the developer, because they get to define the prompt text, by editing the default text in the operand field. However, before editing the text in the field, Prompt must be selected from the *Operand* drop list, or Web Intelligence will assume that it is a constant operand type.

Once Prompt is selected from the *Operand* list, a new smaller button will appear on the query filter, which can be seen in the upper-right of the graphic page. This is the *Prompt Properties* button. In the Properties dialog, we can edit the Prompt Text, by editing the text in the Prompt Text field.

We can also set several properties

3. **Prompt with List of Values**: This option will also display the list of values in the Prompt dialog. At first, it may seem like this is always a good idea, but some lists are large and take a long time to populate. In addition, some objects don't really need a list of values. For example, dates or numbers. For these reasons, many report developers may opt not to show a list of values in the prompt dialog.

4. **Keep Last Values Selected**: This option will populate the prompt with the same values that were selected the previous time the document was refreshed. Many people appreciate this option, because they do not have to reselect the operand values.

5. **Select Only From the List:** With this option, the document refresher must select values from the list of values, and will not be allowed to type in a value. This option is often used for security, where the list is limited due to the User of the application when the document is refreshed.

6. **Optional Prompt**: If this option is check, then the operand does not have to be populated. If it is left blank, then the Query Filter is ignored. This option works well when different prompts can be contradictory. For example, City and State. A person could enter a city and get results, but if the person also enters a state, then the city must be in that state. Therefore, it may be best to leave State blank, if a city is entered.

The last option in the dialog is the *Set Default Values* option. Sometimes, we want a prompt to contain default values. For example, maybe the top value of a hierarchy. We populate the default values by either typing in the edit field or selecting values from a list of values. If the *Select Only From List* option is checked, then the edit field will be disabled.

Notes

Result From Another Query

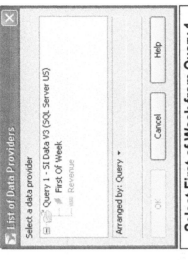

Select First of Week from Query 1

First Of Week	Revenue
5/7/01	925,921
4/30/01	915,899

Query 1 Results

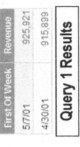

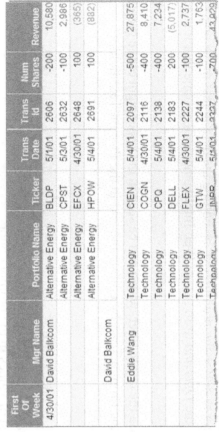

First Of Week	Mgr Name	Portfolio Name	Ticker	Trans Date	Trans Id	Num Shares	Revenue
4/30/01	David Balkcom	Alternative Energy	BLDP	5/1/01	2606	-200	10,580
		Alternative Energy	CPST	5/3/01	2632	-100	2,986
		Alternative Energy	EFCX	4/30/01	2648	100	(365)
	David Balkcom	Alternative Energy	HPOW	5/4/01	2691	100	(882)
	Eddie Wang	Technology	CIEN	5/4/01	2097	-500	27,875
		Technology	COGN	4/30/01	2116	-400	8,410
		Technology	CPQ	5/4/01	2138	-400	7,234
		Technology	DELL	5/4/01	2183	200	(5,017)
		Technology	FLEX	4/30/01	2227	-100	2,737
		Technology	GTW	5/4/01	2244	-100	1,763
		Technology	INPR	5/1/01	2237	-700	43,029

Query 2 Results

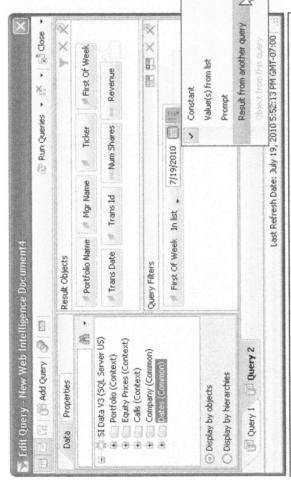

Query 2 - Result from another query

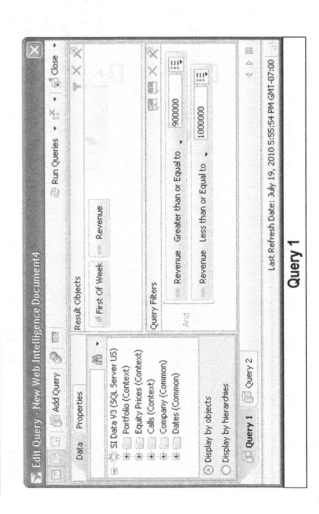

Query 1

Result From Another Query

If we were interested in the weeks that generated more than $900,000, but less than $1,000,000, then we could make a simple query, which is shown in Query1, in the graphic. This query will return the weeks, but can not include any dimension that will divide the Revenues. For example, if we included the Portfolio Name in Query 1, then we no longer would be returning weeks that generated the defined Revenues; we would be returning Portfolios that generated the defined revenue during any week. Therefore, we cannot add such dimension objects to Query 1, as it will change the weeks returned.

We could add another query and ask for Portfolio Name, Manager Name, Ticker, Trans Date, and even the Trans Id. This query will return much finer information than Query 1, but we could not use the Revenue condition that we used in Query 1, because we would be return Trans Id's that generated the defined revenue, and we want this information for the weeks that generated the defined revenue.

To solve this, we select the *Results From Another Query* operand on a First of Week object in a query filter. First of Week represents all dates in a week, because all dates in the week will have the same First of Week. This operand allows us to point the Query Filter to the First of Week in Query 1, even though we are creating the query filter in Query 2. We do this through the List of Data Providers dialog, as shown in the graphic.

In this example, Query 1 generated a list of First of Weeks. The list had a filter that limited the First of Weeks to only weeks where Revenue generated was less than $1,000,000, but greater than $900,000. This list was then used in the query filter in Query 2, to limit the data returned in Query 2, to only the weeks where Revenue was greater than $900,000 and less than $1,000,000.

Notes

Subquery

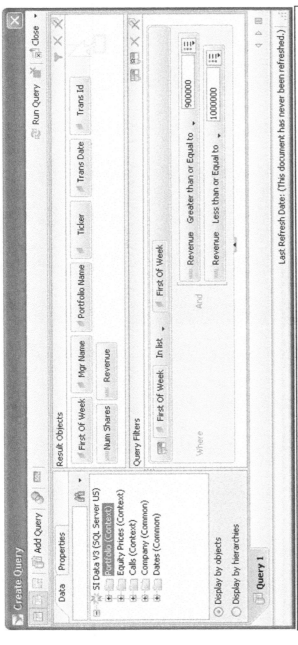

Query with Subquery Filter

Last Refresh Date: (This document has never been refreshed.)

First Of Week	Mgr Name	Portfolio Name	Ticker	Trans Date	Trans Id	Num Shares	Revenue
4/30/01	David Balkcom	Alternative Energy	BLDP	5/1/01	2,606	-200	10,580
		Alternative Energy	CPST	5/3/01	2,632	-100	2,986
		Alternative Energy	EFCX	4/30/01	2,648	100	(365)
		Alternative Energy	HPOW	5/4/01	2,691	100	(882)
	David Balkcom						

First Of Week	Mgr Name	Portfolio Name	Ticker	Trans Date	Trans Id	Num Shares	Revenue
	Eddie Wang	Technology	CIEN	5/4/01	2,097	-500	27,875
		Technology	COGN	4/30/01	2,116	-400	8,410
		Technology	CPQ	5/4/01	2,138	-400	7,234
		Technology	DELL	5/4/01	2,183	200	(5,017)
		Technology	FLEX	4/30/01	2,227	-100	2,737
		Technology	GTW	5/4/01	2,244	-100	1,763
		Technology	JNPR	5/1/01	2,327	700	43,929

Query Results

Subquery

In the previous example, *Result from another query*, we learned that we could use another query in a document to supply the list of values for a list operand in a query. This is a good solution, because it allows the list to be based on logic independent of the query. In this example, we do the same thing, but we use a subquery instead of a separate query.

The subquery is usually independent of the main query, and this allows it to return a list of values that are not affected by the objects in the result objects pane. For example, suppose that we wanted the transaction details for all the transactions during the weeks that generated between $900,000 and $1,000,000. In the previous example, we created a list of weeks where this revenue range was true. However, the query only returned the First of the Week and Revenue. If we were to include the Trans Id in the Result objects for the query, then we would return Trans Id's where the revenue condition was true.

With a subquery, the logic is similar to: *Select details, where Trans Id In List (**Select First of Week Where Revenue Between 900,000 and 1,00,000**).* In this case, the subquery needs nothing from the main query to return the values in the list. The advantage to the subquery over the *Result from Another Query* method is that only one query is needed, and therefore there are no synchronization issues.

Exercise: Subquery (Details From Summary Condition)

1. Create a query with First of Week, Portfolio Name, Mgr Name, Ticker, Trans Date, Trans Id, Num Shares and Revenue. (If we were to add a condition on Revenue in this query, then it would apply to revenue on a transaction resolution, not on a week.)

2. Create the Subquery

   a. Click the Add a subquery button on the Query Filter bar.

   b. Drag the First of Week object to the field before and after the In List operator on the subquery filter object.

   c. Drag the Revenue object onto the subquery object, onto the rect under the First of Week objects. Change the operator to *Greater Than or Equal to*, and then enter 900000 into the edit field on the Revenue filter object.

   d. Drag another Revenue object next to the Revenue object on the subquery condition. Change the operator to *Less Than or Equal to*, and then enter 1000000 into the edit field on the Revenue filter object.

   e. Make sure that the two Revenue objects are related with the And operator, as seen in the graphic.

3. Click the *Run Query* button.

Notes
_____

Database Ranking

Query Filters

Query Filters

Rank Types

| Top | ▾ | 5 | ▾ | ▼ | Ticker | Based on | Revenue |

Top
Bottom
% Top
% Bottom

To ... her ... defined filters here or drag objects or to define custom filters.

Can Prompt for N

| Top | ▾ | 5 | ▾ | ▼ | Ticker | Based on | Revenue |

Constant
Prompt

To filter the ... here or u... filters here or drag objects ine custom filters.

Database Ranking in Query Filters Pane

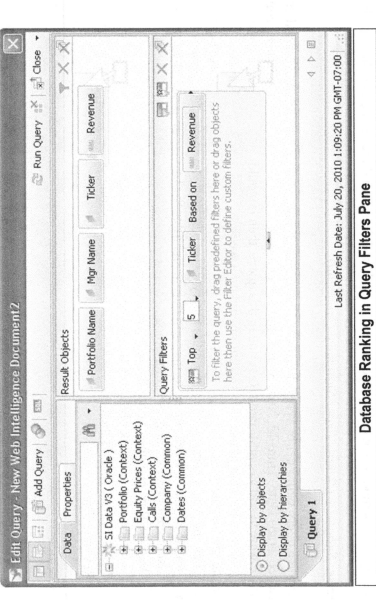

Edit Query - New Web Intelligence Document2

Add Query | ⚙ Run Query | ✗ | 📋 Close ▾

Data | Properties

- SI Data V3 (Oracle)
  - Portfolio (Context)
  - Equity Prices (Context)
  - Calls (Context)
  - Company (Common)
  - Dates (Common)

◉ Display by objects
○ Display by hierarchies

Query 1

Result Objects

| Portfolio Name | ▼ Mgr Name | ▼ Ticker | Revenue |

Query Filters

| Top | ▾ | 5 | ▾ | ▼ | Ticker | Based on | Revenue |

To filter the query, drag predefined filters here or drag objects here then use the Filter Editor to define custom filters.

Last Refresh Date: July 20, 2010 1:09:20 PM GMT-07:00

Query Results

Portfolio Name	Mgr Name	Ticker	Revenue
Biotech	Maria Castro	MRK	4,190
DOW 30	Sean Wilkenson	KO	54,995
DOW 30	Sean Wilkenson	MRK	60,300
Media	Kathy James	YHOO	99,821
Technology	Eddie Wang	CSCO	51,920
Technology	Eddie Wang	RMBS	42,770

Database Ranking

Sometimes, we want a subquery that is not based on constant values, but based on rankings. We cannot do this with a subquery in Web Intelligence, unless we know the dimension values that are the top ranked values for the dimension. With Web Intelligence, we can do this with a Database Ranking in the Query Filters section of the Query Panel.

To create the ranking, we start by clicking the *Add a Database Ranking* button in the Query Filters toolbar, which will add the database ranking object to the Query Filters section. We can choose to rank the Top, Bottom, % Top, or % Bottom. We can also hardcode the number (Top or Bottom) to return. For example, Top 10. However, in some cases, it may be best to let the report refresher decide how many to return. In these cases, we can choose Prompt for the value of N.

Database rankings are independent of the objects in the Result Objects section. Therefore, the Result Objects will have no affect on the values returned by the ranking.

Exercise: Database Ranking

1. Create a query with Portfolio Name, Mgr Name, Ticker, and Revenue.
2. Create the Database Ranking
   a. Click the *Add a Database Ranking* button in the Query Filters section of the Query Panel.
   b. Select Top, on the Database Ranking object, as the ranking type.
   c. Enter 5 into the number to be returned.
   d. Drag Ticker into the dimension field.
   e. Drag Revenue into the measure field.
   f. We could add filters to the ranking, by dropping objects into the rectangle under the rank logic section of the object. But, in this example, we are not adding any filters on the rank.
3. Click the Run Query button.

Notes

Combination Queries

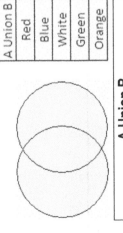

A Union B
Red
Blue
White
Green
Orange

A Union B

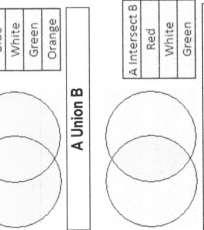

A Intersect B
Red
White
Green

A Intersect B

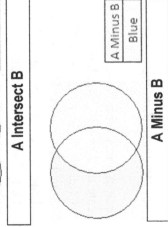

A Minus B
Blue

A Minus B

Data Set A	Data Set B
Red	Red
Blue	White
White	Orange
Green	Green

Set A & B

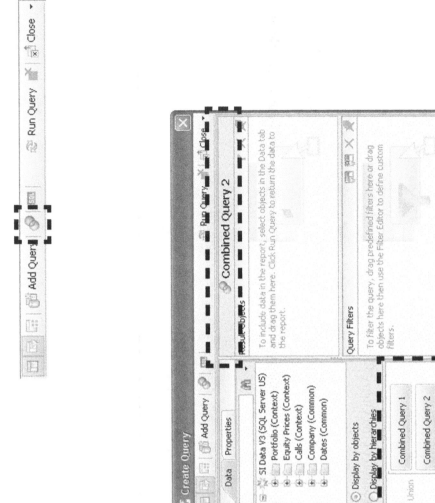

Combination Query in Query Panel

Combination Queries

Combination queries allow us to combine sets of data retrieved by queries on the same universe. We can use three different types of logic to combine the results of the queries - Union, Intersect, and Minus.

Union: Linearly concatenates sets of data. It does this by concatenating the first column of a query to the first column of the other query, then the second columns, the third columns, and so forth. There must be the same number of columns in both queries, and the data type of the columns must be the same. Therefore, we can union Dates to Dates, Numbers to Numbers, and Text to Text. If there is no corresponding column in one of the queries, then a Null object can be used as a place holder (Ask your designer to create a Null object).

Intersect: Will intersect sets of data, and return the data that is the same in all sets. The sets must have the same number of columns, and the data types of the columns must be the same.

Minus: Will minus sets of data, and return the reminder of the first set. The sets must have the same number of columns, and the data types of the columns must be the same.

An example of each of the combination logics is shown in the graphic. In this example, we are working with two sets of data - Data Set A & Data Set B. The diagrams in the graphic are known as Venn diagrams, and the darker shade is the part of the data that is returned after the logic is applied.

Notes

Union Query Example

Portfolio Name	Year Num	Num Transactions	Revenue
Biotech	2000	91	(369,888)
Technology	2001	317	1,059,497

Query Results

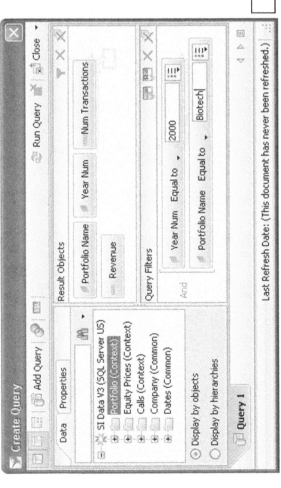

First Query

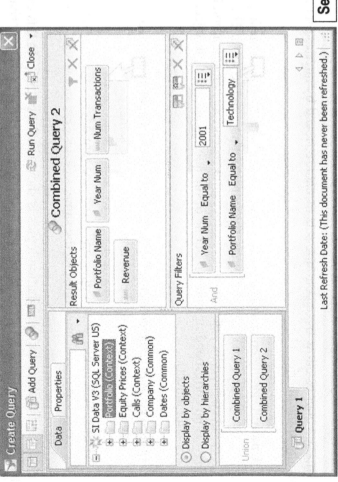

Second Query

Union Query Example

In this example, we want to create a data set for a manager that switched portfolios after the first year of trading. There are other ways to do this query, but the example does illustrate how a union query works.

Exercise: Union Query

3. Create a query with Portfolio Name, Year Num, Num Transactions, and Revenue.
4. Create a Query Filter: Portfolio Name Equal to BioTech And Year Num Equal to 2000.
5. Click the *Add a Combined Query* button in the Query Panel.

   a. Now there are two queries associated with the query - Combined Query 1 and Combined Query 2. To switch between the two queries, we click on one of the query objects in the lower-left of the Query Panel.

   b. Also notice that the Combined Query 2 is prepopulated with the same objects from Combined Query 2. In this case, we do not want to change the objects, as we are just changing the Query Filter. However, in many cases, we will change the objects, so why are they there? They are there to remind us that we must have the same number and types of columns, as in Combined Query 1.

4. In Combined Query 2, create a Query Filter: Portfolio Name Equal to Technology And Year Num Equal to 2001.
5. Click the *Run Query* button.

Notes

Intersect Query Example

Company	Ticker
HWP	HWP
Intel Corporation	INTC
International Business Machines Corporation	IBM
Microsoft Corporation	MSFT
United Technologies Corporation	UTX

Query Results

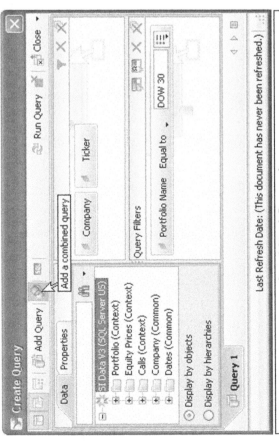

Combined Query 1

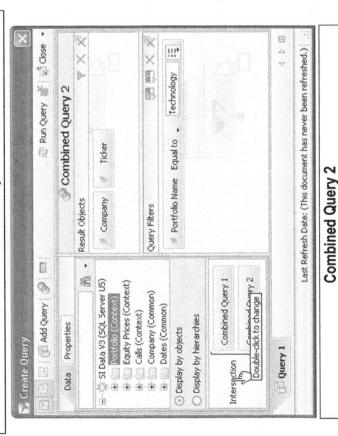

Combined Query 2

Intersect Query Example

In this example, we are going to determine which DOW 30 companies were also traded by the Technology portfolio. We are going to use an Intersect query by first creating a list of DOW 30 companies, and then intersecting this list with a list of Technology companies.

Exercise: Union Query

3. Create a query with Company and Ticker.
4. Create a query filter: Portfolio Name Equal to DOW 30.
5. Click the *Add a Combined Query* button in the Query Panel.
6. The default combined query is a union query, since most combined queries are unions (I will talk about this in the next example). Therefore, we must change the query to an Intersect query. To do this, we double-click on the combined query operator in the lower-left portion of the Query Panel. This will toggle the operator from Union to Intersect, from Intersect to Minus, from Minus to Union, and so forth.
7. Create a query filter: Portfolio Name Equal to Technology
8. Click the Run Query button.
9. Select the Companies we Traded context. (We have to do this, because we selected no measures (context specific objects) in the query.)

Notes

Intersect Subquery Example

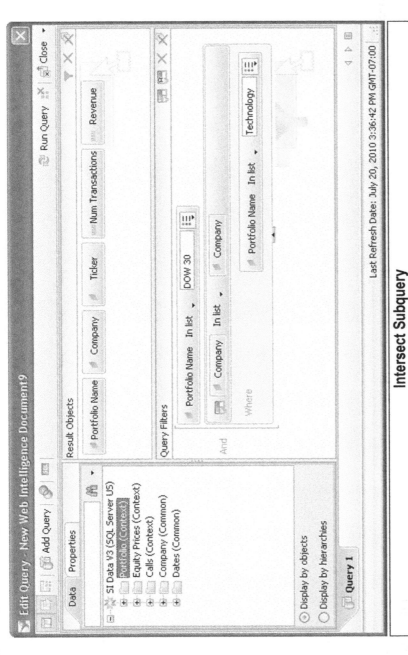

Intersect Subquery

Portfolio Name	Company	Ticker	Num Transactions	Revenue
DOW 30	HWP	HWP	44	(468)
DOW 30	Intel Corporation	INTC	52	5,850
DOW 30	International Business Machines Corporation	IBM	47	116,773
DOW 30	Microsoft Corporation	MSFT	50	86,513
DOW 30	United Technologies Corporation	UTX	55	47,666

Query Results

Intersect Subquery Example

In the previous example, we intersected two data sets and found the intersection of companies that were in both DOW 30 and Technology. In that example, I said that the intersection queries were not done that often. The reason for this statement is that if we add more dimensions to the query, then the probability of an intersection gets less. For example, if we added Portfolio Name to the queries, then we would retrieve no rows, because in Query 1, the Portfolio Name is DOW 30, and in Query 2, the Portfolio Name is Technology. Therefore, there is no intersection.

In this example, we use a subquery to return the companies in the Technology portfolio. We then use the And operator to intersect the list of DOW 30 companies with the list of Technology companies. This technique allows us to place any objects in the Result Objects section. Therefore, we can retrieve much more detail than with the Intersect query. In this example, we added Portfolio Name, Num Transactions, and Revenue.

Exercise: Intersect Subquery

3. Create a query with Portfolio Name, Company, Ticker, Num Transactions, and Revenue.
4. Create a query filter: Portfolio Name Equal to DOW 30.
5. Create Subquery
   a. Click the Add a Subquery button.
   b. Place the Company object in both object spots on the Subquery filter object.
   c. Drag Portfolio Name onto the Condition Rectangle under the Company dimensions.
   d. Select In List or Equal to for the operator.
   e. Enter Technology as the operand.
4. Click Run Query.
5. Select the Companies that we Traded context (This is for the subquery, since there are no context defining objects).

Notes

Intersect Subquery Union Example

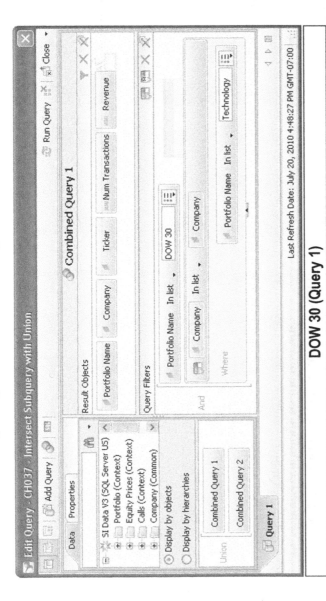

DOW 30 (Query 1)

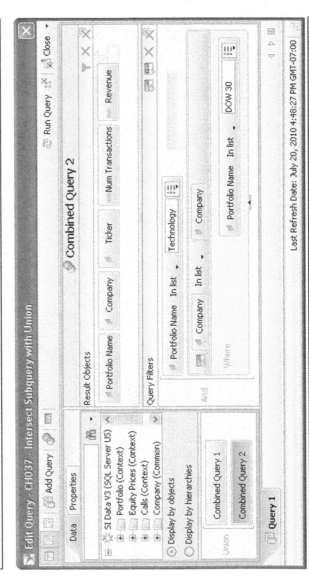

Technology (Query 2)

Ticker	DOW 30		Technology	
	Num Transactions	Revenue	Num Transactions	Revenue
HWP	44	(468)	23	(40,451)
IBM	47	116,773	16	14,250
INTC	52	5,850	23	(5,696)
MSFT	50	86,513	23	12,982
UTX	55	47,666	20	20,730

Query Results

Intersect Subquery Union Example

The previous example did allow us to retrieve more details than the Intersect combination query. However, we only retrieved the details for the DOW 30 portfolio. We knew that the companies were traded for both the DOW 30 and Technology portfolios, but since the main query had a query filter limiting it to only the DOW 30 portfolio, we got no details for the Technology portfolio.

In this example, we create the same query as in the previous example (Intersecting Subquery), and in addition, we also create a query that returns the Technology details. We use the combination Union query to combine the results from both queries. By the way, there is another way to accomplish this, which is to use the Results from Another Query operand. I will leave it up to you to figure out how to use this operand.

Exercise: Intersect Subquery Union Query

3. Create a query with Portfolio Name, Company, Ticker, Num Transactions, and Revenue.
4. Create a query filter: Portfolio Name Equal to DOW 30.
5. Create Subquery
   a. Click the Add a Subquery button.
   b. Place the Company object in both object spots on the Subquery filter object.
   c. Drag Portfolio Name onto the Condition Rectangle under the Company dimensions.
   d. Select In List or Equal to for the operator.
   e. Enter Technology as the operand.
4. Click the Add a Combined Query button in the Query Panel, and leave the Result Objects as they are.
5. Create a query filter: Portfolio Name Equal to Technology.
6. Create Subquery
   a. Click the Add a Subquery button.
   b. Place the Company object in both object spots on the Subquery filter object.
   c. Drag Portfolio Name onto the Condition Rectangle under the Company dimensions.
   d. Select In List or Equal to for the operator.
   e. Enter DOW 30 as the operand.
6. Click Run Query

Notes

Minus Query Example

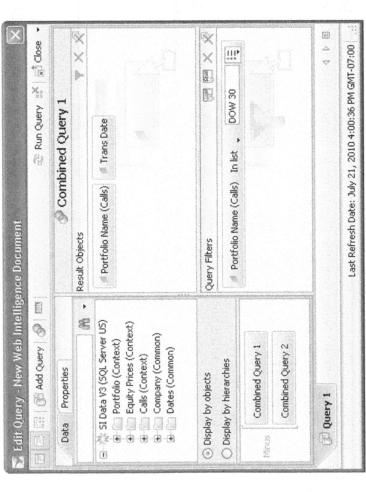

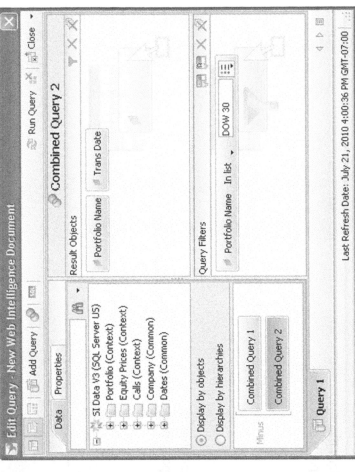

Portfolio Name (Calls)	Trans Date
DOW 30	7/5/00
DOW 30	7/7/00
DOW 30	7/10/00
DOW 30	7/11/00
DOW 30	4/1/01

Add Query Button in Query Panel

Minus Query Example

In this example, we are going to find out the dates that the portfolio manager for the DOW 30 portfolio made calls, but no transactions. We are going to do this by creating a list of all call dates for the portfolio, and then subtract the portfolio transaction dates from the call date list.

Exercise: Minus Query

3. Create a query with Portfolio Name (Calls) (From the Calls Class) and Trans Date.
4. Create a query filter: Portfolio Name (Calls) Equal to DOW 30.
4. Click the Add a Combined Query button in the Query Panel.
5. Replace the Portfolio Name (Calls) object with Portfolio Name from Portfolio Transactions.
6. Create a query filter: Portfolio Name Equal to DOW 30.
7. Click Run Query.

Notes

Minus Subquery

Minus Subquery (Not in List)

Call Id	Trans Date	Industry	Call Duration	Ticker	Contact Name	Contact Title
2	7/7/00	Metals	15	AA	Belda, Alain J.P.	CEO
					Kelson, Richard	CFO
	*Met with Mr. Belda and Mr. Kelson.*					
6	7/7/00	Finance	42	AXP	Goeltz, Richard	CFO
					Golub, Harvey	CEO
	*Robert and Sean discussed Mr. Golub's views on credit default and their clients.*					
9	7/10/00	Airlines	30	BA	Condit, Philip	CEO
					Sears, Michael	CFO
	*We were very lucky to talk to both Mr. Condit and Mr. Sears.*					
15	7/11/00	Industrial	14	CAT	Barton, Glen	CEO
					McPheeters, F. Lynn	CFO
	*Called to tell Mr. Barton and Ms. McPheeters that we were excited that we were starting a fund that would include Caterpillar.*					
17	7/5/00	Chemical	20	DD	Charles O. Holliday Jr.	CEO
					Richard R. Goodmanson	COO
	*Called to see if I could get any clues about future business.*					
18	7/7/00	Media	45	DIS	Michael D. Eisner	CEO
					Robert A. Iger	COO
					Thomas O. Staggs	CFO
	*Called to get clarification on last month's earnings announcement.*					
21	4/1/01	Chemical	14	EK	Daniel A. Carp	CEO
					Patricia F. Russo	COO
	*Called to see if they believed that this was the bottom.*					
39	7/7/00	Biotechnology	55	MRK	Judy C. Lewent	CFO
					Raymond V. Gilmartin	CEO
	*Today, I called to see if their cholesterol drugs Zocor and Mevacor were doing well and if there was any new competition.*					

Query Results

Minus Subquery

In the previous example, we used the Minus Combination Query to determine the dates that the DOW 30 manager made phone calls, but no transactions. These dates were: 7/5/2000, 7/7/2000, 7/10/2000, 7/11/2000, and 4/1/2001. This is all the information we got, because if we added dimensions to the queries, then we would not get the exact results. In fact, we probably would have gotten no data, as there are little intersections between Call and Transaction data.

In this example, we use a subquery to find the same five dates, but we can also find out more about the calls. The report is specially formatted, because there are more than one contact on a call. I will not explain how I formatted the report, and will leave it up to you as an exercise.

Exercise: Minus Subquery

3. Create a query with Ticker, Industry, Contact Name, Contact Title, Trans Date, Call Notes, Call Id, and Call Duration.
4. Create a query filter: Portfolio Name (Calls) Equal to DOW 30.
4. Create Subquery
    a. Click the Add a Subquery button in the Query Panel.
    b. In the first Dimension field, place Portfolio Name (Calls) and Trans Date.
    c. In the second Dimension field, place Portfolio Name and Trans Date.
    d. Drag the Portfolio Name object to the filter rectangle and select In List for the operator, and DOW 30 for the operand.
5. Click the Run Query button.

We placed a Portfolio Name filter on the subquery. While this is not necessary, because we added the Portfolio Name (Calls) condition, it does make the query more efficient by limiting the list to only DOW 30 transaction dates. Also, we used two dimensions in the subquery - Portfolio Name and Trans Date. We did this to because we wanted the dates for the specific portfolio and not just the transaction dates.

Notes

Summary

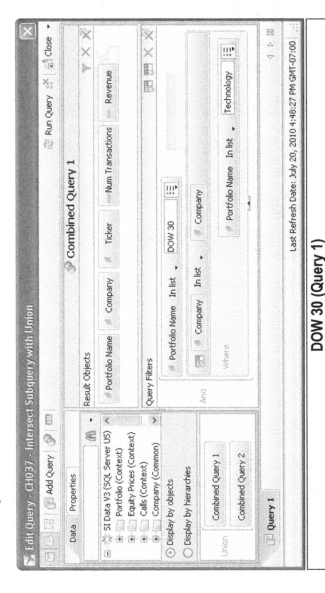

DOW 30 (Query 1)

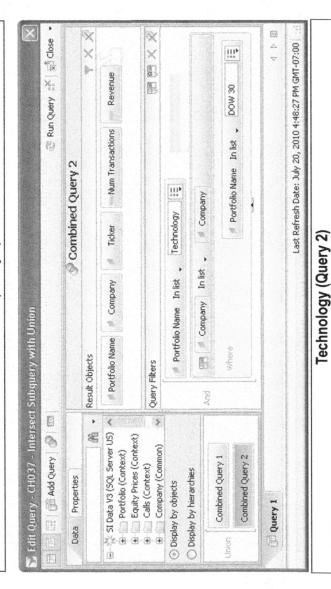

Technology (Query 2)

Ticker	DOW 30		Technology	
	Num Transactions	Revenue	Num Transactions	Revenue
HWP	44	(468)	23	(40,451)
IBM	47	116,773	16	14,250
INTC	52	5,850	23	(5,696)
MSFT	50	86,513	23	12,982
UTX	55	47,666	20	20,730

Query Results

Summary

In this chapter, we learned how to limit data in a query to just the data that we are interested in. We used simple designer defined query filters and we also used more complex subqueries. The trick to defining the filters for your queries is to think about the data that you want to return as a data set that is derived from a larger set. For example, the database contains all of the available data in the universe. Most of the time you are not interested in all of the data, so you must consider what makes the data that you want distinct from the larger data set.

For example, if you are interested in making a payroll report, then you are probably only interested in active employees. So a simple filter, such as Employee State Equal to Active, should work fine. Suppose that you are interested in the details of a summary, such as the previous week totals. Then you could use a subquery that will allow you to access the details, while using a summary condition.

Quite often, people want to see the past performance with the projected performance. Usually, we can union the past to the future, and then graph the results as continuous through the future. There is so much that we can do, and I hope that this chapter has shown you that it is possible and that there are many ways to isolate the data of interest from a much larger data set.

Notes

Creating Documents with Business Objects Web Intelligence XI V3

Chapter 6: Formulas, Variables, and Functions

Introduction

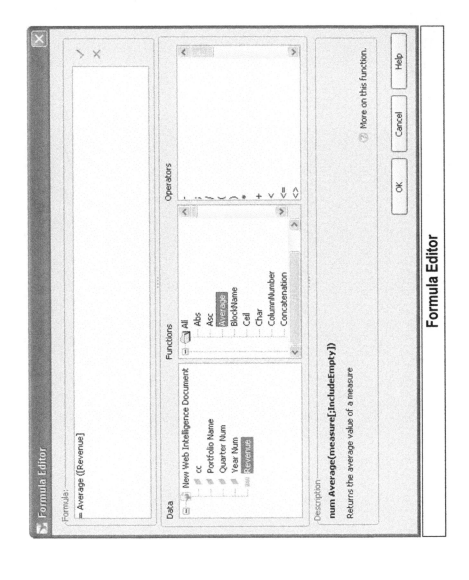

Formula Editor

Introduction

When we create a data provider, we retrieve data from a data source, such as a database. This data is interesting and it is great that we can retrieve such data. However, in some cases we need to use formulas to help us turn the data into information. For example, in the previous chapter, we used the *NoFilter* function. This function allowed us to compare the filtered values to the total in the report. We also used the *IF* function to group dimensions into smaller groups, such as half years.

Web Intelligence comes with many very useful functions that allow us to turn data from a database into very powerful information. In this chapter we are going to discuss creating formulas and variables, using the Web Intelligence functions.

I would also like to mention here that many people have called functions an advanced topic, and usually only present this information to 'Power Users'. I greatly disagree with this assumption and present topic here in this text on the same level as any other topic. As you can see from the previous chapters, if one explores any topic at deep enough levels, then it can be considered advanced. This means that there are functions and formulas that are easier to understand than others. Therefore, we cannot call it an advanced topic. So, please approach this chapter with an open mind and a will to learn. It just may be very interesting and you may be very good at such things.

Notes

Formulas

| 6/21/10 | = CurrentDate() |

| 1 | = Page() |

| Administrator | = CurrentUser() |

| **Quarterly Financial Report** | = "Quarterly Financial Report" |

| Current Date: 6/21/10 | = "Current Date: " + CurrentDate() |

| Page 1 of 6 | = "Page " + Page + " of " + "Number of Pages"() |

| Current User: Administrator | = "Current User: " + CurrentUser() |

| 2000 - 03 | = FormatNumber([Year Num]; "0000") + " - " + FormatNumber([Quarter Num]; "00") |

Portfolio Name	Year Num	Revenue
Alternative Energy	2000	(89,221)
Alternative Energy	2001	303,886
Biotech	2000	(369,888)
Biotech	2001	449,314
DOW 30	2000	(4,385,413)
DOW 30	2001	5,736,866
Finance	2000	(507,101)
Finance	2001	574,563
Media	2000	(465,394)
Media	2001	386,854
Technology	2000	(1,116,767)
Technology	2001	1,059,497
	Sum:	131,433

= Average([Revenue])

Portfolio Name	Year Num	Revenue
Alternative Energy	2000	(89,221)
Alternative Energy	2001	303,886
Biotech	2000	(369,888)
Biotech	2001	449,314
DOW 30	2000	(4,385,413)
DOW 30	2001	5,736,866
Finance	2000	(507,101)
Finance	2001	574,563
Media	2000	(465,394)
Media	2001	386,854
Technology	2000	(1,116,767)
Technology	2001	1,059,497
	Sum:	1,577,196

= Sum([Revenue])

Formulas

Formulas are a method of requesting information. The data provider of a report provides data from a data source. With this data we can build report structures, such as tables, crosstabs, and charts. Formulas allow us to enhance this data by providing information, such as sums and averages. We can also enhance the entire report by providing such information as page numbers, dates, and the current user of the documents.

Every report contains formulas, even ones with just a simple table, as each field in the table will contain a formula similar to: = *[Object]*. We manipulate these simple formulas with functions and strings, as in = *Sum ([Object]*, or = *"Sum is: " + Sum ([Object])*. The better we get at manipulating and creating formulas, the more impressive our reports become. And, one of the main reasons we make reports is to make an impression.

Formulas help our reports become more powerful, more informative, and more impressive.

Notes

Creating Formulas

5

= 5

Hi

= "Hi"

2,577,196

= [Revenue] + 1000000

Examples of Valid Syntax

#syntax

= Hi

Web Intelligence

Invalid identifier 'hi' at position 2. (WIS 10022)

[Close]   [Help]

Example of Invalid Syntax

= [Revenue] + 1000000

Press Ctrl+Enter to show Formula Editor

In Cell Edit

Creating Formulas

Many people find creating formulas difficult, because formulas are created following rules of format. These rules are called syntax. In order for a formula to work, it must have proper syntax. For example, the first character of every formula in Web Intelligence is an equal (=) sign. This tells Web Intelligence that the content of a cell is a formula.

In addition, all text must be enclosed in double quotes. In order for Web Intelligence to recognize text, the text must be enclosed in double quotes. Web Intelligence will assume that the text is some sort of identifier (object), and if this object does not exist, then you will receive a #syntax error. Web Intelligence assigns #syntax errors to cells when it cannot interpret a formula in a cell. However, Web Intelligence usually displays the error dialog before the faulty formula can be committed to a cell.

Another rule of syntax is that all variables must be enclose within square brackets, as seen in the = [Revenue] + 1000000, formula. The square brackets tell Web Intelligence that the text in the brackets represents an object name in the report.

One method of creating a formula is to double-click on a cell and type in a formula. This method works well when creating quick modifications, such as adding 1000000 to [Revenue], because we do not have to know the exact spelling or case of any objects or functions. We are simply adding a number to an object that is already in the formula. We can also use this method to quickly type in text, such as report titles and labels.

However, if we want to create more complicated formulas, then the in-cell editing is just too constrained in both size and available features. Web Intelligence offers us two other methods of editing formulas - the Formula Bar and the Formula Editor. We will visit these methods on the following pages.

Notes

Formula Toolbar

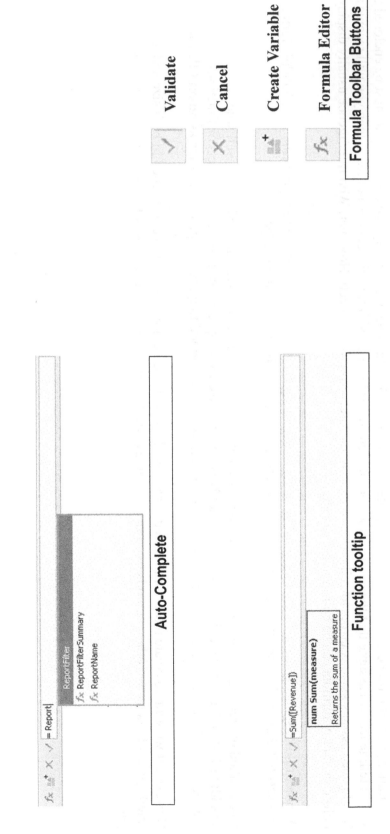

= [Revenue] + 1000000

Formula Toolbar

= Report

ReportFilter
ReportFilterSummary
ReportName

Auto-Complete

=Sum([Revenue])

num Sum(measure)
Returns the sum of a measure

Function tooltip

Validate

Cancel

Create Variable

Formula Editor

Formula Toolbar Buttons

View Structure

Formula Toolbar

To display the formula toolbar, click the *Show / Hide Formula Toolbar* button on the Reporting toolbar.

The formula toolbar offers a wider space to edit formulas, then the in-cell edit approach. In addition, Web Intelligence will offer auto-complete choices as you are typing. This helps in the spelling of available functions, because all you have to know is the first letters to get auto-complete started, then you can just highlight the proper function and press the [Enter] key.

If you see a function on a report that is unfamiliar, then you may use the formula toolbar to give you information on the function. To do this, click on the cell with the formula, and then place the cursor over the function in the formula toolbar. Web Intelligence will pop up a tooltip with information on the function.

There are also four buttons associated with the formula toolbar, which are: Validate, Cancel, Create Variable, and Formula Editor. The *Validate* button will check a formula's syntax. If it is not correct, then an error dialog will be displayed and the offending characters in the formula will be highlighted yellow. The *Cancel* button will cancel any changes made through the formula toolbar, up to any validate if there were any. The *Create Variable* button allows you to package the current formula up into a variable. We will discuss variables in a few pages. The *Formula Editor* button will launch the Formula Editor populated with the contents of the Formula toolbar. We will discuss the Formula Editor on the next page.

Notes

Formula Editor

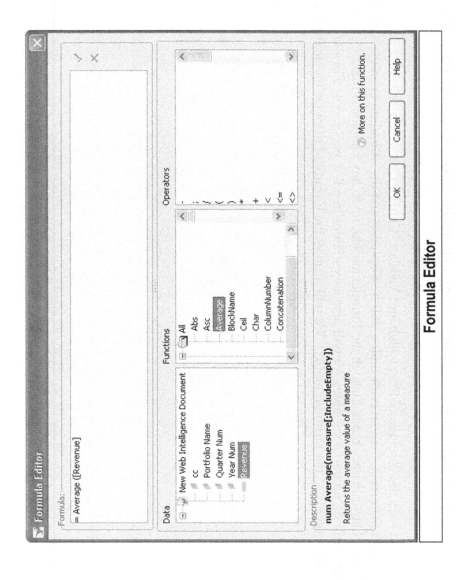

Formula Editor

Formula Editor

So far, we have edited formulas in their cells and in the formula toolbar. Both of these methods are good for quick, short edits, but when we need more involved edits, we use the Formula Editor dialog. To open the Formula Editor, we click the *Formula Editor* button in the Formula toolbar. The Formula Editor allows us to create formulas using a list of available *Data* (Variables and Objects), a list of *Functions*, and a list of *Operators*. To create a formula we use a combination of keystrokes and the available objects in the lists. This helps us by not only showing us what is available, but the correct syntax and arguments. Arguments are values passed to functions within the parentheses that are associated with the function. The formula that will be returned to a cell is the formula in the Formula edit field.

Data: This list is all of the available objects and variables in a document. The objects come from the data provider and variables are packaged formulas. We will learn more about variables in a few pages.

Functions: Lists of the available functions in Web Intelligence. This list is categorized into the following sections: All (all available functions), Aggregate, Character, Data & Time, Document, Data Provider, Misc., Logical and Numeric.

> **Note**: There is a way to create custom functions, but that goes beyond the scope of this book. At the time of this writing, the custom functions document could be found by Googling "xi31_sp2_webi_calc_ext_en.pdf."

Operators: Web Intelligence as many operators. It has the basic +, -, *, and so forth. It also has many internal operators, such as ForEach, In, Linear, Where, and many more. We will discuss many of these operators in this chapter.

Notes

Formula Editor: Description

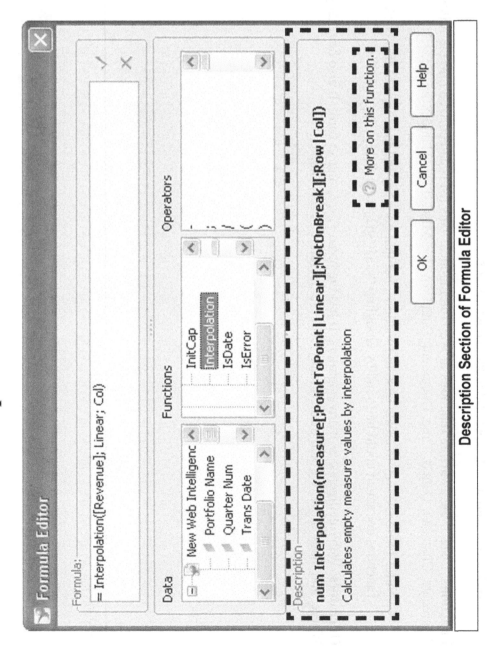

Formula Editor

Formula:
= Interpolation([Revenue]; Linear; Col)

Data

- New Web Intelligenc
- Portfolio Name
- Quarter Num
- Trans Date

Functions

- InitCap
- Interpolation
- IsDate
- IsError

Operators

Description

num Interpolation(measure[;PointToPoint|Linear][;NotOnBreak][;Row|Col])

Calculates empty measure values by interpolation

⑦ More on this function.

OK   Cancel   Help

Description Section of Formula Editor

Web Intelligence Rich Client help

Interpolation

Description
Calculates empty measure values by interpolation

Function Group
Numeric

Syntax
num Interpolation(measure; [interpolation_method]; [NotOnBreak]; [Row|Col])

Input

[measure]	Any measure
interpolation_method	The interpolation method (optional): • PointToPoint - point-to-point interpolation. This is the default interpolation method when you do not supply the argument. • Linear - linear regression with least squares interpolation
NotOnBreak	Prevents the function from resetting the calculation on block and section breaks (Optional.)
Row	Col	The calculation direction (optional)

Output
The list of values returned by the measure with missing values supplied by interpolation

Example
Interpolation([Value]) supplies the following missing values using the default point-to-point interpolation method:

Day	Value	Interpolation([Value])
Monday	12	12
Tuesday	14	14
Wednesday		15
Thursday	16	16
Friday		17
Saturday		18
Sunday	19	19

Notes
- Interpolation is particularly useful when you create a line graph on a measure that contains missing values. By using the function you ensure that the graph plots a continuous line rather than disconnected lines and points.

More on this function.

Return Type: num
Function Name: Interpolation
Arguments: (measure;[interpolation_method];[NotOnBreak];[Row|Col]

Function Description Elements

Formula Editor: Description

One of the great advantages of the Formula Editor is that we can see descriptions of selected functions and operators, which help us to understand the purpose of the selected element and how we should use it. To see a description, select the function or operator in a list, and then observe the *Description* section of the dialog.

For functions, the description will include the return type, function name, and the argument types that the function expects. The return type must be compatible with other elements of the formula. For example, if you want the cosign of the value that another function returns, then the other function must return a number. For example, = Cos (Interpolation ([Revenue]))

In this example, we are asking for the cosign of the interpolation of Revenue.

There are required arguments and optional arguments. Required arguments are arguments that must be supplied for the function to work. For example, = ToNumber("250"). The function needs a text input in order to output the number version of the text. Optional arguments are enclosed with square brackets in the function description. For example, the Interpolation function has interpolation_method as an optional argument. The available methods are PointToPoint or Linear. To calculate the interpolation, Web Intelligence must use one of these methods. The method argument is optional, because Web Intelligence will use the PointToPoint method, if no method is entered. This means the PointToPoint is the default method that the function will use.

If more information is needed, then simply click on the *More on this function* link, located in the lower-right of the dialog. This will open up a browser with a complete function or operation description, as shown in the graphic.

Notes

Variables

Variable Editor Dialog

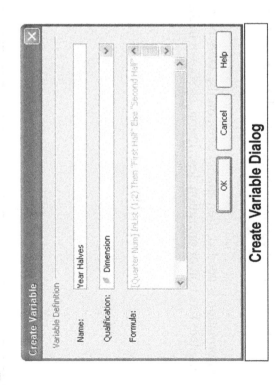

Create Variable Dialog

Variables

Variables are packaged formulas. We use variables for various reasons that include simplifying formulas, by packaging subcomponents of the formula. For example (Sum ([Revenue]) Where ([Year Num] = 2001) - (Sum ([Revenue]) Where ([Year Num] = 2000), could become [Current Year Rev] - [Previous Year Rev], by packaging the two components of the formula.

We also use variables to package parts of more complicated formulas will not work in the context of the formula, as the variable parts will calculate before the other components of the formula. For example, we had to use this formula in earlier versions of Web Intelligence:

    Variable Name: Current Date
    Variable Formula: = UserResponse ("Enter Current Date")
    Used in Formula: = ToDate ([Current Date]; INPUT_DATE)

We can create variables using two different dialogs:

Create Variable Dialog: This dialog is called from the Formula Toolbar, and it will create a formula from the contents of the toolbar. With this dialog, we can only name and qualify the variable, as the formula is already defined. This dialog is usually used to create variables from formulas that are already working in a column of a report structure.

Variable Editor: This dialog is very similar to the Formula Editor, except that we can name and qualify the formula to create a variable. This dialog is called from the *Variable Editor* button on the Reporting toolbar. This dialog is usually used to create formulas that are not yet part of an existing report structure, as when it is displayed it will not be populated with an existing formula.

Notes

Finding and Editing Variables

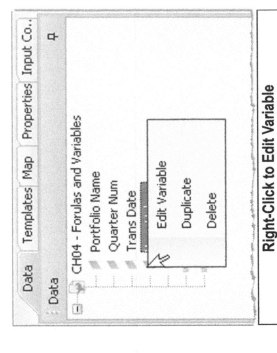

Variable Tooltip Includes Formula

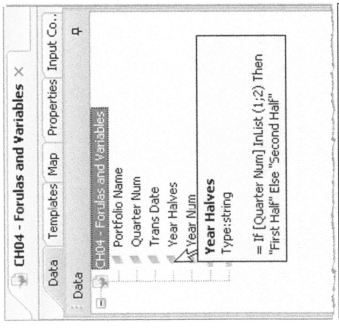

Object Tooltip has no Formula

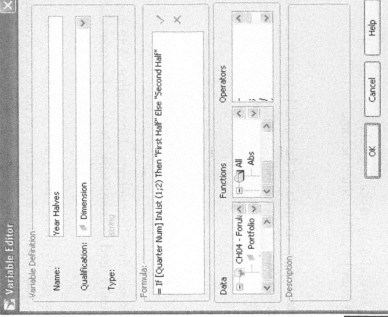

Right-Click to Edit Variable

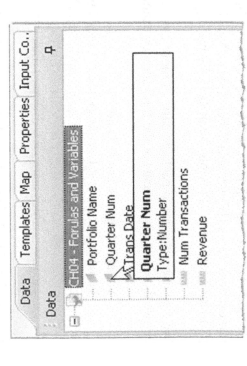

**Edit Variable Calls
Variable Editor**

Finding and Editing Variables

Once a variable is created it looks and acts as an object, so they are difficult to discern from objects. This is why people often refer to variables as objects, and objects as variables. To find variables, just place your mouse cursor over the objects in the Data tab and observe the tooltips. Tooltips for variables will contain the formula for the variable. This is sort of a quick reference that allows you to observe the formula without editing the variable. Data objects that were provided from the query will not have formulas associated with them, as the formulas were created in the universe.

> **Note:** If the Universe Developer thinks it of interest for Report Designers to see the formula that an object is based on, then the designer will usually include the formula in the object description, and this description will be included in the tooltip of the object. If the description is only the formula, then the description can make the object appear to be a variable.

Right-click on a variable in the Data tab to Edit, Duplicate, or Delete the variable. Choosing edit will launch the Variable Editor populated with the variable. Double-clicking on the variable will also launch the Variable Editor dialog. We may want to duplicate an object and then make modifications to the duplicate, as this is a quick method to make similar variables. You can use the pop-up menu to delete variables, or you can select them in the Data tab and press the [Delete] key.

Notes

IF-Then Statement

Alt Portfolio Name	Portfolio Name	Year Num	Year Half	Revenue
Temp Portfolio #1	Alternative Energy	2000	Second Half	(89,221)
	Alternative Energy	2001	First Half	242,357
	Alternative Energy	2001	Second Half	61,529
	Biotech	2000	Second Half	(369,888)
	Biotech	2001	First Half	153,796
	Biotech	2001	Second Half	295,519
Temp Portfolio #1			Sum:	294,090

Alt Portfolio Name	Portfolio Name	Year Num	Year Half	Revenue
Temp Portfolio #2	DOW 30	2000	Second Half	(4,385,413)
	DOW 30	2001	First Half	1,670,800
	DOW 30	2001	Second Half	4,066,066
	Finance	2000	Second Half	(507,101)
	Finance	2001	First Half	330,180
	Finance	2001	Second Half	244,383
Temp Portfolio #2			Sum:	1,418,915

Alt Portfolio Name	Portfolio Name	Year Num	Year Half	Revenue
Temp Portfolio #3	Media	2000	Second Half	(465,394)
	Media	2001	First Half	165,135
	Media	2001	Second Half	221,719
	Technology	2000	Second Half	(1,116,767)
	Technology	2001	First Half	537,883
	Technology	2001	Second Half	521,614
Temp Portfolio #3			Sum:	(135,810)
			Sum:	1,577,196

Table Using If-Than Staements

Alt Portfolio Name #1 = If [Portfolio Name] InList ("Alternative Energy","Biotech") Then "Temp Portfolio #1" Else (If [Portfolio Name] InList ("DOW 30";"Finance") Then "Temp Portfolio #2" Else "Temp Portfolio #3")

Alt Portfolio Name #2 =If [Portfolio Name] InList ("Alternative Energy","Biotech") Then "Temp Portfolio #1" ElseIf [Portfolio Name] InList ("DOW 30";"Finance") Then "Temp Portfolio #2" Else "Temp Portfolio #3"

Year Half = If [Quarter Num] InList (1;2) Then "First Half" Else "Second Half"

If-Then Statement

The if statement is one of the most powerful statements in any programming language, because it allows decisions to be made. We have already used the If statement to create a Year Half grouping. The formula for that was: = **If** *[Quarter Num] InList (1;2)* **Then** *"First Half"* **Else** *"Second Half"*. In this formula, we are testing to see if Quarter Num is in the list of (1;2). If it is, then we output "First Half". If it is not (Else), then we output "Second Half." Therefore, this statement is binomial in nature, as it has two outputs.

If-then statements can have more than two outputs by embedding the statements in either the true or the false portions of the statement. For example, suppose that we have a temporary management situation at our company, because many managers went on vacation. The managers that stayed agreed to managing the other's portfolios. We could use the following to accomplish this in our report.

= *If [Portfolio Name] InList ("Alternative Energy";"Biotech") Then "Temp Portfolio #1" Else (If [Portfolio Name] InList ("DOW* **30";"Finance") Then "Temp Portfolio #2" Else "Temp Portfolio #3"**)

In this formula, we embedded another If-Then statement in the Else portion of an If statement. Some people will use the ElseIf statement:

= *If [Portfolio Name] InList ("Alternative Energy";"Biotech") Then "Temp Portfolio #1"* **ElseIf [Portfolio Name] InList ("DOW** **30";"Finance") Then "Temp Portfolio #2"** *Else "Temp Portfolio #3"*

Exercise: If-Then Example

6. Create a query with Portfolio Name, Year Num, Quarter Num, and Revenue.
7. Click on any Quarter in the Quarter Num column. Click the Show/Hide Formula Toolbar button to show the Formula Editor button on the Formula toolbar to show the Formula Editor dialog.
8. Enter the following formula, and then click OK to apply the formula.
   = *If [Quarter Num] InList (1;2) Then "First Half" Else "Second Half"*
9. Insert a column to the left of Portfolio Name, and enter the following formula:
   =*If [Portfolio Name] InList ("Alternative Energy";"Biotech") Then "Temp Portfolio #1" ElseIf [Portfolio Name] InList ("DOW 30";"Finance")* *Then "Temp Portfolio #2" Else "Temp Portfolio #3"*

Notes

_____

Aggregate Functions

Portfolio Name	Year Num	Quarter Num	Num Transactions	Num Transactions
Alternative Energy	2000	3	42	= Sum ([Num Transactions])
		4	36	= Sum ([Num Transactions])
	2000	Sum:	78	= Sum ([Num Transactions])
	2001	1	49	= Sum ([Num Transactions])
		2	36	= Sum ([Num Transactions])
		3	11	= Sum ([Num Transactions])
	2001	Sum:	96	= Sum ([Num Transactions])
Alternative Energy		Sum:	174	= Sum ([Num Transactions])

Portfolio Name	Year Num	Quarter Num	Num Transactions	Num Transactions
Biotech	2000	3	43	= Sum ([Num Transactions])
		4	48	= Sum ([Num Transactions])
	2000	Sum:	91	= Sum ([Num Transactions])
	2001	1	37	= Sum ([Num Transactions])
		2	45	= Sum ([Num Transactions])
		3	11	= Sum ([Num Transactions])
	2001	Sum:	93	= Sum ([Num Transactions])
Biotech		Sum:	184	= Sum ([Num Transactions])

Portfolio Name	Year Num	Quarter Num	Num Transactions	Num Transactions
DOW 30	2000	3	322	= Sum ([Num Transactions])
		4	353	= Sum ([Num Transactions])
	2000	Sum:	675	= Sum ([Num Transactions])
	2001	1	369	= Sum ([Num Transactions])
		2	372	= Sum ([Num Transactions])
		3	75	= Sum ([Num Transactions])
	2001	Sum:	816	= Sum ([Num Transactions])
DOW 30		Sum:	1,491	= Sum ([Num Transactions])
		Sum:	1,849	= Sum ([Num Transactions])

The Sum Formula is Identical on Every Row

Aggregate Functions

Aggregate functions operate on sets of data. For example, the Sum or Average of all numbers in a set. Sets of numbers in Web Intelligence are determined by the context of the structure where the function is placed. In the graphic, the Sum formula is identical on every row in the report, including the break and report footers. Even though the formula is identical, the sums are different. This is because Web Intelligence is grouping the numbers to be sum'ed in different contexts, which are defined by the dimension objects in the report.

The dimension objects in a report define the data contexts for aggregate functions. For example, in the graphic we have four different contexts: Table context, Portfolio Name break context, Portfolio Name - Year Num break context, and the Row context.

Table Context: Is the grand total at the bottom of the table (Table Footer), and this context contains all of the Num Transactions in the table.

Portfolio Name Context: Is the break footer, where the portfolio total is displayed.

Portfolio Name - Year Num context: Is the Year Num Break, but this break is within the Portfolio Name break. Therefore, the context is defined by both Portfolio Name and Year Num.

Row Context: The row is the lowest granularity of the table. It is defined by all dimensions in the table.

We can look at these aggregation contexts in two different ways. One way is to think that the row is the basic unit and they add up to create the other contexts. The other, is to think about the table context being divided up by different groups of dimensions. You should think about it both ways, as later we will use context operators to manipulate the contexts in a report, which will allow us to create aggregates that operate on other contexts, besides the default contexts created by the structure of a table.

Notes

Aggregates and Measures

Default Table with Sum

Portfolio Name	Year Num	Revenue
Alternative Energy	2000	(89,221)
Alternative Energy	2001	303,886
Biotech	2000	(369,888)
Biotech	2001	449,314
DOW 30	2000	(4,385,413)
DOW 30	2001	5,736,866
Finance	2000	(507,101)
Finance	2001	574,563
Media	2000	(465,394)
Media	2001	386,854
Technology	2000	(1,116,767)
Technology	2001	1,059,497
	Sum:	1,577,196

Re-Aggregated Table with Sum

Portfolio Name	Revenue
Alternative Energy	214,665
Biotech	79,426
DOW 30	1,351,453
Finance	67,462
Media	(78,540)
Technology	(57,270)
	1,577,196

Portfolio Sums by Break

Portfolio Name	Year Num	Revenue
Alternative Energy	2000	(89,221)
	2001	303,886
	Sum:	214,665
Biotech	2000	(369,888)
	2001	449,314
	Sum:	79,426
DOW 30	2000	(4,385,413)
	2001	5,736,866
	Sum:	1,351,453
Finance	2000	(507,101)
	2001	574,563
	Sum:	67,462
Media	2000	(465,394)
	2001	386,854
	Sum:	(78,540)
Technology	2000	(1,116,767)
	2001	1,059,497
	Sum:	(57,270)

| 1,577,196 | = Average ([Revenue]) |

Report Context Average

| 131,433 | = Average ([Revenue] ForEach ([Portfolio Name]; [Quarter Num])) |

Portfolio Name - Quarter Num Context Average

Table Context Average

Portfolio Name	Year Num	Revenue
Alternative Energy	2000	(89,221)
Alternative Energy	2001	303,886
Biotech	2000	(369,888)
Biotech	2001	449,314
DOW 30	2000	(4,385,413)
DOW 30	2001	5,736,866
Finance	2000	(507,101)
Finance	2001	574,563
Media	2000	(465,394)
Media	2001	386,854
Technology	2000	(1,116,767)
Technology	2001	1,059,497
	Average	131,433

| 131,433 | = Average ([Revenue]) |

Aggregates and Measures

Measures are different from the other two data objects in Web Intelligence, because they contain an aggregate function. This aggregate function helps them to conform to changing contexts in a report. Remember, in the previous example that the same aggregate function yielded differing results when placed in different contexts in a report. In the *Default Table* graphic, we have the total Revenue for each portfolio, for two different years. This is the default data that was returned with the query. In the *Re-Aggregated Table* graphic, the Year Num column has been deleted from the table, but not from the query. This caused the Portfolio Names to consolidate, because there is no reason to see each name twice in the absence of Year Num. The Revenue object adjusted by simply summing the two two row values for each portfolio to create one sum that can be placed on each row of the newly re-aggregated table. The *Portfolio Sums with Breaks* graphic, shows both contexts' totals, and you can see that the totals in the re-aggregated table are correct.

Since each measure usually has an aggregate function assigned to it, this aggregate must calculate before any external aggregate calculates. In the *Table Context Average* graphic, we have the average of all the revenues in the table placed in the table footer, which is 131,433. This works, because the measure's default aggregate conforms to the table's context and then the average is calculated. Now, look at the *Report Context Average* graphic, which is a free-standing cell with the same formula that the table used to calculate the average. Its average is not the same as the table's average, because the default aggregate calculated first, and then the average aggregate calculated. This means that it summed to the report, which is 1,577,196, and then averages this one number, which is the same as the sum.

To get the free-standing cell average to calculate, as desired, we must somehow tell Web Intelligence the context for which the average aggregate will be calculated. In the graphic, this is done with the *ForEach* operator. The *ForEach* operator tells Web Intelligence to sum the Revenues into Portfolio Name - Quarter Num totals, of which there will be twelve totals, as in the table. Then, Web Intelligence simply averages this vector of Revenue totals to get the 131,433 value.

Notes

Interpolation

number Interpolation(measure; [interpolation_method]; [NotOnBreak]; [Row|Col])

	Biotech	DOW 30	Finance	Technology
7/17/00		(124,538)	(10,575)	(15,638)
7/18/00	(9,500)	(142,875)		(35,763)
7/19/00	(12,675)	(59,475)		(95,266)
7/20/00		(158,025)		(20,000)
7/21/00	(6,381)	(105,038)	(21,250)	(76,972)
7/24/00		(144,963)	(42,825)	(140,704)

= [Revenue]

	Biotech	DOW 30	Finance	Technology
7/17/00	(61,905)	(124,538)	(10,575)	(15,638)
7/18/00	(9,500)	(142,875)	(68,127)	(35,763)
7/19/00	(12,675)	(59,475)	(68,606)	(95,266)
7/20/00	(63,341)	(158,025)	(69,085)	(20,000)
7/21/00	(6,381)	(105,038)	(21,250)	(76,972)
7/24/00	(64,298)	(144,963)	(42,825)	(140,704)

= Interpolation(([Revenue]); Linear; Col)

	Biotech	DOW 30	Finance	Technology
7/17/00	(6,325)	(124,538)	(10,575)	(15,638)
7/18/00	(9,500)	(142,875)	(13,244)	(35,763)
7/19/00	(12,675)	(59,475)	(15,913)	(95,266)
7/20/00	(9,528)	(158,025)	(18,581)	(20,000)
7/21/00	(6,381)	(105,038)	(21,250)	(76,972)
7/24/00	(65,459)	(144,963)	(42,825)	(140,704)

= Interpolation(([Revenue]); PointToPoint; Col)

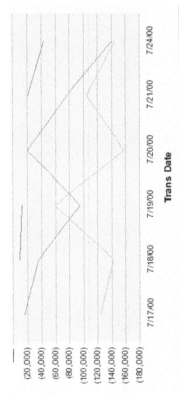

Default Chart with Incomplete Series Lines

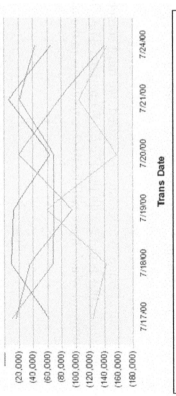

Series Completed with Linear Interpolation

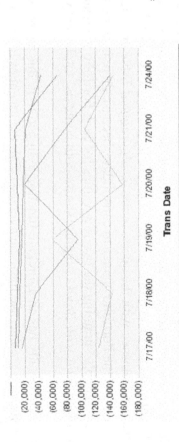

Series Completed with PointToPoint Interpolation

Interpolation

Interpolation will calculate missing values from a set of data, which is not always necessary and should only be used when one is sure that the data is missing and not null. For example, we have a length of 200 meters. We know that something moved a certain number of meters each week to get to this distance of 200 meters. We also know that it moved for 10 weeks, and we have the distances that it moved for 6 of the weeks. We do not have the distances for 4 of the weeks, but we know that it must have moved, because the final distance is 200. We can use interpolation to fill in the missing weeks, so charts made from the data will appear to be continuous.

In the graphic, we should not use interpolation, because we know that there was no revenue generated on days with no revenue. However, it is the best data that is available to show you how interpolation works. The Default Chart has incomplete series that is represented by lines that do not span the entire length of the chart. We can use one of two methods to calculate the missing data to complete the lines - Linear (Default) or PointToPoint. Linear uses linear regression with least squares, and Point to Point uses the absolute differences between the known data to complete the lines.

The function takes four arguments, of which three are optional. The first argument is the measure to operate on. The second is the interpolation method, which can be Linear or PointToPoint. Linear is the default. The interpolation will reset on breaks, sections, and, in our case, columns or rows in crosstabs. If you do not want the function to reset on these report elements, then include the NotOnBreak argument. Crosstabs can calculate across rows or down columns. Row is the Default, which would not work for our crosstab, so in our crosstab, we used the Col argument. However, since the chart is grouped by Dates, and not Portfolio Names, the charts use the Row argument.

Notes

Running Aggregates

number RunningSum([measure];[Row|Col];[(reset_dimensions)])

Portfolio Name	Year Num	Month Num	Num Transactions	Yearly Running Sum	Running Yearly Percentage	Portfolio Running Sum	Running Portfolio Percentage
Alternative Energy	2000	7	8	8	10%	8	5%
Alternative Energy		8	19	27	35%	27	16%
Alternative Energy		9	15	42	54%	42	24%
Alternative Energy		10	10	52	67%	52	30%
Alternative Energy		11	14	66	85%	66	38%
Alternative Energy		12	12	78	100%	78	45%
	2000		78	78	100%	78	45%

Portfolio Name	Year Num	Month Num	Num Transactions	Yearly Running Sum	Running Yearly Percentage	Portfolio Running Sum	Running Portfolio Percentage
Alternative Energy	2001	1	15	15	16%	93	53%
Alternative Energy		2	15	30	31%	108	62%
Alternative Energy		3	19	49	51%	127	73%
Alternative Energy		4	15	64	67%	142	82%
Alternative Energy		5	12	76	79%	154	89%
Alternative Energy		6	9	85	89%	163	94%
Alternative Energy		7	11	96	100%	174	100%
	2001		96	96	100%	174	100%

Table with Running Aggregates

Yearly Running Sum: =RunningSum([Num Transactions]; ([Year Num]))

Running Yearly Percentge: =RunningSum([Num Transactions]; ([Year Num])) / [Num Transactions] In ([Year Num])

Portfolio Running Sum: =RunningSum([Num Transactions])

Running Portfolio Percentage: =RunningSum([Num Transactions]) / [Num Transactions] In Block

Running Aggregate Formulas

Running Aggregates

Running aggregates aggregate as numbers are accumulated. This means that each new number creates a new set of numbers for a calculation. For example, consider a running average, where the formula for each output would be (x1)/1, (X1+X2)/2, (X1+X2+X3)/3, (X1+X2+ ... +Xn)/n. Running aggregates display how a final number is reached. In the graphic, we have the Number of Transactions for each month for the Alternative Energy portfolio, which is in the Num Transactions column. Notice the Yearly Running Sum column, where the Num Transactions are accumulated with each new row. The running sum is calculated as 8, 8+19=27, 8+19+15=42, and so forth. This example shows you that the sort order is very important for running aggregates, because they calculate down a column or across a row.

Notice the Running Yearly Percentage column, which displays the accumulated percentage throughout the year. This formula is simply the running sum divided by the total number of transactions for the year. We derived this denominator using the *In()* operator that allows us to get the total number of transactions in a context. In this case, the context is Year Num. You can see the formula in the graphic. We will formally discuss context operators later in this book.

The Running Aggregates take up to three arguments, which are the measure object, the calculation direction, and reset dimension objects. The measure is simply a column of numbers for the running aggregate. The calculation direction can be row or col, as in a crosstab or chart, the calculation can be down columns or across rows. The reset dimension(s) is a list of dimensions, separated by semicolons and enclosed in parentheses. The running aggregates will accumulate numbers until a dimension in the reset list changes, and then it will purge and start over with the measures associated with the new dimension values. In the graphic, we reset on Year Num - = *RunningSum([Num Transactions]; ([Year Num]))*

Notes

Percentage Function

Portfolio Name	Company	Num Transactions	Portfolio Percentage	Report Percentage
Alternative Energy	Active Power, Inc.	16	9%	1%
	AstroPower, Inc.	23	13%	1%
	Ballard Power Systems Inc.	24	14%	1%
	Capstone Turbine Corporation	27	16%	1%
	Electric Fuel Corporation	19	11%	1%
	FuelCell Energy, Inc.	24	14%	1%
	H Power Corp.	19	11%	1%
	Plug Power Inc.	22	13%	1%
Alternative Energy		174	6%	6%

Portfolio Name	Company	Num Transactions	Portfolio Percentage	Report Percentage
Biotech	Amgen Inc.	25	14%	1%
	Chiron Corporation	20	11%	1%
	Deltagen, Inc.	17	9%	1%
	Genome Therapeutics Corp.	21	11%	1%
	Genzyme Corporation	22	12%	1%
	Merck & Co., Inc.	21	11%	1%
	Pfizer Inc	22	12%	1%
	Pharmacopeia, Inc.	19	10%	1%
	Quest Diagnostics Incorporated	17	9%	1%
Biotech		184	7%	7%

Portfolio Name	Company	Num Transactions	Portfolio Percentage	Report Percentage
DOW 30	Alcoa Inc.	52	3%	2%
	American Express Company	38	3%	1%

Percentage Function in Table

Percentage Function

The Percentage function calculates the percentage of a sum of a set of numbers that a number represents. For example, Active Power, Inc. has 16 transactions, which is 9% of the Alternative Energy portfolios total number of transactions. The calculation for the percentage is 16/174, where 174 is the total number of transactions for the portfolio.

When we add up all of the percentages from the Portfolio Percentage column, in the Alternative Energy break, the total should be 100%. However, it is not 100%, in the graphic. This is because the calculation is context specific, and in the break it returns the percentage of the table total that the break total represents, which is 174/2680 = 0.0649 or 6.49%. We could simply replace the 6% with a 100%, since we know that it will always be 100%. Or we could use a formula, such as = *[Num Transactions] / [Num Transactions] In ([Portfolio Name])*, which simply divides the total in the row by the total in the Portfolio Name break.

Notice that the right-most column has the report percentage that the row Num Transactions represents. We calculated this with the formula: = *Percentage([Num Transactions]) In Report*. Also, notice that the total of these report percentages equal the break total that was incorrect in the previous paragraph's example.

The Percentage function takes up to three arguments. The first is the measure for the calculation. The second is optional, and it is supposed to tell Web Intelligence to take the break into consideration. However, in my studies, it seems to have no affect on the outcome of the calculation. The third optional argument is the col or row argument that tells the function to go across rows or columns in crosstabs and charts.

Exercise: Percentage Function

6. Create a query with Portfolio Name, Company, and Num Transactions.
7. Place a break on Portfolio Name, and then insert two columns to the right of Num Transactions.
8. In the first inserted column, enter the following formula: = *Percentage([Num Transactions])*.
9. In the second inserted column, enter: = *Percentage([Num Transactions]) In Report*.
10. Sum the values in Num Transactions, and the new new columns.

Notes

Numeric Functions - Rank

number Rank(measure; (dimensions); [TOP|BOTTOM]; [(reset_dimensions)])

Portfolio Name	Company	Company Rank	Revenue
Alternative Energy	Active Power, Inc.	4	19,648
	AstroPower, Inc.	7	3,620
	Ballard Power Systems Inc.	5	14,998
	Capstone Turbine Corporation	2	52,855
	Electric Fuel Corporation	8	(2,507)
	FuelCell Energy. Inc.	1	90,575
	H Power Corp.	6	7,438
	Plug Power Inc.	3	28,038
	Total		214,665

#1 Company	FuelCell Energy, Inc.		90,575
Remainding Companies			124,090
#1 Company %			73%

Portfolio Name	Company	Company Rank	Revenue
Biotech	Amgen Inc.	4	2,106
	Chiron Corporation	3	18,956
	Deltagen, Inc.	7	(3,501)
	Genome Therapeutics Corp.	9	(6,343)
	Genzyme Corporation	2	35,390
	Merck & Co., Inc.	8	(4,190)
	Pfizer Inc	5	943
	Pharmacopeia, Inc.	6	(2,182)
	Quest Diagnostics Incorporated	1	38,247
	Total		79,426

#1 Company	Quest Diagnostics Incorporated		38,247
Remainding Companies			41,179
#1 Company %			93%

Portfolio Name	Company	Company Rank	Revenue
DOW 30	Alcoa Inc.	2	172,813
	American Express Company	25	1,348
	AT&T Corp.		

Companies Ranked with Rank Function

Numeric Functions - Rank

Numeric functions operate on a single number, rather than sets of numbers as aggregate functions do. Examples of Numeric functions are Cos, Sin, Tan, Abs, Log, Power, and so forth. Each of these functions takes a single number and operate on it to return a result. This is true of all numeric functions, save for the Rank function, which must operate on a set of data to return the rank of a value.

In the previous chapter, we learned that we could use the Rank filter to show only the top or bottom values in a report structure. The Rank function, in this chapter, allows us to rank dimensions based on a measure without hiding any of the values in the report structure. The table in the graphic ranks the companies in each portfolio. Notice that the rank function has no effect on the sort or values that are shown in the report. We then added three extra rows to the footer to highlight the top company and its share of the portfolio revenue.

The Rank function takes up to four arguments. The first argument is the measure that is used to calculate the rank. The second is the dimension(s) to rank. If a single dimension is entered, then that dimension will define the context for the rank. If multiple dimensions are entered, then those dimensions will define the context for the rank. The third argument is Top or Bottom. Top will assign #1 to the highest value measure and Bottom will assign #1 to the lowest value measure.

Notes

_____

Numeric Functions - ToNumber

number ToNumber(string number_string)

Portfolio Name	Company	Previous Year	Curr Year MTD
Alternative Energy	Active Power, Inc.	(17,569)	27,098
	AstroPower, Inc.	2,809	(10,098)
	Ballard Power Systems Inc.	(16,380)	20,134
	Capstone Turbine Corporation	7,635	36,532
	Electric Fuel Corporation	(9,571)	3,588
	FuelCell Energy, Inc.	9,343	(85,510)
	H Power Corp.	(24,469)	(9,001)
	Plug Power Inc.	(41,019)	35,828
Alternative Energy	Sum:	(89,221)	18,571

Portfolio Name	Company	Previous Year	Curr Year MTD
Biotech	Amgen Inc.	(126,995)	31,525
	Chiron Corporation	(47,800)	23,416
	Deltagen, Inc.	(9,844)	(14,188)
	Genome Therapeutics Corp.	(18,432)	1,931
	Genzyme Corporation	(51,588)	48,336
	Merck & Co., Inc.	14,812	(90,350)
	Pfizer Inc	(29,257)	(22,838)
	Pharmacopeia, Inc.	(30,991)	12,086
	Quest Diagnostics Incorporated	(69,795)	(2,000)
Biotech	Sum:	(369,888)	(12,082)

Portfolio Name	Company	Previous Year	Curr Year MTD
DOW 30	Alcoa Inc.	(259,238)	(14,113)
	American Express Company	(35,700)	(12,888)

MTD and Whole Previous Year

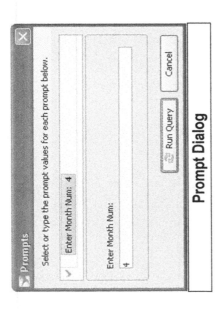

Prompt Dialog

ToNumber(UserResponse("Enter Month Num:"))

ToNumber used with UserResponse

Numeric Functions - ToNumber

The ToNumber function takes a string input and converts it to a number. At first, this seems a little strange, because a person may think, "Why not use a number in the first place?" The answer to this is that we don't always have a choice as to the type of a variable. For example, the UserResponse function will return the value that is entered into the Prompt dialog when a report is refreshed. The UserResponse function always returns a text string. If we wanted to use the UserResponse function to supply a number input to another function, then we would have to use the *ToNumber* function to convert the text string to a number. We did this in the report in the graphic that separates the data on a report into Previous Year and Current Month to Date.

Exercise: Percentage Function

6. Create a query with Portfolio Name, Company, Year Num, Month Num, and Revenue.
7. Create the Query Filter
   a. Drag Month Num dimension into the Query Filters section of the query Panel.
   b. Change the operator to *Greater Than or Equal To.*
   c. Select Prompt as the operand.
   a. Drag Another Month Num dimension into the Query Filters section of the query Panel.
   b. Change the operator to *Less Than.*
   c. Select Prompt as the operand.
   d. Make sure that the operator relating the two query filters is the *Or* operator.
3. Run the Query.
4. Click the *Variable Editor* toolbar button.
   a. Name the variable: *Is 2001 MTD.*
   b. Qualify the variable as: Dimension.
   c. Formula is: *= If [Month Num] <= ToNumber(UserResponse("Enter Month Num:")) And [Year Num] = 2001 Then 1 Else 0*
5. Change the Revenue Header to: Previous Year. Change the formula to: = *[Revenue] Where ([Year Num]=2000).*
6. Insert a column to the right or Previous Year.
7. Header Text: Curr Year MTD. Formula is: = *[Revenue] Where (Is 2001 MTD]=1)*

___

Notes

Character Functions

Formula	Output
= Asc ("T")	84
= Cha r(84)	T
= Fill ("A"; 8)	AAAAAAAA
= FormatDate (CurrentDate(); "MM/dd/yyyy")	06/25/2010
= InitCap ("alternative energy")	Alternative energy
= WordCap ("alternative energy")	Alternative Energy
= Left ("Alternative Energy"; 3)	Alt
= Pos ("Alternative Energy"; " ")	12
= Left ("Alternative Energy" ; Pos ("Alternative Energy"; " "))	Alternative
= LeftPad ("88"; 8; "0")	00000088
=Fill ("0"; 8-Length("88")) + "88"	00000088
= LeftTrim (" Schmidt Ink")	Schmidt Ink
= Length ("David Balkcom")	13
= Left ("David Balkcom"; Length ("David Balkcom") - (Pos ("David Balkcom"; " ") + 2))	David
= Match ("David Balkcom"; "David Balkcom")	1 (True)
= Substr ("David Balkcom"; 7; 7)	Balkcom
= Substr ("David Balkcom"; Pos ("David Balkcom"; " ") + 1; Length (Right ("David Balkcom"; " ") + 1; Length (Right ("David Balkcom";Pos ("David Balkcom"; " ") + 1)))	Balkcom
= Right ("David Balkcom"; Length ("David Balkcom") - Pos ("David Balkcom"; " ") + 1	Balkcom

Various String Formulas

= "Current Date: " + FormatDate (CurrentDate(); "Mmm/dd/yyyy")

= "Revenue Is: " + FormatNumber ([Revenue]; "#,##0")

= "Manager: " + [Mgr Name]

Concatenating Text Strings

Character Functions

Character functions are very important, as they allow us to manipulate text in our reports. There are many times that text from the data source is not in the form that we want it to be. For example, maybe we want only the last name of a manager, but the data source has the full name. We can use the Right or SubString function to isolate just the last name for our report. As seen in the graphic, in the last three rows in the table.

We can use the Match function to search for text values. For example, = *If Match("David Balkcom"; [Mgr Name]) Then "It's David!"* Sometimes, we want to export our report to MS Excel, but when we do there seems to be too many rows in the spreadsheet. This is because there were embedded line returns in a cell of the document. This usually happens with address objects, because they want the cells to be formatted as they would appear on an envelope. However, when we export to Excel, we don't want these line returns in our addresses. To remove the line returns, we can use a formula similar to: = *Replace ([Address Field]; char(13); "")*, where char(13) is the line feed and it is replaced by a space "".

There are some examples of character functions and how to use them in the graphic. Character functions are fun, because it is similar to a puzzle, in that you know what the output should look like, but you have to combine the functions in such a way, in order to achieve the output. We will see how we solved some of the examples on the next page.

Notes

Explanation of Examples

1) = FormatDate (CurrentDate(); "MM/dd/yyyy")

    Notice Capital M's for Month

2) = Left ("Alternative Energy"; 3)
   = Pos ("Alternative Energy"; " ")
   = Left ("Alternative Energy" ; Pos ("Alternative Energy"; " "))

    Using the Pos and Left Functions

3) = LeftPad ("88"; 8; "0")
   =Fill ("0"; 8-Length("88")) + "88"

    LeftPad and Fill

4) = Length ("David Balkcom")
   = Left ("David Balkcom"; Length ("David Balkcom") - (Pos ("David Balkcom"; " ") + 2))

    Using Length and Pos with Left

5) = Substr ("David Balkcom"; 7; 7)
   = Substr ("David Balkcom"; Pos ("David Balkcom"; " ") + 1; Length (Right ("David Balkcom"; " ") + 1; Length (Right ("David Balkcom"; " ") + 1))
   = Right ("David Balkcom"; Length ("David Balkcom") - Pos ("David Balkcom"; " ") + 1)

    All Three Formulas Return "Balkcom"

Explanation of Examples

1. Notice the capital M in the date format. Capital M is for Month, where lower case m is for minutes. Also, notice that the *CurrentDate* function is used as the first argument. This demonstrates that we can pass functions as arguments to other functions.

2. The *Left* function will return the specified number of leftmost characters of a text string. This Text string is usually a dimension object. The *Pos* function will return the position of a specified character, which in this case is a space. We can use the *Pos* function as the second argument in the *Left* function to specify how many characters to return. Here we isolated the first word of Alternative Energy.

3. The output of the *LeftPad* and *Fill* functions in the example are identical.

   a. *LeftPad* will pad the left side of a character string, until a certain number of characters is reached, which in this case is 8 characters.

   b. The Fill function will repeat a character a specified number of times. In this case, we want the final number of characters to be 8, but in order to achieve this, we must know how many characters are in the original string. In our case, the original string is "88", which is two characters, but we may not always know this. Therefore, to determine the number of characters for the *Fill* function, we use the length function to determine the length of the original string, and then subtract this length from 8, which is the desired final length. Then we Fill the number of characters and concatenate it to the original string with the plus (+) operator.

4. In this set, we use the Length function in the *Left* function. The Length function will return the number of characters in its string argument. In the *Left* function, Length determines the length of the string: "David Balkcom". It then uses the *Pos* function to determine where the space between the first and last names occurs. The position of the space is subtracted from the length of the two names, and two is added to the difference. This value is then passed into the Left function in the number of characters to return argument.

5. All three formulas in this set return "Balkcom."

   a. The first of the three returns 7 characters starting with the 7 character in the string. In fact, they all do this, but the first uses absolute (constant) numbers for the starting position and the length.

   b. The second function uses the *Pos* function to determine the starting position of Balkcom. It does this by searching for the space before the last name and then adding 1 to point to the first character of the last name. It then uses the *Length*, *Right*, and *Pos* functions to determine the length of the last name. Since we know the starting position of the last name, and the last name is the last characters in the text, then it does not matter if we specify too many characters to retrieve the last name. This is why many people will just use some large number, such as 50, for the last argument. Then the formula will look like: = *Substr ("David Balkcom", Pos ("David Balkcom", " ") + 1; 50)*

   c. The third formula uses the Right function to retrieve the last name. It can do this, because the last name is the rightmost characters. It uses the same *Length*, *Right* and *Pos* formula as the second example did.

Notes

Format Functions versus Format Number

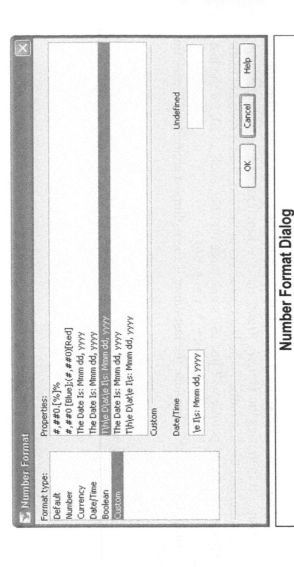

Number Format Dialog

First Of Month	Revenue
The Date Is: Apr 01, 2001	113,306
The Date Is: Aug 01, 2000	(1,832,371)
The Date Is: Dec 01, 2000	(796,460)
The Date Is: Feb 01, 2001	609,760
The Date Is: Jan 01, 2001	911,394
The Date Is: Jul 01, 2000	(3,008,431)
The Date Is: Jul 01, 2001	5,410,828
The Date Is: Jun 01, 2001	(287,497)
The Date Is: Mar 01, 2001	(1,171,716)
The Date Is: May 01, 2001	2,924,905
The Date Is: Nov 01, 2000	(583,157)
The Date Is: Oct 01, 2000	(1,275,482)
The Date Is: Sep 01, 2000	562,116

Formatted to Text with FormatDate()

"The Date Is: " + FormatDate([First Of Month]; "Mmm dd, yyyy")

First Of Month	Revenue
T12183 DAMt183 I0: Jul 01, 2000	(3,008,431)
T12214 DAMt214 I0: Aug 01, 2000	(1,832,371)
T12245 DAMt245 I0: Sep 01, 2000	562,116
T12275 DAMt275 I0: Oct 01, 2000	(1,275,482)
T12306 DAMt306 I0: Nov 01, 2000	(583,157)
T12336 DAMt336 I0: Dec 01, 2000	(796,460)
T121 DAMt1 I0: Jan 01, 2001	911,394
T1232 DAMt32 I0: Feb 01, 2001	609,760
T1260 DAMt60 I0: Mar 01, 2001	(1,171,716)
T1291 DAMt91 I0: Apr 01, 2001	113,306
T12121 DAMt121 I0: May 01, 2001	2,924,905
T12152 DAMt152 I0: Jun 01, 2001	(287,497)
T12182 DAMt182 I0: Jul 01, 2001	5,410,828

Format Number with No Escapes

The Date Is: Mmm dd, yyyy

First Of Month	Revenue
The Date Is: Jul 01, 2000	(3,008,431)
The Date Is: Aug 01, 2000	(1,832,371)
The Date Is: Sep 01, 2000	562,116
The Date Is: Oct 01, 2000	(1,275,482)
The Date Is: Nov 01, 2000	(583,157)
The Date Is: Dec 01, 2000	(796,460)
The Date Is: Jan 01, 2001	911,394
The Date Is: Feb 01, 2001	609,760
The Date Is: Mar 01, 2001	(1,171,716)
The Date Is: Apr 01, 2001	113,306
The Date Is: May 01, 2001	2,924,905
The Date Is: Jun 01, 2001	(287,497)
The Date Is: Jul 01, 2001	5,410,828

Format Number with Escapes

Th\e D\at\e I\s: Mmm dd, yyyy

Format Functions versus Format Number

We have seen that FormatDate will format a date and change the date from date type to text. This allows it to be concatenated to a text string, such as an identifier. In this case the identifier is "The Date Is:." We have also learned, in the Report Structures chapter, that we can format the contents of cells with the Format Number dialog.

In this example, we want to prefix the date with the label – "The Date Is:." In the *Formatted to Text* graphic, we use the *FormatDate* Function to format the date, and then we concatenate the result to the label. The output looks very nice, except that it does not sort properly, as it is now text and sorts in alpha-numeric order, not in chronological order. Therefore, this method does not work well when the date is in a column of a table that needs to be sorted by date. It does work well in free-standing cells and people typically use it for the refresh date of a report, as in the following:

= "Report Refresh Date: " + FormatDate (LastExecutionDate(): "Mmm dd, yyyy")

The Number Format dialog allows us to place text in the format field of the dialog. The *Format Number with No Escapes* graphic, shows the output if we simply use "The Date Is: Mmm dd, yyyy" format. The reason the output is so strange, is because the format string contains formatting characters. For example, the 'h' in 'The' is the format character for hour. So, in the graphic, I created this format string in the 12th hour of the day, becuase the 'h' in 'The' has been replaced with the number 12.

The *Format Number with Escapes* graphic, the 'h' in the format string is preceded by a backslash (\). This backslash is known as an escape character, and it tells Web Intelligence not to treat the next character as a format character, but to simply interprete it as text. In this example, we preceded all of the known format characters with a backslash, except the characters that are used to actually format the date portion of the string. Notice that the advantage to this method is that the dates still sort as dates. If you do not know all of the format characters, then you can just put a backslash in front of every text character in the format string, as in the following:

"\T\h\e \D\a\t\e \I\s\: Mmm dd, yyyy"

Notes

Chapter 6: Formulas, Variables, and Functions - 311

Date Functions

Column	Formula
Day of Month	= DayName ([Trans Date])
Day # of Month	= DayNumberOfMonth ([Trans Date])
Last Day of Month	= LastDayOfMonth ([Trans Date])
Days in Month	= DayNumberOfMonth (LastDayOfMonth ([Trans Date]))
% of Month Used	= DayNumberOfMonth ([Trans Date]) / DayNumberOfMonth (LastDayOfMonth ([Trans Date]))
Accumulated % Transactions	= RunningSum ([Num Transactions]; ([First Of Month]) / [Num Transactions] In ([Year Num];[Month Num]))
Days Remaining in Month	= DaysBetween ([Trans Date]; LastDayOfMonth ([Trans Date]))
Day # of Week	= DayNumberOfWeek ([Trans Date])
% of Week Used	= DayNumberOfWeek ([Trans Date])/5
Day # of Year	= DayNumberOfYear ([Trans Date])
% of Year Used	= DayNumberOfYear ([Trans Date])/365
Date Next Week	= RelativeDate ([Trans Date]; 7)
Date Previous Week	= RelativeDate ([Trans Date]; -7)

Date Formulas from Table

Trans Date	Day of Month	Day # of Month	Last Day of Month	Days in Month	% of Month Used	Accumulated % Transactions	Days Remaining in Month	Day # of Week	% of Week Used	Day # of Year	% of Year Used	Date Next Week	Date Previous Week
7/13/00	Thursday	13	7/31/00	31	42%	25%	18	4	80%	195	53%	7/20/00	7/6/00
7/14/00	Friday	14	7/31/00	31	45%	32%	17	5	100%	196	54%	7/21/00	7/7/00
7/17/00	Monday	17	7/31/00	31	55%	38%	14	1	20%	199	55%	7/24/00	7/10/00
7/18/00	Tuesday	18	7/31/00	31	58%	44%	13	2	40%	200	55%	7/25/00	7/11/00
7/19/00	Wednesday	19	7/31/00	31	61%	50%	12	3	60%	201	55%	7/26/00	7/12/00
7/20/00	Thursday	20	7/31/00	31	65%	53%	11	4	80%	202	55%	7/27/00	7/13/00
7/21/00	Friday	21	7/31/00	31	68%	61%	10	5	100%	203	56%	7/28/00	7/14/00

Date Formulas in Table

Date Functions

Date functions help us to make powerful reports, because we can do calculations based on time. In the beginning of databases, usually only the transaction date was stored in the tables. This was okay, but we had to use date functions to derive such calculations as in the table of the graphic. Then, as data warehousing became more popular, people started storing many date derivatives, such as the number of days in a month. This date data is usually stored in a Date table. If you edit a query made with the SI Data universe, used to make the example reports, then you will see a date class in the provider. This date class has many different date derivatives, such as Day of Month, Last Day of Month, First Day of Month, and so forth. However, most date tables do not carry all of the possible date derivatives needed to make reports. This is where the Date Functions in Web Intelligence are necessary, to create date derivatives that are not in the database.

In the example, we used:

Day of Month: Uses *DayName* to return the day name of the date.
Day # of Month: Uses the *DayNumberOfMonth* function to return the day number of the month.
Last Day of Month: Uses the *LastDayOfMonth* function to return the last day of a month for a date.
Days In Month: This is not a function, but a combination of *DayNymberOfMonth* and *LastDayOfMonth*.
% of Month Used: Also not a function, but a combination of *DayNumberOfMonth* and *LastDayOfMonth*
Acc % Transactions: This formula is helpful to determine how the monthly transactions grew relative to the month growth.
Days Remaining in Month: This is *DaysBetween* the *CurrentDate* and the end of the month. Should be 1 - **% of Month Used.**
Day # of Week: Uses the *DayNumberOfWeek* function to determine the day number of the week. Monday is #1.
% of Week Used: Day # of Week divided by 5. Can use to make sure weekly growth is consistent. 20% on Monday, 40% on Tuesday...
Day # of Year: Uses the *DayNumberOfYear* function to return the day number of the year.
% of Year Used: Day # of Year divided by 365. Can use to make sure yearly growth is consistent.
Date Next Week: Uses the *RelativeDate* function to calculate the date seven days after the Trans Date.
Date Previous Week: Uses the *RelativeDate* function to calculate the date seven days before the Trans Date.

Notes

Date Function Example

Revenue Goals

Portfolio Name	Year End	Monthly	Weekly
Biotech	130,000	70,000	16,000
Technology	(20,000)	160,000	38,000

Biotech

Portfolio Name	Trans Date	Revenue	% Year Used	Acc Yearly Revenue	% Year Goal	% Month Used	Acc Monthly Revenue	% Monthly Goal	First of Week	% Week Used	Acc Weekly Revenue	% Weekly Goal
Biotech	6/4/01	14,658	80%	40,312	37%	0.13	14,657.5	21%	6/4/01	20%	14,657.5	92%
	6/6/01	36,248	81%	76,559	70%	0.2	50,905	73%	6/4/01	60%	50,905	318%
	6/8/01	(4,775)	82%	71,785	65%	0.27	46,130.5	66%	6/4/01	100%	46,130.5	288%
	6/12/01	9,950	84%	81,735	74%	0.4	56,080.5	80%	6/11/01	40%	9,950	62%
	6/13/01	(36,288)	85%	45,447	41%	0.43	19,793	28%	6/11/01	60%	(26,338)	(165)%
	6/18/01	9,230	87%	54,677	50%	0.6	29,023	41%	6/18/01	20%	9,230	58%
	6/20/01	(5,426)	88%	49,251	45%	0.67	23,597	34%	6/18/01	60%	3,804	24%
	6/21/01	38,022	89%	87,273	79%	0.7	61,619	88%	6/18/01	80%	41,826	261%
	6/22/01	28,268	89%	115,541	105%	0.73	89,886.5	128%	6/18/01	100%	70,093.5	438%
	6/25/01	(19,175)	91%	96,366	88%	0.83	70,712	101%	6/25/01	20%	(19,175)	(120)%
	6/26/01	32,178	91%	128,544	117%	0.87	102,889.5	147%	6/25/01	40%	13,003	81%
	6/27/01	25,252	92%	153,796	140%	0.9	128,141.5	183%	6/25/01	60%	38,255	239%

Technology

Portfolio Name	Trans Date	Revenue	% Year Used	Acc Yearly Revenue	% Year Goal	% Month Used	Acc Monthly Revenue	% Monthly Goal	First of Week	% Week Used	Acc Weekly Revenue	% Weekly Goal
Technology	6/1/01	(16,441)	78%	538,133	489%	0.03	-16,441	(10)%	5/28/01	100%	(16,441)	(43)%
	6/4/01	(48,300)	80%	489,833	445%	0.13	-64,741	(40)%	6/4/01	20%	(48,300)	(127)%
	6/5/01	(4,570)	80%	485,263	441%	0.17	-69,311	(43)%	6/4/01	40%	(52,870)	(139)%
	6/6/01	14,431	81%	499,693	454%	0.2	-54,880.5	(34)%	6/4/01	60%	(38,440)	(101)%
	6/7/01	20,049	81%	519,742	472%	0.23	-34,831.5	(22)%	6/4/01	80%	(18,391)	(48)%
	6/8/01	1,540	82%	521,282	474%	0.27	-33,292	(21)%	6/4/01	100%	(16,851)	(44)%
	6/11/01	510	84%	521,792	474%	0.37	-32,782	(20)%	6/11/01	20%	510	1%
	6/12/01	19,830	84%	541,622	492%	0.4	-12,952	(8)%	6/11/01	40%	20,340	54%
	6/13/01	(1,266)	85%	540,356	491%	0.43	-14,218	(9)%	6/11/01	60%	19,074	50%
	6/14/01	51,197	85%	591,553	538%	0.47	36,979	23%	6/11/01	80%	70,271	185%
	6/15/01	(8,066)	86%	583,487	530%	0.5	28,913	18%	6/11/01	100%	62,205	164%
	6/18/01	22,020	87%	605,507	550%	0.6	50,933	32%	6/18/01	20%	22,020	58%
	6/19/01	(4,496)	88%	601,011	546%	0.63	46,437	29%	6/18/01	40%	17,524	46%
	6/21/01	(19,984)	89%	581,027	528%	0.7	26,453	17%	6/18/01	80%	(2,460)	(6)%
	6/22/01	(4,175)	89%	576,852	524%	0.73	22,278	14%	6/18/01	100%	(6,635)	(17)%
	6/25/01	(6,191)	91%	570,661	519%	0.83	16,087	10%	6/25/01	20%	(6,191)	(16)%
	6/26/01	(12,072)	91%	558,589	508%	0.87	4,015	3%	6/25/01	40%	(18,263)	(48)%
	6/27/01	(10,919)	92%	547,670	498%	0.9	-6,903.5	(4)%	6/25/01	60%	(29,182)	(77)%
	6/28/01	(2,985)	92%	544,685	495%	0.93	-9,888.5	(6)%	6/25/01	80%	(32,167)	(85)%
	6/29/01	(6,802)	93%	537,883	489%	0.97	-16,690.5	(10)%	6/25/01	100%	(38,969)	(103)%

Date Function Example

In this example, we are going to analyze two portfolio's progress for the year 2001, through the month of June. We are going to see if they met their Yearly, Monthly and Weekly progress goals. We are going to look at every day that a trade was made by the portfolio, to see how the day affected the progress for that period's goal. To do this, we are going to use a lot of the Web Intelligence skills that we have learned. In addition, we will have to use a context operator, which we will learn more about later in the next chapter. To start this exercise, we have to create a query.

1. Create a new document with a query that contains Portfolio Name, Trans Date, First of Month, First of Week, and Revenue. Include two Query Filters - *Year Num Equal to 2001*, and *Portfolio Name In List Biotech; Technology*.

    a. Drag the query objects into the Result Objects section of the Query Panel.

    b. Create Year Num Filter:

    Drag Year Num into the Query Filters section of the panel
    Select Equal to from the Operator drop list on the filter object.
    Type 2001 into the Operand portion of the filter object.

    c. Create Portfolio Name Filter:

    Drag the Portfolio Name object into the Query Filters section of the panel
    Select In List from the Operator drop list.
    Click on the down arrow on the right potion of the filter object and select *Value(s) from list.*
    Double-click Biotech and Technology, and then click the OK button to dismiss the *List of Values* dialog.

    d. Click the Run Query button.

Notes

Date Function Example (Variables)

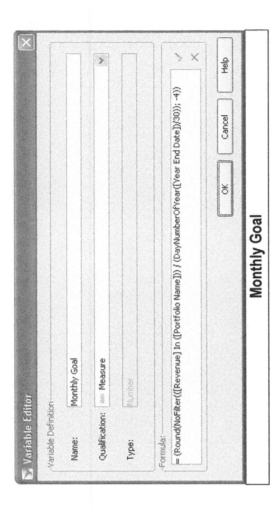

Year End Date

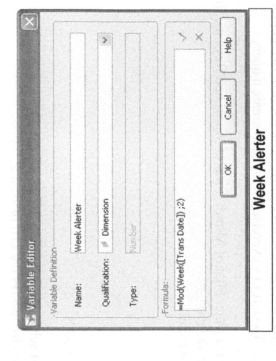

Monthly Goal

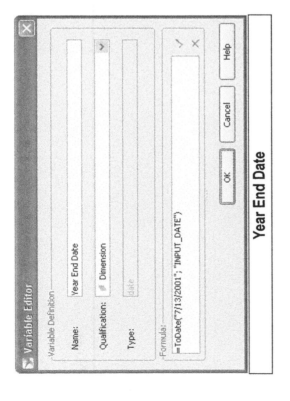

Year End Goal

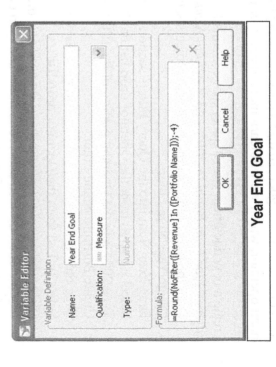

Week Alerter

Date Function Example (Variables)

2. Create the following four variables

a. We need this variable for the end of year formulas, since our end of year is not 12/31. Notice that we use a date string (text) and then convert the string to a date using the ToDate function. Also, notice that we are using a keyword, INPUT_DATE, for the format string in the function.

Name: Year End Date

Qualification: Dimension

Formula: = *ToDate ("7/13/2001"; "INPUT_DATE")*

b. This is the year end goal calculation for each portfolio. We are going to place a filter on the report that only displays the month of June. Therefore, to get the entire year's revenue for our calculation, we need to use the NoFilter function. Notice the *In ([Portfolio Name])* part of the function. This tells Web Intelligence to use the entire revenue for a portfolio, regardless of the context where the variable is place.

Name: Year End Goal

Qualification: Measure

Formula: = *Round (NoFilter ([Revenue] In ([Portfolio Name]));-4)*

c. This formula divides the yearly revenue from (b) by the number of months in our year that ends on 7/13/2010. We calculated the number of months by first finding out the day number of the year, and then by dividing this day number by thirty. We used the DayNumberOfYear function to return the day number for our year-end date.

Name: Monthly Goal

Qualification: Measure

Formula: = *Round (NoFilter (([Revenue] In ([Portfolio Name]) / (DayNumberOfYear ([Year End Date])/30)); -4)*

d. This formula is similar to the monthly goal formula, but we divide the numerator by the number of weeks in the year, which is calculated by dividing the day number of the year end date by 7.

Name: Weekly Goal

Qualification: Measure

Formula: = *Round (NoFilter (([Revenue] In ([Portfolio Name]) / (DayNumberOfYear ([Year End Date])/7)); -3)*

e. We need this variable to create an Alerter that will help identify the weeks in the report.

Name: Week Alerter

Qualification: Dimension

Formula: = *Mod (Week ([Trans Date]) ;2)*

Notes

Date Function Example (Tables)

Revenue Goals Table

Portfolio Name	Revenue Goals		
	Year End	Monthly	Weekly
Biotech	450,000	70,000	16,000
Technology	1,060,000	160,000	38,000

Inserting Revenue Goal Variables

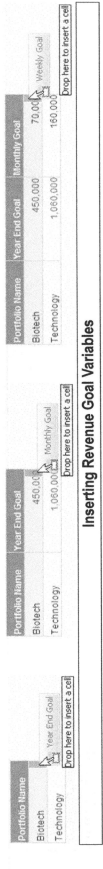

Portfolio Name	Year End Goal	Monthly Goal	Weekly Goal
Biotech	450,000	70,000	
Technology	1,060,000	160,000	

Drop here to insert a cell

Portfolio Name	Year End Goal	Monthly Goal
Biotech	450,000	
Technology	1,060,000	

Drop here to insert a cell

Portfolio Name	Year End Goal
Biotech	450,000
Technology	1,060,000

Drop here to insert a cell

Portfolio Name
Biotech
Technology

Year End Goal — Drop here to insert a cell

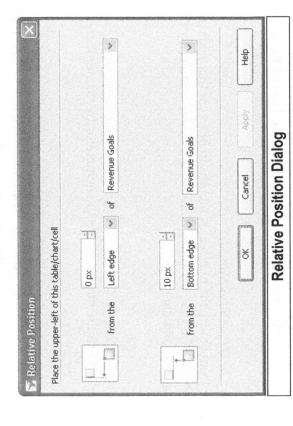

Relative Position Dialog

Relative Position

Place the upper-left of this table/chart/cell

0 px — from the — Left edge — of — Revenue Goals

10 px — from the — Bottom edge — of — Revenue Goals

OK   Cancel   Apply   Help

Table so Far

Portfolio Name	Trans Date	Revenue	Acc Yearly Revenue	% Year Used	% Year Goal	Acc Monthly Revenue	% Month Used	% Monthly Goal	First of Week	% Week Used	Acc Weekly Revenue	% Weekly Goal
Biotech	1/2/01	(2,250)										
Biotech	1/3/01	(3,360)										
Biotech	1/4/01	36,950										

Date Function Example (Tables)

3. Create the Goals table, which is the small table above the larger table.
   a. Delete all columns from the default table, except the Portfolio Name column.
   b. Insert Year End Goal, Monthly Goal, and Weekly Goal.
   c. Insert a row above the header row, selecting any cell in the table header, and then clicking the *Insert Row Above* toolbar button.
   d. Merge all of the cells in the newly added header row, by selecting the cells, and then clicking on the *Merge / Split Cells* toolbar button.
   e. Double-click on the merged row, and then type *Revenue Goals* into the cell. Center the text by clicking the Align Center button.
   f. Double-click on the column headers and type *Year End*, *Monthly*, and *Weekly*, as seen in the graphic.
   g. Click on the edge of the table to select it, and then Name the table *Revenue Goals* on the Properties tab.

4. Create the Detail Table
   a. Drag Portfolio Name, Trans Date, and Revenue from the data tab, to just under the Revenue Goals table.
   b. Set a break on Portfolio Name.
   c. Position the new table relative the Revenue Goals, by first selecting the table, and then clicking the small button on the Relative Position property, in the Page Layout properties of the Property tab.
   d. Insert 12 empty columns in the table, by clicking on the Revenue column, and then clicking the Insert Column After button 12 times.

5. Create the column headers for the new columns
   a. Insert the following column header text into the new columns: *% Year Used*, *Acc Yearly Revenue*, and *% Year Goal*. Skip a column, and then *% Month Used*, *Acc Monthly Revenue*, and *% Monthly Goal*. Skip a column, and then *First of Week*, *% Week Used*, *Acc Weekly Revenue*, and *% Weekly Goal*.

6. Group the New columns into Year, Month, and Week groups.
   a. Insert a row above the header, by selecting any cell in the header, and then clicking the Insert Cell Above button.
   b. Create the Year Header group by selecting the empty header cells above *% Year Used*, *Acc Yearly Revenue*, and *% Year Goal*, and then by clicking the Split / Merge Cells button on the toolbar. Type Year into the merged cells.
   c. Skip a column, and then merge the three header cells above *% Month Used*, *Acc Monthly Revenue*, and *% Monthly Goal*. Type Month into the merged cells.
   d. Skip a column, and then merge the four header cells above *First of Week*, *% Week Used*, *Acc Weekly Revenue*, and *% Weekly Goal*. Type week into the merged cells.

7. Center align and wrap text all header cells.

Notes

Date Function Example (Formulas)

% Year Used = DayNumberOfYear([Trans Date]) / DayNumberOfYear ([Year End Date])

Acc Yearly Revenue = NoFilter(RunningSum([Revenue];([Portfolio Name])))

% Year Goal = NoFilter(RunningSum([Revenue];([Portfolio Name]))) / [Year End Goal]

Year Group Functions

% Month Used = DayNumberOfMonth ([Trans Date]) / DayNumberOfMonth (LastDayOfMonth([Trans Date]))

Acc Monthly Revenue = RunningSum ([Revenue]; ([Portfolio Name]))

% Monthly Goal = RunningSum ([Revenue]; ([Portfolio Name])) / [Monthly Goal]

Month Group Functions

First of Week = [First Of Week]

% Week Used = DayNumberOfWeek ([Trans Date])/5

Acc Weekly Revenue = RunningSum ([Revenue];([Portfolio Name]; [First Of Week]))

% Weekly Goal = RunningSum ([Revenue];([Portfolio Name]; [First Of Week])) / [Weekly Goal]

Week Group Functions

Date Function Example (Formulas)

The formulas in this example demonstrate how to achieve powerful results by combining simple formulas.

The Year Group Formulas include the three formulas shown in the graphic. The *% Year Used* formula calculates how much of the year has been consumed. We calculate this percentage by first finding the day number of the year for Trans Date, and then dividing this number by the total number of days in our business year. We use the DayNumberOfYear function to find these day numbers. Notice that we are using the Year End Date variable that we created in the beginning of this exercise. The *Acc Yearly Revenue* is calculated by summing all of the revenues for that portfolio up to the Trans Date on the row. We accomplish this with the RunningSum function, which resets at each portfolio. We need the NoFilter function to look at all dates in the data provider, because the report has a filter that only displays the month of June. The *% Year Goal* simply divides the Acc Yearly Revenue by our Year End Goal variable that we created in the beginning of this exercise.

The Month Group Formulas are almost identical to the Year Group Formulas, except there is no NoFilter function in the formulas. Without this function, the RunningSum functions will only aggregate the non-filtered (visible) revenues in the report, which are the month of June values.

The Week Group Formulas include a new formula, which is the First of the Week. We need this to identify the week. Also, notice that we did not derive this value from the existing date, but we included it in our query. The date table in our database has many date derivatives, such as First of Week. Before using any date functions, you should always check to see if the date derivative is available in your universe. In this group, the RunningSum must reset at both Portfolio Name and FirstOfWeek, as we want to accumulate week revenues.

8. Enter the formulas in the graphic into their respective fields in the report. When you create the percentage formulas, the cell may contain 0's or 1's, until they are formatted as percentages with the Cell Format dialog.

Notes

Date Function Example (Alerter)

Trans Date	Week Alerter
1/2/01	1
1/3/01	1
1/4/01	1
1/5/01	1
1/8/01	0
1/9/01	0
1/11/01	0
1/12/01	0
1/16/01	1

= Mod (Week ([Trans Date]) ;2)

Week Alerter Variable

Week			
First of Week	% Week Used	Acc Weekly Revenue	% Weekly Goal
6/4/01	20%	14,657.5	92%
6/4/01	60%	50,905	318%
6/4/01	100%	46,130.5	288%
6/11/01	40%	9,950	62%
6/11/01	60%	(26,338)	(165)%
6/18/01	20%	9,230	58%
6/18/01	60%	3,804	24%
6/18/01	80%	41,826	261%
6/18/01	100%	70,093.5	438%
6/25/01	20%	(19,175)	(120)%
6/25/01	40%	13,003	81%
6/25/01	60%	38,255	239%

Week			
First of Week	% Week Used	Acc Weekly Revenue	% Weekly Goal
5/28/01	100%	(16,441)	(43)%
6/4/01	20%	(48,300)	(127)%
6/4/01	40%	(52,870)	(139)%
6/4/01	60%	(38,440)	(101)%
6/4/01	80%	(18,391)	(48)%
6/4/01	100%	(16,851)	(44)%
6/11/01	20%	510	1%
6/11/01	40%	20,340	54%
6/11/01	60%	19,074	50%
6/11/01	80%	70,271	185%
6/11/01	100%	62,205	164%
6/18/01	20%	22,020	58%
6/18/01	40%	17,524	46%
6/18/01	80%	(2,460)	(6)%
6/18/01	100%	(6,635)	(17)%
6/25/01	20%	(6,191)	(16)%
6/25/01	40%	(18,263)	(48)%
6/25/01	60%	(29,182)	(77)%
6/25/01	80%	(32,167)	(85)%
6/25/01	100%	(38,969)	(103)%

Shade Every Other Week

Alerter Editor

Alerter name: Week

Description:

Sub-Alerter

Filtered object or cell
Week Alerter

Operator
Equal to

Operands
0

If the above is true, then display: Cell contents

Format ...

Formula

Add Sub-Alerter   Remove Sub-Alerter

OK   Cancel   Help

Alerter Editor for our Alerter

Date Function Example (Alerter)

We have a break on Portfolio Name, and that separates the portfolios. We also have only one year and one month, which makes Year and Month sections of the report easy to discern. However, we have multiple weeks, within the month. We do not have a break on week, as we may think that the flow of the report is better without the interruptions in the Year and Month sections of the table. We also have a running sum that resets on every new week, so if we are reading the report, we will appreciate being able to discern when a new week begins. Instead of breaks, in this example, we have decided to use an Alerter to shade every other week in the table. To identify every other week, we created the Week Alerter variable that is zero for even week numbers and 1 for odd week numbers. We used the Mod and Week functions to create this formula.

Now that we have an identifier for the weeks, we can place an Alerter that will format even weeks with a light shaded background. In order for this to look good, we are also going to remove the default alternate row shading in the table.

9. Create the Alerter
    a. Select any data cell (not the header) in the % Weekly goal column.
    b. Click the *Alerters* Toolbar button, to display the Alerters dialog.
    c. Click the *New* button, to display the Alerter Editor dialog.
    d. Name the Alerter Week.
    e. in the Filtered Object or Cell field, select the Week Alerter variable. Operator is *Equal to.* Operand is *0.*
    f. Click the *Format...* button, and set the Font Color to Default and the Background Color to a light shade.
    g. Click the OK's to dismiss all dialogs and apply the Alerter to the % Weekly Goal column.
    h. Apply the Alerter to each of the Week Group columns, by first clicking on any data cell in the column, then clicking on the *Alerters* toolbar button, and lastly selecting the Alerter in the list and clicking the OK button to apply the Alerter.

10. Remove the Alternate Row Shading format
    a. Click on the edge of the table to select it.
    b. Click on the Properties tab to activate it. Select White (255, 255, 255) for the Alternate Row / Column color.

Wow, that was a large example, right in the middle of the formulas chapter. Is this author nuts! Maybe, but that's another topic. However, I put this example here to show you what can be done with all of these wonderful functions that we are learning. I hope that this great report inspires you to create similarly powerful reports on your business data.

_____

Notes

Logical Functions

Even	Returns true (1), if a number is even. Even(6) = 1
Odd	Returns false (0), if a number is even. Odd(6) = 0
IsDate	Returns true (1), if the result of a formula or variable is a date.
IsError	Returns true (1), if the result of a formula or variable is an error.
IsLogical	Returns true (1), if variable returns a boolean value.
IsNull	Returns true (1), if variable or formula returns a NULL value.
IsNumber	Returns true (1), if variable or formula returns a number data type.
IsString	Returns true (1), if variable of formula returns a string (text) value.
IsTime	Returns true (1), if variable or formula returns a time data type.

Logical Functions

Logical functions return true (1) or false (0). We use them to test data, such as is there an error? Is this value Null? Is the value odd or even? In the previous example, we used the Mod function to determine if the week number was odd or even. In this example, we can just use the Even function. Then, the Week Alerter variable formula could be *Even (Week ([Trans Date]))*, instead of *Mod (Week ([Trans Date]); 2)*. The difference between these two formulas is that the Even function returns true (1) when the row is even, and the Mod function returns false (0) when the row is even. To fix this, we could use the Odd function, *Odd (Week ([Trans Date]))*, which would return false (0) when the row is even, just as the *Mod* function did. I wanted to point this out, because so many people try to remember the exact code that someone used to create a formula, instead of just trying to think about what they are trying to accomplish. So, I showed you three ways to determine if a row number is even.

Logical functions are used in Alerters, as just pointed out. They are also used with If-Then statements. For example, If IsError([x]/[y]) Then 0 Else [x]/[y]. This formula will place a zero in a cell, if there is an error in the division. By the way, if there is an error, and we don't check it as shown, then Web Intelligence will place #Div in the cell, which signifies a division error.

Logical functions are known as binomial or Boolean functions, because they return only one of two values, which are True or False.

Notes

Document Functions

| Document Author: Administrator | = "Document Author: " + DocumentAuthor() |

| Document Creation Date: 6/21/10 | = "Document Creation Date: " + DocumentCreationDate() |

| Document Creation Time: 3:50:08 PM GMT-07:00 | = "Document Creation Time: " + DocumentCreationTime() |

| 3:50:08 PM | = DocumentCreationTime() |

| Document Creation Time: 3:50:08 PM | = "Document Creation Time: " + FormatDate(DocumentCreationDate(); "h:mm:ss A") |

| Last Save Date: 7/1/10 | = "Last Save Date: " + DocumentDate() |

| Last Save Time: 9:43:47 AM GMT-07:00 | = "Last Save Time: " + DocumentTime() |

| Document not completely refreshed | = If DocumentPartiallyRefreshed() Then "Document not completely refreshed" |

```
*** Query Name:Query 1 ***

  ** Query Properties:
     Universe:SI Data V3 (SQL Server US)
     Last Refresh Date:7/1/10 4:33 PM
     Last Execution Duration: 1
     Number of rows: 2,673
     Retrieve Duplicate Row: ON

  ** Query Definition:
     Result Objects: Portfolio Name, Year Num, Quarter Num,
Trans Date, Revenue, Num Transactions, Month Num, Company,
First of Month
```

Query Summary Function

Document Functions

The Document functions return information about a document. The first field in the graphic returns the document's author. I have concatenated The *DocumentAuthor* function with a label to identify the data on the document. This is preferable to using separate cells for the label and data.

With document creation date and time, I have also concatenated labels to the data. The *DocumentCreationDate* function returns a Date data type, where the *DocumentCreationTime* returns a Time data type. When we concatenate the results of these two functions to a string, then Web Intelligence must format the data into strings. With the date, it simply converted the data to m/d/yy, which is acceptable in many cases. However, it uses a much different format for the time, which includes the Greenwich Mean Time offset, as can be seen in the graphic. We cannot use the *FormatDate* function to format this time, because it is not a date. However, since the *DocumentCreationDate* function returns a date, with a time component, then we can use the *FormatDate* function to extract the time component, as seen it the graphic. There are also functions to return the date and time that the document was last saved.

The *DocumentPartiallyRefreshed* function is very important. I will usually include this function on every report that I create, using the formula in the graphic (= *If DocumentPartiallyRefreshed() Then "Document not completely refreshed")*. A document may not completely retrieve a dataset from a data source. There are various reasons for this, including exceeding the maximum number of rows that a data provider can return, or even the refresh being interrupted by pressing the [ESC] key. The reason that the formula is so important is that we do not want anybody to see a printed report of partial data, as they make incorrect assumptions based on the incomplete data set. This formula can be placed in a free-standing cell in the footer or header of a report.

The remaining functions in this group can be accessed through the Free-standing cell templates, as discussed in the Report Structures chapter. These are the summary functions - *DrillFilters()*, *PromptSummary()*, *QuerySummary()*, *ReportFilter()*, and *ReportFilterSummary()*.

Notes

Data Provider Functions

Query 1 - SI Data V3 (SQL Server US)   = **DataProvider ([Company])**

Universe	=UniverseName(DataProvider([Company]))

Query 1 - SI Data V3 (SQL Server US)

2,673	=NumberOfRows(DataProvider([Company]))
1	=LastExecutionDuration(DataProvider([Company]))

Query 1 - SI Data V3 (SQL Server US)	=DataProviderType(DataProvider([Company]))
7/1/10	=LastExecutionDate(DataProvider([Company]))
9:33:51 AM	=LastExecutionTime(DataProvider([Company]))

Biotech; Technology

= UserResponse (DataProvider ([Trans Date]); "Enter Portfolio Name:")
= UserResponse ("Enter Portfolio Name:")

```
SELECT
PORTFOLIO.PortfolioName,
SIDATE.YEAR_NUM,
SIDATE.QTR_NUM,
SIDATE.FULL_DATE,

Sum(( PORTFOLIOTRANSACTIONS.PRICE ) *
( PORTFOLIOTRANSACTIONS.NUM_SHARES )) * (-1),

Count( Distinct PORTFOLIOTRANSACTIONS.TRANS_ID),
SIDATE.MONTH_NUM,
COMPANY.COMPANY,
SIDATE.FIRST_OF_MONTH
FROM
COMPANY INNER JOIN PORTFOLIOTRANSACTIONS ON
(PORTFOLIOTRANSACTIONS.TICKER=COMPANY.TICKER)
INNER JOIN PORTFOLIO ON
(PORTFOLIO.PortfolioID=PORTFOLIOTRANSACTIONS.PORTFILIO_NUM)
INNER JOIN SIDATE ON
(SIDATE.FULL_DATE=PORTFOLIOTRANSACTIONS.TRANS_DATE)

GROUP BY
PORTFOLIO.PortfolioName,
SIDATE.YEAR_NUM,
SIDATE.QTR_NUM,
SIDATE.FULL_DATE,
SIDATE.MONTH_NUM,
COMPANY.COMPANY,
SIDATE.FIRST_OF_MONTH
```

=DataProviderSQL(DataProvider([Company]))

Data Provider Functions

The data provider of a document supplies the data. They can be based on Text Files, Microsoft Excel Files, Web Services, or, as in our case, Universes. There can be one or more data providers in a document. Often times, we need to know information about these data providers. For example, the Last Execution Date, the Universe Name that a provider uses, the Number of Rows that a provider uses, the User Response to prompts when the data provider was refreshed, and so forth. Most of the data provider functions expect the name of the data provider to be an argument. However, most of us do not know the name of the provider, and even if we did, we may not spell it correctly. So, Web Intelligence has provided a function that will return the name of a data provider, and this function is *DataProvider* ([obj]). The DataProvider function accepts an object for an argument, and it will return the name of the data provider that provided the object to the document.

We are showing many of the Data Provider functions in the graphic. Notice in all of the functions, we have included the *DataProvider*([obj]) argument, even though this argument is optional in many of them. The DataProvider argument is optional, because most documents only contain one data provider, so why identify it when using data provider functions. However, if there is more than one data provider, then it is probably best to include it. I have the UserResponse with and without the DataProvider argument. The reason for this is if the prompt text (operand) is the same for both data providers, then there is no need to state the data provider name.

The *NumberOfRows* function is good when used with the *DocumentPartiallyRefreshed* function, because if the document is partially refreshed, then the NumberOfRows function will return the number of rows that the provider returned. If this number is equal to the maximum rows that a provider can return, then you know that the provider is trying to return too much data. If the number is less, then you know that something interrupted the document while it was refreshing.

We can make Prompted Queries by selecting Prompt as a query filter's operand. When a document is refreshed, the refresher enters a value for the operand. Once, a report is ran and printed, it is very important to know what value the refresher entered into the prompt dialog. We can use the *UserResponse* function to return this information to the report. For this function to work properly, we must enter the prompt text exactly as it is in the prompt operand of the query filter. For example, *Enter value(s) for Portfolio Name:*. The simpler the prompt text is, then the better it is, because fewer errors will be made when using the *UserResponse* function. If the prompt filter is created in the query, and not the universe, then you can edit the query and copy the text from the filter operand. Notice in the graphic that one *UserResponse* includes the Data Provider name, and the other does not. However, they both work fine. This is true even when there is more than one data provider, since if the text is the same, then the values should be identical for each provider.

Notes

Misc. Functions

Row (LineNumber()) and Column (ColumnNumber()) Numbers

	Jul 2000	Aug 2000	Sep 2000	Oct 2000	Nov 2000	Dec 2000
	3	4	5	6	7	8
Alternative Energy (3)	8	19	15	10	14	12
Biotech (4)	4	22	17	21	12	15
DOW 30 (5)	89	112	121	134	112	107
Finance (6)	4	11	9	10	8	3
Media (7)	9	12	10	7	11	13
Technology (8)	34	57	35	49	47	52

RowIndex()

Portfolio Name	RowIndex()
Alternative Energy	0
Alternative Energy	1
Alternative Energy	2
Alternative Energy	3
Alternative Energy	4
Alternative Energy	5
Alternative Energy	6
Alternative Energy	7

Using RelativeValue to Calculate Profit/Loss

Quarter Num	Portfolio Name	Revenue	Previous Year Revenue	Quarter Profit/Loss
1	Alternative Energy	14,341		
	Biotech	(119,552)		
	DOW 30	330,350		
	Finance	77,166		
	Media	52,981		
	Technology	(5,848)		
			Sum:	

Quarter Num	Portfolio Name	Revenue	Previous Year Revenue	Quarter Profit/Loss
2	Alternative Energy	228,017	14,341	213,676
	Biotech	273,348	(119,552)	392,899
	DOW 30	1,340,450	330,350	1,010,100
	Finance	253,014	77,166	175,848
	Media	112,154	52,981	59,173
	Technology	543,731	(5,848)	549,579
			Sum:	2,401,275

Quarter Num	Portfolio Name	Revenue	Previous Year Revenue	Quarter Profit/Loss
3	Alternative Energy	61,529	228,017	(166,488)
	Biotech	295,519	273,348	22,171
	DOW 30	4,066,066	1,340,450	2,725,616
	Finance	244,383	253,014	(8,631)
	Media	221,719	112,154	109,565
	Technology	521,614	543,731	(22,117)
			Sum:	2,660,115
			Sum:	5,061,390

Profit/Loss Formula

= If Not (IsNull (RelativeValue([Revenue]; ([Quarter Num]);-1))) Then [Revenue] - RelativeValue([Revenue]; ([Quarter Num]);-1)

Misc. Functions

Miscellaneous functions are functions that could not be categorized into the other category folders. They include the *If-Then*, *NoFilter*, and *Page* functions that we have already used in other examples. These three functions are very powerful and a majority of all reports include these functions. Other functions in this category include *ForceMerge* and *Previous*, two important functions that we will do examples in the following pages.

Miscellaneous functions also include *LineNumber*, *ColumnNumber*, and *RowIndex*. *LineNumber* will numerate the rows in a table, as can be seen in the crosstab. Notice that the rows start at three, because the header is two rows. The same is true for the *ColumnNumber* function in the graphic, which numerates the columns. The *RowIndex* does not numerate the rows in a report structure, it numerates the rows in a data provider. Therefore, these numbers are independent of the report structure where the function is placed. Notice in the *RowIndex* graphic that the Alternative Energy portfolio repeats many times, because the *RowIndex* is stopping the Dimension values from rolling up (aggregating).

Another powerful miscellaneous function is the *RelativeValue()* function. This function allows you to get previous/next values based on a numeric offset from the current row. It also synchronizes the previous values using a slicing dimension. In this example, we are using [Quarter Num] as the slicing dimension. This means that the RelativeValue function will retrieve the previous Quarter Num's Revenue for the dimension values on the current row, which in this case is Portfolio Name. In this example, we used the function to determine quarterly profit/loss. The Profit/Loss formula in this example is prefixed with the following: *= If Not(IsNull(RelativeValue([Revenue]; ([Quarter Num]);-1))) Then....* This part of the formula is determining if there was a previous revenue for the current row, which in this case, there was no previous revenue for the first quarter of the year.

Force Merge

Data Provider #1

Portfolio Name	Mgr Name
Alternative Energy	David Balkcom
Biotech	Maria Castro
DOW 30	Sean Wilkenson
Finance	Robert Denning
Media	Kathy James
Technology	Eddie Wang

Data Provider #2

Portfolio Name	Revenue
Alternative Energy	214,665
Biotech	79,426
DOW 30	1,351,453
Finance	67,462
Media	(78,540)
Technology	(57,270)

Portfolio Names are Merged

Data | Templa.. | Map | Propert.. | Input ..

Data

- CH04 - Force Merge Example
  - Mgr Name
  - Portfolio Name
    - Portfolio Name(Query 1)
    - Portfolio Name(Query 2)
  - Revenue

Forced Merge

Mgr Name	Revenue
David Balkcom	214,665
Eddie Wang	(57,270)
Kathy James	(78,540)
Maria Castro	79,426
Robert Denning	67,462
Sean Wilkenson	1,351,453

Revenues are all Equal

Mgr Name	Revenue
David Balkcom	1,577,196
Eddie Wang	1,577,196
Kathy James	1,577,196
Maria Castro	1,577,196
Robert Denning	1,577,196
Sean Wilkenson	1,577,196

Force Merge

Reports can contain more than one data provider. We create multiple data providers to pull data from different sources, and then create reports reflecting the diverse data. In this example, we have two data providers - Data Provider #1 (DP1) and Data Provider #2 (DP2). DP1 contains two objects: Portfolio Name and Mgr Name. Each Portfolio has only one manager. Therefore, if a manager is identified, then we know the portfolio that the manager is responsible for. The second data provider, DP2, also has two objects: Portfolio Name and Revenue.

The two data providers are linked on Portfolio Name, as can be seen in the *Portfolio Names are Merged* graphic. This means that if we make a report with Portfolio Name from DP1 and Revenue from DP2, the report would be correct, as the Portfolio Names are merged.

The problem comes when we try to create a report with Mgr Name from DP1 and Revenue from DP2, because Web Intelligence does not recognize the relationship between Revenue and Mgr Name. Therefore, the Revenue for the entire report is simply reported in each row of the table. By looking at the tables, we know that David Balkcom manages the Alternative Energy portfolio, and therefore David should have 214,665 associated with him in the Mgr Name - Revenue table.

To notify Web Intelligence that this relationship exists, we can use the *ForceMerge()* function with the Revenue object. The formula in this example is: =*ForceMerge([Revenue])*. The *ForceMerge* function only works with multiple data provider documents that have these sorts of indirect relationships. It is similar to the *MultiCube()* function in Desktop Intelligence.

Notes

Misc. Function Example

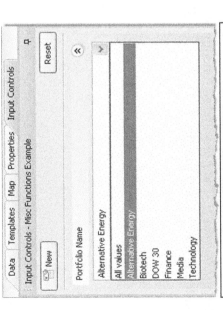

Input Control for Example

Report for Example

Misc. Functions Example

It's time for another example that will use many of the functions that we have already learned. In this example, we will calculate the 3-day moving average for a selected portfolio, and then we will compare that average to the 3-day moving average of the transactions for the entire company.

We will first start with creating the query and tables.

1. Build a new document with Portfolio Name, First of Month, and Num Transactions.
2. In the Default table, Insert three columns to the right of Num Transactions.
3. Enter the column headers into the three new columns: 3-Month Moving Average, 3-Month Company Moving Average, % Moving Average.
4. Format the First of Month, by right-clicking on any date in the column, and selecting *Format Number* from the pop-up menu. Select the Date/Time Format type, and then click the Custom option. Enter Mmm yyyy into the Date/Time Format edit field.
5. Slide the default table down a little on the report to make room for the Parameters table. To do this, click on the edge of the table and drag it a few inches down the report.
6. Create the Parameters tables
   a. Drag the Vertical table template, from the Templates tab, and drop it near the top left of the report.
   b. Insert four columns and two rows, by selecting the default data row in the table and clicking the *Insert Column to the Right* three times, and the *Insert Row Below* button three times.
   c. Type *Portfolio Name:* in the first cell of the first row. Enter the formula, *=ReportFilter([Portfolio Name])*, into the second cell on the first row. All portfolios will be displayed, until we actually place a filter on the report.
   d. Type *Refresh Date:* under the *Portfolio Name:* cell. Enter the formula, *=LastExecutionDate()*, to the right of the *Refresh Date:* label.
   e. Type *Author:* under the *Refresh Date:* cell. Enter the formula, *=DocumentAuthor()*, to the right of the *Author:* label.
   f. Type *Created On:* under the *Author:* cell. Enter the formula, *=DocumentCreationDate()*, to the right of the *Created on:* label.
   g. Type *Current User:*, above the *Created On:* cell. Enter the formula, *=CurrentUser()*, to the right of the *Current User:* cell.
   h. Name the Parameters table, by first selecting the table, and then naming it *Parameters* in the Name field of the Properties tab.
7. Position the data table relative to the Parameters table
   a. Click on the edge of the table to select it, and then expand the Page Layout section of the Properties tab.
   b. Click the little button (…) next to the Relative Position field to launch the Relative Position dialog.
   c. Place the data table 0 px from the Left edge of Parameters, and -5 px from the Bottom edge of Parameters.

Notes

Misc. Function Example (Page 2)

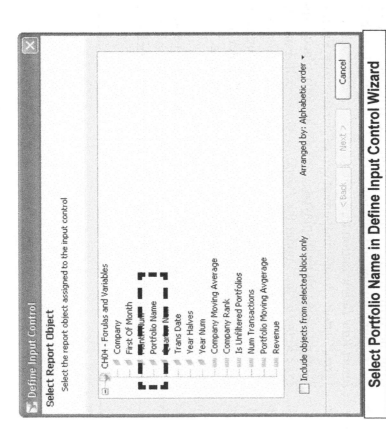

Select Portfolio Name in Define Input Control Wizard

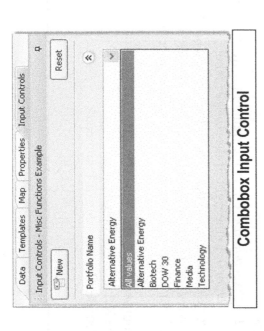

Combobox Input Control

Portfolio Moving Average

= ([Num Transactions] + Previous ([Num Transactions];([Portfolio Name]);1) + Previous ([Num Transactions];([Portfolio Name]);2)) / 3

Company Moving Average

= **NoFilter** (([Num Transactions] *In ([First Of Month])* + Previous([Num Transactions];([Portfolio Name]);1) *In ([First Of Month])* +
Previous([Num Transactions];([Portfolio Name]);2) *In ([First Of Month])*)) / 3

Misc. Functions Example (Page 2)

In the previous page, we used a parameters table to display the parameters of the report. This is preferred to individual cells, because it is difficult to insert new cells, or to modify the structure of the cells. This parameters table can go in the body of the report or in the header or footer of the report. If I place it in the body, and there is more than one page, then I will usually repeat it on each page, using the Page Layout properties.

8. Add the Input Control
    a. Activate the Input Controls tab by clicking on it, and then click the New button.
    b. Select Portfolio Name form the Select Report Object step of the Define Input Control wizard, and then Click the *Next >* button.
    c. In the Single Value section, select Combo box, and then Click the *Next >* button.
    d. On the Assign Report Elements step of the wizard, choose Report Body, and then Click the *Finish* button.
    e. Choose a Portfolio Name from the combo box.
9. Create the Formulas for 3-Day Moving Averages
    a. Portfolio Moving Average
        = ([Num Transactions] + Previous ([Num Transactions];([Portfolio Name]);1) + Previous ([Num Transactions];([Portfolio Name]);2)) / 3
    b. Company Moving Average
        =NoFilter([Num Transactions] In ([First Of Month]) + Previous([Num Transactions];([Portfolio Name]);1) In ([First Of Month]) + Previous([Num Transactions];([Portfolio Name]);2) In ([First Of Month]))) / 3

The Portfolio Moving Average formula in step 9a, adds the current row Num Transactions to the two previous rows's Num Transactions, and then divides this sum by three. We use the *Previous* function to get the Num Transactions from the previous rows. In our example, the *Previous* function has three arguments. The first argument is Num Transactions, which is the value that we are fetching. The second argument is the reset dimension. This argument tells the function not to get previous values from a different Portfolio Name. Since we are using the Input Control to limit the report to one portfolio name, we could exclude the reset dimension. However, it is best to use it, because somebody may remove the input control at a later date. The final argument tells the function how many rows to look back. We want the current, one row back, and two rows back.

The Company Moving Average formula is similar, except we want all of the portfolio name's num transactions for each First Of Month value. To do this, we use *In ([First Of Month])* to expand the context to all portfolios, and the *NoFilter* function to include the number of transactions from the filtered portfolios.

Notes

Misc. Function Example (Page 3)

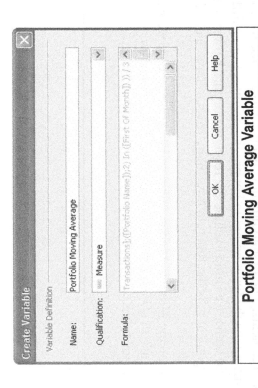

Create Variable

Variable Definition

Name: Portfolio Moving Average

Qualification: Measure

Formula: Transactions)/(Portfolio Name)),2) In ([First Of Month]))) / 3

[OK] [Cancel] [Help]

Portfolio Moving Average Variable

= "Page " + Page() + " of " + NumberOfPages() + " "

Page 1 of 1

Portfolio Name	First Of Month	Num Transactions	3-Month Moving Average	3-Month Company Moving Avg	% Moving Average
Alternative Energy	Jul 2000	8	2.67	49.33	5%
Alternative Energy	Aug 2000	19	9	127	7%
Alternative Energy	Sep 2000	15	14	196	7%
Alternative Energy	Oct 2000	10	14.67	223.67	7%
Alternative Energy	Nov 2000	14	13	214	6%
Alternative Energy	Dec 2000	12	12	212.33	6%
Alternative Energy	Jan 2001	15	13.67	207	7%
Alternative Energy	Feb 2001	15	14	202	7%
Alternative Energy	Mar 2001	19	16.33	215	8%
Alternative Energy	Apr 2001	15	16.33	207.67	8%
Alternative Energy	May 2001	12	15.33	222	7%
Alternative Energy	Jun 2001	9	12	214.33	6%
Alternative Energy	Jul 2001	11	10.67	205.67	5%

First Two Rows are Incorrect

Portfolio Name	First Of Month	Num Transactions	3-Month Moving Average	3-Month Company Moving Avg	% Moving Average
Alternative Energy	Jul 2000	8			
Alternative Energy	Aug 2000	19			
Alternative Energy	Sep 2000	15	14	196	7%
Alternative Energy	Oct 2000	10	14.67	223.67	7%
Alternative Energy	Nov 2000	14	13	214	6%
Alternative Energy	Dec 2000	12	12	212.33	6%
Alternative Energy	Jan 2001	15	13.67	207	7%
Alternative Energy	Feb 2001	15	14	202	7%
Alternative Energy	Mar 2001	19	16.33	215	8%
Alternative Energy	Apr 2001	15	16.33	207.67	8%
Alternative Energy	May 2001	12	15.33	222	7%
Alternative Energy	Jun 2001	9	12	214.33	6%
Alternative Energy	Jul 2001	11	10.67	205.67	5%

Values Removed From First Two Rows

Misc. Functions Example (Page 3)

To find the % Moving Average value, we must divide the Portfolio Moving Average by the Company Moving Average. The formulas that we used to create these averages are a little long and a little cumbersome. It would probably not be a good idea to divide one formula by the other, as this can cause errors, or at the very least make the formula difficult to understand. For this reason, we will encapsulate both formulas into variables, and then simply divide one variable by the other.

10. Create the Variables
    a. Click on any body cell in the 3-Month Moving Average column.
        Click the Create Variable button on the Formula bar, and name the variable Portfolio Moving Average.
    b. Click on any body cell in the 3-Month Company Moving Average column.
        Click the Create Variable button on the Formula bar, and name the variable Company Moving Average.

11. Insert the % Moving Average formula into the last column: = *[Portfolio Moving Average]/[Company Moving Average]*

12. Format the value using the Number Format dialog. Format it as a percent.

We now have one final step. Notice that the first two rows of the table have 3-day moving averages, when they should not, as there are not previous values for these rows. For example, the first 3-Month Moving Average value of 2.67, is simply the Num Transactions (8) divided by 3. This is not a three month average, as this is just one month divided by three. To fix this, we are only going to calculate the average, if a num transactions value exists for two months prior.

13. Prefix the formulas in the last three columns with: = *If Not (IsNull(Previous([Num Transactions];([Portfolio Name]);2))) Then*. This will make the three formulas similar to:

= *If Not (IsNull (Previous([Num Transactions];([Portfolio Name]);2))) Then [Portfolio Moving Average]*
= *If Not (IsNull (Previous([Num Transactions];([Portfolio Name]);2))) Then [Company Moving Average]*
= *If Not (IsNull (Previous([Num Transactions];([Portfolio Name]);2))) Then [Portfolio Moving Average]/[Company Moving Average]*

14. Add the Page Number to the report
    a. Drag the Blank Cell template, from the Free-standing cells templates, to the footer.
    b. Insert the following formula: = *"Page " + Page() + " of " – NumberOfPages() + " "*

Notes

Summary

Report Parameters

Portfolio Name: Alternative Energy	
Refresh Date: 7/1/10	Current User: Administrator
Author: Administrator	Created On: 6/21/10

Portfolio Name	First Of Month	Num Transactions	3-Month Moving Average	3-Month Company Moving Avg	% Moving Average
Alternative Energy	Jul 2000	8			
Alternative Energy	Aug 2000	19			
Alternative Energy	Sep 2000	15	14	196	7%
Alternative Energy	Oct 2000	10	14.67	223.67	7%
Alternative Energy	Nov 2000	14	13	214	6%
Alternative Energy	Dec 2000	12	12	212.33	6%
Alternative Energy	Jan 2001	15	13.67	207	7%
Alternative Energy	Feb 2001	15	14	202	7%
Alternative Energy	Mar 2001	19	16.33	215	8%
Alternative Energy	Apr 2001	15	16.33	207.67	8%
Alternative Energy	May 2001	12	15.33	222	7%
Alternative Energy	Jun 2001	9	12	214.33	6%
Alternative Energy	Jul 2001	11	10.67	205.67	5%

Miscellaneous Functions Example

Portfolio Name	Trans Date	Revenue	Year			Month			Week			
			% Year Used	Acc Yearly Revenue	% Year Goal	% Month Used	Acc Monthly Revenue	% Monthly Goal	First of Week	% Week Used	Acc Weekly Revenue	% Weekly Goal
Biotech	6/4/01	14,658	80%	40,312	9%	0.13	14,657.5	21%	6/4/01	20%	14,657.5	92%
	6/6/01	36,248	81%	76,559	17%	0.2	50,905	73%	6/4/01	60%	50,905	318%
	6/8/01	(4,775)	82%	71,785	16%	0.27	46,130.5	66%	6/4/01	100%	46,130.5	288%
	6/12/01	9,950	84%	81,735	18%	0.4	56,080.5	80%	6/11/01	40%	9,950	62%
	6/13/01	(36,288)	85%	45,447	10%	0.43	19,793	28%	6/11/01	60%	(26,338)	(165)%
	6/18/01	9,230	87%	54,677	12%	0.6	29,023	41%	6/18/01	20%	9,230	58%
	6/20/01	(5,426)	88%	49,251	11%	0.67	23,597	34%	6/18/01	60%	3,804	24%
	6/21/01	38,022	89%	87,273	19%	0.7	61,619	88%	6/18/01	80%	41,826	261%
	6/22/01	28,268	89%	115,541	26%	0.73	89,886.5	128%	6/18/01	100%	70,093.5	438%
	6/25/01	(19,175)	91%	96,366	21%	0.83	70,712	101%	6/25/01	20%	(19,175)	(120)%
	6/26/01	32,178	91%	128,544	29%	0.87	102,889.5	147%	6/25/01	40%	13,003	81%
	6/27/01	25,252	92%	153,796	34%	0.9	128,141.5	183%	6/25/01	60%	38,255	239%

Date Functions Example

Summary

In this chapter we learned how to create formulas in Web Intelligence. We learned how to package these formulas into objects called variables. We then learned how to use many of the available functions to create formulas and variables that help to create very powerful reports.

Many people refer to people that understand the contents of this chapter as power users. This is why I present this chapter in the same context as all chapters in this book, because I do not want you to think that power users are the only people that can create such formulas and variables. In fact, I want you to think that you can do this as well as anybody else.

At first these topics may seem a little intimidating, but isn't almost anything in life a little intimidating at first? I hope that you have read all the pages in this chapter and understand the material. If you do not, then please go back and have another look. You will see that it is not really that bad. I know, because I am also a consultant, and basically my job is to work myself out of a job by transferring my knowledge to others. When I first arrive at most jobs, the employees need me so much, and they keep asking me redundant questions, because they are unsure of themselves. However, I am bored near the end of most jobs, because they do not really need me anymore and they are quite capable of creating the formulas necessary for their reports. Once in a while, they may not understand how to accomplish something, as I am also. When this happens, search the web. There is a great forum site at www.ForumTopics.com. Here, many questions are posted and answered. In fact, most questions are answered within a day.

Notes

_____

Chapter 7: Calculation Contexts

Introduction

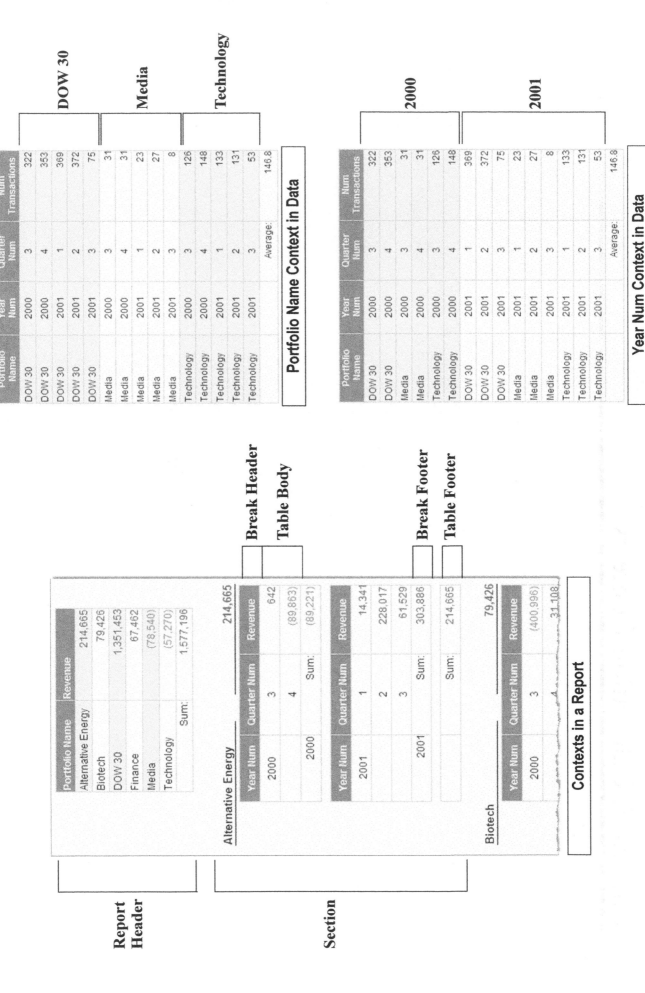

Report Header

Section

Break Header
Table Body
Break Footer
Table Footer

Contexts in a Report

Portfolio Name	Year Num	Quarter Num	Num Transactions
DOW 30	2000	3	322
DOW 30	2000	4	353
DOW 30	2001	1	369
DOW 30	2001	2	372
DOW 30	2001	3	75
Media	2000	3	31
Media	2000	4	31
Media	2001	1	23
Media	2001	2	27
Media	2001	3	8
Technology	2000	3	126
Technology	2000	4	148
Technology	2001	1	133
Technology	2001	2	131
Technology	2001	3	53
		Average:	146.8

Portfolio Name Context in Data

Portfolio Name	Year Num	Quarter Num	Num Transactions
DOW 30	2000	3	322
DOW 30	2000	4	353
Media	2000	3	31
Media	2000	4	31
Technology	2000	3	126
Technology	2000	4	148
DOW 30	2001	1	369
DOW 30	2001	2	372
DOW 30	2001	3	75
Media	2001	1	23
Media	2001	2	27
Media	2001	3	8
Technology	2001	1	133
Technology	2001	2	131
Technology	2001	3	53
		Average:	146.8

Year Num Context in Data

Introduction

For anything to make sense, it must be placed in its proper context. For example, if I told you 100,000, this number probably would not mean too much to you, because you do not know what it is referring to. If I told you that was the raise that you were getting, then you would greatly appreciate this number. If I told you that was your utility bill, then you would be greatly alarmed. So, numbers taken in context mean more than numbers without a context.

In this chapter, we are going to learn about contexts in data and in reports. We are going to learn how to manipulate these contexts in order to achieve the calculations that we desire.

Notes

Contexts

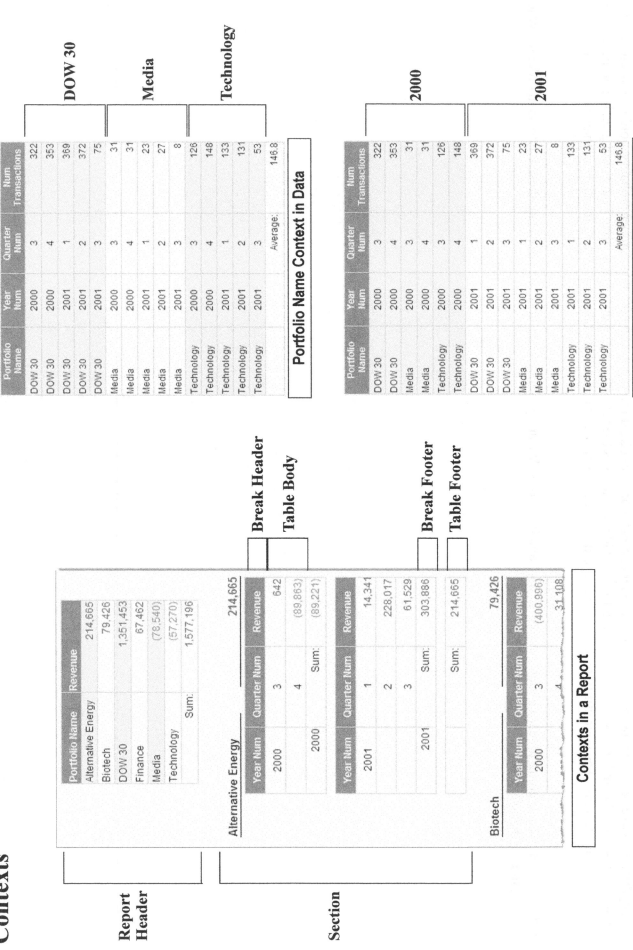

Portfolio Name Context in Data

Year Num Context in Data

Contexts in a Report

Contexts

Contexts are subsets of data within a data set. In the upper-right table, the data is divided into three subsets - one for each Portfolio Name in the data. If we were interested in the Portfolio Name subsets, we may refer to the sets as *In ([Portfolio Name])*, which would allow us to group the Num Transactions values into three sets. In the lower-right table, we've used the Year Num context to create two sets within the data, which we could refer to as *In ([Year Num])*. Therefore, in these two tables, we see that there at least three different contexts: Portfolio Name, Year Num, and the default context of each row. This means if someone asks for an Average Num Transactions value, we will have to ask for which context they want the average. The default average would simply be the average of all row values, which is 146.8. The Portfolio Name average is: $(1,491 + 120 + 5991)/3 = 1,101$. The Year Num average is: $(1,011 + 1,191)/2 = 734$.

So contexts exist within any dataset with dimension values, as we can create subsets identified by the dimension values. One last example could be, suppose that there is a room with three people in it. The total cash of all three people in the room is $100. This is the room context, which could also be called the report context, since it includes all money in the room. Now, suppose that Ralph has $45, James has $32, and Debbie has $23. This could be considered the person context, since we have divided the total among the people in the room.

Reports also divide the report total among the structures in the report. In a report, we can have the report header, sections, breaks, and rows. All of which divide the report total into subsets. In the *Contexts in a Report* graphic, we see the divisions created by the default contexts of the report. The total of all revenue in the report is 1,577,196. Any number is not equal to this total is in a context defined by some combination of dimension values. For example, the 303,886 number is defined by Alternative Energy & 2001, which is in the Portfolio Name & Year Num context.

In this chapter, we are going to learn how to get context totals into contexts, other than their default contexts. We may do this to create percentages, such as Revenue/(Revenue in Report), which would divide the default context revenue by the report total revenue.

Notes

Input/Output Contexts

Portfolio Name	Year Num	Quarter Num	Revenue	X
Biotech	2000	3	(400,996)	31,108
Biotech	2000	4	31,108	31,108
Biotech	2001	1	(119,552)	543,731
Biotech	2001	2	273,348	543,731
Biotech	2001	3	295,519	543,731
Technology	2000	3	(740,160)	31,108
Technology	2000	4	(376,607)	31,108
Technology	2001	1	(5,848)	543,731
Technology	2001	2	543,731	543,731
Technology	2001	3	521,614	543,731

Maximum Quarter In Year Num (Output Context)

$X = Max\ ([Revenue])\ In\ ([Year\ Num])$

Portfolio Name	Year Num	Quarter Num	Revenue	Y
Biotech	2000	3	(400,996)	(1,486,656)
Biotech	2000	4	31,108	(1,486,656)
Biotech	2001	1	(119,552)	1,508,812
Biotech	2001	2	273,348	1,508,812
Biotech	2001	3	295,519	1,508,812
Technology	2000	3	(740,160)	(1,486,656)
Technology	2000	4	(376,607)	(1,486,656)
Technology	2001	1	(5,848)	1,508,812
Technology	2001	2	543,731	1,508,812
Technology	2001	3	521,614	1,508,812

Maximum Sum In Year Num (Input Context)

$Y = Max\ ([Revenue]\ In\ ([Year\ Num]))$

Year Num	Revenue
2000	(1,486,656)
2001	1,508,812

Year Num Sums

Input/Output Contexts

Contexts in Web Intelligence can be manipulated by using context operators. We have seen this with the use of the *In* operator in previous examples. Before we see all of the context operators and what they can do, let's first explore how the contexts can be manipulated. In the two top tables in the graphic, we have a default context of Portfolio Name, Year Num, and Quarter Num. This means that all of the Revenues are aggregated to this context level by default. For example, we know that Biotech generated 31,108 in the third quarter of 2000.

Now suppose that you wanted to put the maximum for the each year in the last column. We have titled these columns, X & Y. You would have to define what you mean by year. Notice that we have two different, but similar, formulas in the graphic.

$$X = Max ([Revenue]) In ([Year Num]) \text{ and } Y = Max([Revenue] In ([Year Num]))$$

The difference between these formulas is that in the formula for X, the *In ([Year Num])* is outside of the Max function's parentheses. Web Intelligence calls this the Output context. In the formula for Y, the *In ([Year Num])* is within the Max function's parentheses, and Web Intelligence calls this the Input context. I find this labeling of input and output confusing and I will present it in a different way. I think that so many people don't really understand this labeling and just continue to teach it until it is so convoluted that nobody understands it.

In the formula for X, the *In ([Year Num])* is outside of the Max function's parentheses, which means that Web Intelligence (WI) will look at the revenues in the default context and keep the values as they are in the table. WI will then group the revenues into two groups - one for each year. Then the max will return the maximum revenue from the group for the year on the row. For example, the revenues for the year 2000 are: (400,886); 31,108; (740,160), and (376,607). The maximum for this group is 31,108, as shown in the table in every row where year is 2000.

In the formula for Y, *In ([Year Num])* is within the Max function's parentheses, which means that WI will create two sums - one for each year. Notice, in the X formula, WI created two groups, not two sums. It creates these sums, because Sum is the default aggregate function for the Revenue measure object. This can be seen in the small *Year Num Sums* table, in the graphic. Then WI simply returns the max for each year to the respected rows. Since there is only one value for each year, the Max = the Sum.

So, when the *In()* operator is inside a function's parentheses, the measure will be allowed to aggregate to the level of the objects in the *In()* operator's argument list. When the *In()* operator is outside of the parentheses, the *In()* operator will create groups from which to operate.

Notes

Input/Output Contexts (Page 2)

Portfolio Name	Year Num	Quarter Num	Revenue	X
Biotech	2000	3	(400,996)	31,108
Biotech	2000	4	31,108	31,108
Biotech	2001	1	(119,552)	295,519
Biotech	2001	2	273,348	295,519
Biotech	2001	3	295,519	295,519
Technology	2000	3	(740,160)	(376,607)
Technology	2000	4	(376,607)	(376,607)
Technology	2001	1	(5,848)	543,731
Technology	2001	2	543,731	543,731
Technology	2001	3	521,614	543,731

Maximum Quarter In Year Num - PortfolioNum

X = Max ([Revenue]) In ([Year Num];[Portfolio Name])

Portfolio Name	Year Num	Quarter Num	Revenue	Y
Biotech	2000	3	(400,996)	(369,888)
Biotech	2000	4	31,108	(369,888)
Biotech	2001	1	(119,552)	449,314
Biotech	2001	2	273,348	449,314
Biotech	2001	3	295,519	449,314
Technology	2000	3	(740,160)	(1,116,767)
Technology	2000	4	(376,607)	(1,116,767)
Technology	2001	1	(5,848)	1,059,497
Technology	2001	2	543,731	1,059,497
Technology	2001	3	521,614	1,059,497

Maximum Year Num - Portfolio Num

Y = Max ([Revenue] In ([Year Num];[Portfolio Name]))

Portfolio Name	Year Num	Revenue
Biotech	2000	(369,888)
	2001	449,314
Biotech		

Portfolio Name	Year Num	Revenue
Technology	2000	(1,116,767)
	2001	1,059,497
Technology		

Examples of Valid Syntax

Input/Output Contexts (Page 2)

Here is another look at the same data. This time we are going to examine what happens when we place both Year Num and Portfolio Name in the $In()$ operator's argument list.

In the formula for X, we placed Portfolio Name & Year Num in the argument list. By the way, the order does not matter. Web Intelligence used this list to create groups (buckets) of values. These values are the values in the context of Portfolio Name & Year Num. For example, the group defined by Biotech & 2000 has two values - (400,996) and 31,108, of which 31,108 is the maximum. Web Intelligence assigns 31,108 to both rows with Biotech & 2000. This can be seen in the upper-left table, in the graphic.

In the formula for Y, Web Intelligence aggregates the values defined by the dimensions Portfolio Name & Year Num. This turns out to be four values, which can be seen in the lower table of the graphic. For example, Biotech & 2000 has one value of (369,888). Then, Web Intelligence assigns one of the four values to their respective rows defined by the dimensions that defined the sums. This can be seen in the upper-right table, in the graphic. Notice that rows with Biotech & 2000 have the value of (369,888).

Therefore, when the $In()$ operator is excluded from a function's parentheses, the arguments of the $In()$ operator will form buckets from which to aggregate the values, and then it will assign these values to the rows that included the dimensions from the $In()$ operator's argument list. If the $In()$ operator is within function's parentheses, the arguments of the $In()$ operator will form a new context to which the values will be aggregated by their default functions. This aggregation is demonstrated in the lower table of the graphic. Then, these values will be assigned to their respective rows of the report structure, rows that are defined by the values of the dimensions in the $In()$ operator's argument list.

Notes

Input/Output Contexts (Page 3)

Added In Report to the Input Context

Portfolio Name	Year Num	Quarter Num	Revenue	X
Biotech	2000	3	(400,996)	22,156
Biotech	2000	4	31,108	22,156
Biotech	2001	1	(119,552)	22,156
Biotech	2001	2	273,348	22,156
Biotech	2001	3	295,519	22,156
Technology	2000	3	(740,160)	22,156
Technology	2000	4	(376,607)	22,156
Technology	2001	1	(5,848)	22,156
Technology	2001	2	543,731	22,156
Technology	2001	3	521,614	22,156

X=Max([Revenue] In Report) In ([Year Num];[Portfolio Name])

Added In Report to the Output Context

Portfolio Name	Year Num	Quarter Num	Revenue	Y
Biotech	2000	3	(400,996)	1,059,497
Biotech	2000	4	31,108	1,059,497
Biotech	2001	1	(119,552)	1,059,497
Biotech	2001	2	273,348	1,059,497
Biotech	2001	3	295,519	1,059,497
Technology	2000	3	(740,160)	1,059,497
Technology	2000	4	(376,607)	1,059,497
Technology	2001	1	(5,848)	1,059,497
Technology	2001	2	543,731	1,059,497
Technology	2001	3	521,614	1,059,497

Y=Max([Revenue] In ([Year Num];[Portfolio Name])) In Report

Sum of all Revenues

Portfolio Name	Year Num	Quarter Num	Revenue
Biotech	2001	1	(119,552)
Biotech	2001	2	273,348
Biotech	2000	3	(400,996)
Biotech	2001	3	295,519
Biotech	2000	4	31,108
Technology	2001	1	(5,848)
Technology	2001	2	543,731
Technology	2000	3	(740,160)
Technology	2001	3	521,614
Technology	2000	4	(376,607)
		Sum:	22,156

Sum of all Revenues

Portfolio Name	Year Num	Revenue
Biotech	2000	(369,888)
Biotech	2001	449,314

Portfolio Name	Year Num	Revenue
Technology	2000	(1,116,767)
Technology	2001	1,059,497

Input/Output Contexts (Page 3)

Now, let's do one more thing to these formulas. Let's add In Report to X and Y's output context. Here, I am saying that within a function's parentheses is the input context, and outside of a function's parentheses is the output context. *Report* is a keyword that defines a context. It is the context of the entire report. For example, the maximum revenue in the report is 543,731, which can be found using *Max([Revenue]) In Report* .

In the formula for X, the *In Report* is added to the Input context (within the parentheses), which caused Web Intelligence to aggregate all of the revenues in the report by Revenue's default aggregate, which is sum. Then, Web Intelligence found the max of this single value, which is the sum. So X's formula just returns the sum of all revenues.

In the formula for Y, the *In Report* is added to the Output context (outside the parentheses), which caused Web Intelligence to assign the maximum of the four buckets to all rows in the table. The buckets are defined by the Portfolio Name & Year Num values, of which 1,059,497 is the maximum, which can be seen in the lower-left table, in the graphic.

So the Input context states how to calculate the values, and the output context tells how to distribute the values. By combining these types of contexts, we can create aggregates from any combination of dimensions and assign them to any context defined by combinations of dimensions.

Notes

The In Operator

Portfolio Name	Year Num	Quarter Num	Num Transactions	Num Transactions in Portfolio	Num Transactions in Report	Percent Portfolio Transactions	Percent Report Transactions
Biotech	2000	3	43	184	775	23%	6%
	2000	4	48	184	775	26%	6%
	2001	1	37	184	775	20%	5%
	2001	2	45	184	775	24%	6%
	2001	3	11	184	775	6%	1%
Biotech		Sum:	184				

Portfolio Name	Year Num	Quarter Num	Num Transactions	Num Transactions in Portfolio	Num Transactions in Report	Percent Portfolio Transactions	Percent Report Transactions
Technology	2000	3	126	591	775	21%	16%
	2000	4	148	591	775	25%	19%
	2001	1	133	591	775	23%	17%
	2001	2	131	591	775	22%	17%
	2001	3	53	591	775	9%	7%
Technology		Sum:	591				

| | | Sum: | 775 | | | | |

In Operator Used to Calculate Percentages

Revenue in Portfolio = [Num Transactions] In ([Portfolio Name])
Revenue in Report = [Num Transactions] In Report
Percent Portfolio Transactions = [Num Transactions]/[Num Transactions] In ([Portfolio Name])
Percent Report Transactions = [Num Transactions]/[Num Transactions] In Report

The In Operator

We use the *In()* operator to override existing contexts within a report structure. The table, in the graphic, has a default context of Portfolio Name, Year Num, and Quarter Num. The Num Transactions are aggregated to this default level on each row. We put a break on Portfolio Name, and then summed the Num Transactions to get a total at the Portfolio Name level (in the break footer) and at the table level (in the table footer).

We used the *In()* operator to bring the footer totals up into the body of the table, and unto each row. The formula for the break level total (*Revenue in Portfolio* column) is: = *[Num Transactions] In ([Portfolio Name]).* We do not care if the *In()* operator is in the Input or Output context, because the default aggregate is for Num Transactions is sum. If it was in the Input context, then it would first sum to the portfolio level and then distribute this sum to the rows with the portfolio name. If it was in the output context, it would do exactly the same. The formula for the *Revenue in Report* column is: = *[Num Transactions] In Report.*

To create the percentage columns, we just divide the row revenue by the context revenues using the following formulas: Percent Portfolio Transaction = *[Num Transactions]/[Num Transactions] In ([Portfolio Name]),* and Percent Report Transactions = *[Num Transactions]/[Num Transactions]In Report.* Notice that we did not need parentheses to associate the *In()* operator to its denominator. Some may write the formula as: = *[Num Transactions]/([Num Transactions] In ([Portfolio Name])),* which would yield the same results, but lets others see that the *In()* operator is operating on only the denominator.

Exercise: Use In() Operator

1. Create a query with Portfolio Name, Year Num, Quarter Num, and Num Transactions.
2. Place a break on Portfolio Name.
3. Insert four columns after Num Transactions in default table.
4. Insert the formulas
   a. First Column
      Header: Num Transactions in Portfolio
      Formula: = [Num Transactions] In ([Portfolio Name])
   b. Second Column
      Header: Num Transactions in Report
      Formula: = [Num Transactions] In Report
   c. Third Column
      Header: Percent Portfolio Transactions
      Formula: = [Num Transactions]/[Num Transactions] In
                                              ([Portfolio Name])
   d. Forth Column
      Header: Percent Report Transactions
      Formula: = [Num Transactions]/[Num Transactions] In Report

___

Notes

In Operator Example

Portfolio Name	Year Num	Quarter Num	Num Transactions	Portfolio Yearly Average	Company Yearly Average
Alternative Energy	2000	3	42	87	1,340
	2000	4	36	87	1,340
	2001	1	49	87	1,340
	2001	2	36	87	1,340
	2001	3	11	87	1,340
Biotech	2000	3	43	92	1,340
	2000	4	48	92	1,340
	2001	1	37	92	1,340
	2001	2	45	92	1,340
	2001	3	11	92	1,340
DOW 30	2000	3	322	745.5	1,340
	2000	4	353	745.5	1,340
	2001	1	369	745.5	1,340
	2001	2	372	745.5	1,340
	2001	3	75	745.5	1,340
Finance	2000	3	24	60	1,340
	2000	4	21	60	1,340
	2001	1	34	60	1,340
	2001	2	32	60	1,340
	2001	3	9	60	1,340
Media	2000	3	31	60	1,340
	2000	4	31	60	1,340
	2001	1	23	60	1,340
	2001	2	27	60	1,340
	2001	3	8	60	1,340
Technology	2000	3	126	295.5	1,340
	2000	4	148	295.5	1,340
	2001	1	133	295.5	1,340
	2001	2	131	295.5	1,340
	2001	3	53	295.5	1,340

Company Averages

Row Average:	89.33
Portfolio Average:	446.67
Yearly Average:	1,340
Quarterly Average:	536
Portfolio Yearly Average:	#MULTIVALUE

Averages Table

Portfolio Name	Num Transactions
Alternative Energy	174
Biotech	184
DOW 30	1,491
Finance	120
Media	120
Technology	591
Average:	446.67

Portfolio Avgerage: 446.67

Year Num	Num Transactions
2000	1,225
2001	1,455
Average:	1,340

Yearly Avgerage: 1,340

Year Num	Quarter Num	Num Transactions
2000	3	588
2000	4	637
2001	1	645
2001	2	643
2001	3	167
	Average:	536

Quarterly Avgerage: 536

Portfolio Name	Year Num	Num Transactions
Alternative Energy	2000	78
	2001	96
Alternative Energy	Average:	87
Biotech	2000	91
	2001	93
Biotech	Average:	92
DOW 30	2000	675
	2001	816
DOW 30	Average:	745.5
Finance	2000	45
	2001	75
Finance	Average:	60
Media	2000	62
	2001	58
Media	Average:	60
Technology	2000	274
	2001	317
Technology	Average:	295.5

Portfolio Yearly Averages

Row Average: =Average([Num Transactions])
Portfolio Average:=Average([Num Transactions] In ([Portfolio Name]))
Yearly Average:=Average([Num Transactions] In ([Year Num]))
Quarterly Average:=Average([Num Transactions] In ([Year Num];[Quarter Num]))

In Operator Example

Exercise: In Operator

1. Create a query with Portfolio Name, Year Num, Quarter Num, and Num Transactions.
2. Put a Break on Portfolio Name.
3. Average the Num Transactions, by selecting any value in the column, and then clicking the *Average* toolbar button.
4. Delete the break averages, by right-clicking on one of the break footers (not the table footer), and selecting *Remove>Remove Row.*
5. Insert four rows under the table row. Merge the second and third cells of each footer row. Then enter the labels: Row Average, Portfolio Average, Yearly Average, Quarterly Average, and Portfolio Yearly Average, as shown in the graphic. Also, enter the formulas in the graphic.

Notice that all of the formulas use the Input context to calculate the averages. We use the Input context to calculate the averages. Where the groups are the values of Portfolio Name, Year Num, and Quarter Num. Remember that the measure will first aggregate by its default function, which is sum for Num Transactions, and then the Average function will average the resulting sums. Therefore, Portfolio Average is calculated by first summing the transactions in each portfolio, and then averaging the calculated sums. The *Portfolio Average* table, in the graphic, displays the portfolio sums and portfolio average.

The next trick is to see if we can get the Yearly Average up into the body of the table. We also want to calculate the Portfolio Yearly Average for each portfolio. We will use the *In()* operator, but we cannot use the same formulas from the footer.

6. Insert two columns to the right of Num Transactions. Enter *Portfolio Yearly Average* and *Company Yearly Average* into the new header.
7. In the Company Yearly Average column enter: = *Average([Num Transactions] In ([Year Num])) In Report.*
   This formula is very similar to the one used in the footer. However, we added *In Report* to the output context, which forces it to consider all of the transactions when calculating the average. Therefore, the result is the same 1,340.
8. In the Portfolio Yearly Average column enter: = *Average([Num Transactions] In ([Year Num];[Portfolio Name])) In ([Portfolio Name]).*
   This formula will create sums for each year in a portfolio, and then average the sums. It will only do this within each portfolio.
9. In the table footer, enter the following into the Portfolio Yearly Average field:
   =*Average([Num Transactions] In ([Year Num];[Portfolio Name])) In ([Portfolio Name]).*
   This is the same formula used in step 8, but it yields a #MULTIVALUE, because it is outputting six values (one for each portfolio).

Notes

Context Keywords

In Body: = [Num Transactions] In Body
In Break: = [Num Transactions] In Break
In Block: = [Num Transactions] In Block
In Section: = [Num Transactions] In Section
In Report: = [Num Transactions] In Report

Alternative Energy

Year Num	Quarter Num	Num Transactions	In Body	In Break	In Block	In Section	In Report
2000	3	42	42	78	174	174	2,680
	4	36	36	78	174	174	2,680
2000	Sum:	78					
2001	1	49	49	96	174	174	2,680
	2	36	36	96	174	174	2,680
	3	11	11	96	174	174	2,680
2001	Sum:	96					
	Sum:	174					

Biotech

Year Num	Quarter Num	Num Transactions	In Body	In Break	In Block	In Section	In Report
2000	3	43	43	91	184	184	2,680
	4	48	48	91	184	184	2,680
2000	Sum:	91					
2001	1	37	37	93	184	184	2,680
	2	45	45	93	184	184	2,680
	3	11	11	93	184	184	2,680
2001	Sum:	93					
	Sum:	184					

DOW 30

Year Num	Quarter Num	Num Transactions	In Body	In Break	In Block	In Section	In Report
2000	3	322	322	675	1,491	1,491	2,680

Report with Portfolio Name Sections and Break on Year Num

Context Keywords

The report in the graphic has sections on Portfolio Name. The table has a break on Year Num. Therefore, this report has four different contexts: Body, Break, Section, and Report. Web Intelligence realizes that these contexts are important in many context sensitive formulas, so WI has assigned a keyword to represent each context. We have already used *In Report* in several examples. Now let's look at the others.

Body: The current default context of the formula, which is the context of the cell where it is placed. This keyword is rarely needed, as it is redundant.

Break: The context of the break in the table where the keyword is used. In our example, the break context is (Portfolio Name - Year Num), because the break exists within a section. Therefore, in our case, In Break = In ([Year Num]; [Portfolio Name])

Block: The context of the section where the keyword is placed. In our report, we have sections defined by the Portfolio Name object. Therefore, In Block = In ([Portfolio Name])

Section: Section is the same as Block, but it ignores filters placed on the report structure. So, in our case [Num Transactions] In Section = NoFilter([Num Transactions] In Block).

Report: This is the entire report's context. We use this keyword when we want to operate on the entire set of data in the report.

Notes

ForEach Operator

Portfolio Context

Portfolio Name	Num Transactions	Average Portfolio
Alternative Energy	174	446.67
Biotech	184	
DOW 30	1,491	
Finance	120	
Media	120	
Technology	591	
Average:	446.67	

= Average([Num Transactions] ForEach([Portfolio Name]))

Portfolio - Year Context

Portfolio Name	Year Num	Num Transactions	Average Yearly Portfolio
Alternative Energy	2000	78	223.33
Alternative Energy	2001	96	
Biotech	2000	91	
Biotech	2001	93	
DOW 30	2000	675	
DOW 30	2001	816	
Finance	2000	45	
Finance	2001	75	
Media	2000	62	
Media	2001	58	
Technology	2000	274	
Technology	2001	217	
Average:		223.33	

= Average([Num Transactions] ForEach([Portfolio Name]; [Year Num]))

Portfolio - Year - Quarter Context

Portfolio Name	Year Num	Quarter Num	Num Transactions
Alternative Energy	2000	3	42
	2000	4	36
	2001	1	49
	2001	2	36
	2001	3	11
Alternative Energy		Average:	34.8
Biotech	2000	3	43
	2000	4	48
	2001	1	37
	2001	2	45
	2001	3	11
Biotech		Average:	36.8
DOW 30	2000	3	322
	2000	4	353
	2001	1	369
	2001	2	372
	2001	3	75
DOW 30		Average:	298.2
Finance	2000	3	24
	2000	4	21
	2001	1	34
	2001	2	32
	2001	3	9
Finance		Average:	24
Media	2000	3	31
	2000	4	31
	2001	1	23
	2001	2	27
	2001	3	8
Media		Average:	24
Technology	2000	3	126
	2000	4	148
	2001	1	133
	2001	2	131
	2001	3	53
Technology		Average:	118.2
		Average:	89.33

Portfolio Name	Avgerage Num Transactions
Alternative Energy	34.8
Biotech	36.8
DOW 30	298.2
Finance	24
Media	24
Technology	118.2
	89.33

ForEach Operator

Earlier, we found that the *In()* operator overrode existing contexts in a structure. Now, we are going to find out that the *ForEach()* operator manufactures contexts.

For example, look at the Portfolio Context graphic. In the left table, we have Portfolio and Num Transactions. In the footer of this table, we have the average of all the portfolios in the table. In the table on the right of the graphic, we have removed the Portfolio Name column, but we still want to display the average of all portfolios. We achieved this by using the formula: =Average([Num Transactions] ForEach([Portfolio Name])). The ForEach in this formula creates a bucket for each portfolio, and in each bucket is the sum of the portfolio. Then, the *Average* function averages the bucket values.

The formula in the Portfolio - Year Context graphic is similar. The larger table is averaging the number of yearly transactions for each portfolio. The formula is: = *Average ([Num Transactions] ForEach([Portfolio Name]; [Year Num]))*. In both of these cases, the *ForEach()* operator is creating a context that equals the larger table, by adding the removed columns to the *ForEach()* operator's argument list. This enables the *Average* function to operate on the values at the same resolution as the larger table, even though the context has change, because of the deleted columns.

Exercise: ForEach Exercise

1. Create a query with Portfolio Name, Year Num, Quarter Num, and Num Transactions.
2. Copy the default table to the right of itself.
3. Create Break table in graphic.
   a. Place a break on Portfolio Name
   b. Click on any Num Transactions value, and then click the *Average* toolbar button.
4. Create the Summary table in the graphic
   a. Delete The Year Num and Quarter Num columns from the second table.
   b. Modify the Num Transactions formula to: = *Average ([Num Transactions] ForEach ([Year Num]; [Quarter Num]))*
   c. Modify the Num Transactions header to: Average Num Transactions.

The smaller table should contain the values from the breaks in the larger table.

Notes

ForEach() & In()

Using ForEach() Operator

Portfolio Name	Avgerage Num Transactions
Alternative Energy	34.8
Biotech	36.8
DOW 30	298.2
Finance	24
Media	24
Technology	118.2
	89.33

Row: = Average([Num Transactions] ForEach ([Year Num];[Quarter Num]))
Footer: = Average([Num Transactions] ForEach ([Year Num];[Quarter Num]))

Using In() Operator

Portfolio Name	Avgerage Num Transactions
Alternative Energy	34.8
Biotech	36.8
DOW 30	298.2
Finance	24
Media	24
Technology	118.2
	89.33

Row: = Average([Num Transactions] In ([Year Num];[Quarter Num];[Portfolio Name]))
Footer: = Average([Num Transactions] In ([Year Num];[Quarter Num];[Portfolio Name]))

Portfolio Quarterly Averages

Portfolio Name	Year Num	Quarter Num	Num Transactions
Alternative Energy	2000	3	42
	2000	4	36
	2001	1	49
	2001	2	36
	2001	3	11
Alternative Energy		Average:	34.8
Biotech	2000	3	43
	2000	4	48
	2001	1	37
	2001	2	45
	2001	3	11
Biotech		Average:	36.8
DOW 30	2000	3	322
	2000	4	353
	2001	1	369
	2001	2	372
	2001	3	75
DOW 30		Average:	298.2
Finance	2000	3	24
	2000	4	21
	2001	1	34
	2001	2	32
	2001	3	9
Finance		Average:	24
Media	2000	3	31
	2000	4	31
	2001	1	23
	2001	2	27
	2001	3	8
Media		Average:	24
Technology	2000	3	126
	2000	4	148
	2001	1	133
	2001	2	131
	2001	3	53
Technology		Average:	118.2
		Average:	89.33

ForEach() & In()

Earlier I stated that the *In()* operator overrode contexts and the *ForEach()* operator manufactured contexts. What I should have said is that the *In()* operator does not take into consideration its current context, unless it is defined in the *In()* operator's argument list. For example, *In Report* will operate on all of the values in the entire report, *In ([Portfolio Name])* will operate on the values in each portfolio and ignore any other dimensions in the context.

The *ForEach()* operator will operate on the context defined in its argument, but will still consider the context of where it is placed. For example, in the graphic, we have a large table with a break placed on Portfolio Name. Each break footer contains the average of the Quarter Num's number of transactions in the portfolio break. When we created the summary table, in the *Using ForEach() Operator* graphic, we did not include the Portfolio Name in the *ForEach* operator's argument list. We did not have to, because Portfolio Name is in the table and defines the default context.

However, in the *Using In() Operator* graphic, we had to specifically mention Portfolio Name in the *In()* operator's argument list. If we did not include it, then the *Average* would have returned the average of all quarters, and ignored Portfolio Name's participation in the average. In both the *ForEach()* and *In()* examples, we are creating buckets that are defined by Portfolio Name, Year Num, and Quarter Num. However, we do not have to mention the Portfolio Name in the *ForEach()* operator's argument list, because the default context is not overridden by the dimensions in the argument list.

Notes

ForAll() Operator

Portfolio Name	Year Num	Quarter Num	Num Transactions	Portfolio Percentage
Alternative Energy	2000	3	42	24%
	2000	4	36	21%
	2001	1	49	28%
	2001	2	36	21%
	2001	3	11	6%
Alternative Energy			Sum:	100%
Biotech	2000	3	43	23%
	2000	4	48	26%
	2001	1	37	20%
	2001	2	45	24%
	2001	3	11	6%
Biotech			Sum:	100%
DOW 30	2000	3	322	22%
	2000	4	353	24%
	2001	1	369	25%
	2001	2	372	25%
	2001	3	75	5%
DOW 30			Sum:	100%
Finance	2000	3	24	20%
	2000	4	21	18%
	2001	1	34	28%
	2001	2	32	27%
	2001	3	9	8%
Finance			Sum:	100%

Media	2000	3	31	26%
	2000	4	31	26%
	2001	1	23	19%
	2001	2	27	23%
	2001	3	8	7%
Media			Sum:	100%
Technology	2000	3	126	21%
	2000	4	148	25%
	2001	1	133	23%
	2001	2	131	22%
	2001	3	53	9%
Technology			Sum:	100%
		Row Average:	89.33	
		Portfolio Average:	446.67	
		Yearly Average:	1,340	
		Quarterly Average:	536	

ForAll() Example

Porfolio Average: =Average([Num Transactions] ForAll([Quarter Num]; [Year Num]))
                    =Average([Num Transactions] In ([Portfolio Name]))

Yearly Average: =Average([Num Transactions] ForAll([Portfolio Name];[Quarter Num]))
                    =Average([Num Transactions] In ([Year Num]))

Quarterly Average: =Average([Num Transactions] ForAll([Portfolio Name]))
                    =Average([Num Transactions] In ([Year Num];[Quarter Num]))

ForAll() Operator

You may recognize the report in the graphic, as it is very similar to the report in the *In()* operator example. However, it is created using the *ForAll()* operator, which is the converse of the *In()* operator. When we used the *In()* operator, we specified the dimensions that we wanted to operate on. With the *ForAll* operator, we specify the dimensions in the default context that we want to ignore.

In the above report, the table context is Portfolio Name, Year Num, and Quarter Num. If we want to average the Portfolio Name context, then we use *ForAll([Year Num];[Quarter Num])*. With the *In()* operator, we used *In([Portfolio Name])*. This is why I say one is the converse of the other. With the *ForAll()* operator, we state the dimensions that we want to exclude, and with the *In()* operator, we state the dimensions that we want to include. This probably means that we could use the *In()* operator for almost any formula that uses the *ForAll()* operator. In fact, I can only remember a few times that I have used the *ForAll()* operator in my professional reports.

Notes

Combining Context Operators

Portfolio Name	Year Num	Quarter Num	Num Transactions	Variance from Portfolio Mean	Variance from Report Mean
Alternative Energy	2000	3	42	7.2	-47.33
	2000	4	36	1.2	-53.33
	2001	1	49	14.2	-40.33
	2001	2	36	1.2	-53.33
	2001	3	11	-23.8	-78.33
Biotech	2000	3	43	6.2	-46.33
	2000	4	48	11.2	-41.33
	2001	1	37	0.2	-52.33
	2001	2	45	8.2	-44.33
	2001	3	11	-25.8	-78.33
DOW 30	2000	3	322	23.8	232.67
	2000	4	353	54.8	263.67
	2001	1	369	70.8	279.67
	2001	2	372	73.8	282.67
	2001	3	75	-223.2	-14.33
Finance	2000	3	24	0	-65.33
	2000	4	21	-3	-68.33
	2001	1	34	10	-55.33
	2001	2	32	8	-57.33
	2001	3	9	-15	-80.33
Media	2000	3	31	7	-58.33
	2000	4	31	7	-58.33
	2001	1	23	-1	-66.33
	2001	2	27	3	-62.33
	2001	3	8	-16	-81.33
Technology	2000	3	126	7.8	36.67
	2000	4	148	29.8	58.67
	2001	1	133	14.8	43.67
	2001	2	131	12.8	41.67
	2001	3	53	-65.2	-36.33

Num Transactions Variance from The Report Mean

Variance from Portfolio Mean: = [Num Transactions] - Average ([Num Transactions] ForEach ([Year Num];[Quarter Num])) In ([Portfolio Name])

Variance from Report Mean: = [Num Transactions] - Average ([Num Transactions] ForEach ([Year Num];[Quarter Num])) In Report

Combining Context Operators

In this report, we want to calculate how the current context (row) Num Transactions differs from the portfolio and report average Num Transactions. To do this, we simply subtract the portfolio or report average number of transactions from the number of transactions on the current row.

To calculate the Portfolio Num Transactions, we used the *ForEach()* operator to define the values to average, which is every row in a portfolio. Each row is defined by Portfolio Name, Year Num, and Quarter Num. However, we did not include the Portfolio Name in the argument list. This is because the *ForEach()* operator will not override the current default context. We next add the In ([Portfolio Name]) to the output context, because we want to only average the values within a portfolio. The Report variance is basically the same formula, but with the output context replaced with *In Report*.

Okay, so the ForEach basically separated the values into their default contexts, which is a row. It did this implicitly by not overriding the default context. For example, ForEach([Quarter Num]) is equal to ForEach ([Year Num]) is equal to ForEach ([Portfolio Name];[Year Num];[Quarter Num]). This is true, because we use the ForEach() operator to add to existing contexts, not override them. So, in this case, the following is also true:

Average([Num Transactions] ForEach([Year Num];[Quarter Num]) In ([Portfolio Name]) = Average([Num Transactions]) In ([Portfolio Name])

Because, the arguments in the ForEach() operator do not add anything to the existing context. It simply acknowledges two of the dimensions that created it.

Notes

Combining Context Operators (2)

Portfolio Name	Year Num	Quarter Num	Num Transactions
Alternative Energy	2000	3	42
Alternative Energy	2000	4	36
Alternative Energy	2001	1	49
Alternative Energy	2001	2	36
Alternative Energy	2001	3	11
Media	2001	3	8
Technology	2000	3	126
Technology	2000	4	148
Technology	2001	1	133
Technology	2001	2	131
Technology	2001	3	53
		Average:	89.33

Average of all Quarters is 89.33

Portfolio Name	Year Num	Quarter Num	Num Transactions
Alternative Energy	2000	3	42
Biotech	2000	3	43
DOW 30	2000	3	322
Finance	2000	3	24
Media	2000	3	31
Technology	2000	3	126
		Average:	98

Third Quarter 2000 Average

Year Num	Quarter Num	Average Num Transactions	Report Average Transactions	Difference from Report Average
2000	3	98	89.33	8.67
2000	4	106.17	89.33	16.83
2001	1	107.5	89.33	18.17
2001	2	107.17	89.33	17.83
2001	3	27.83	89.33	-61.5

Average Transactions for Each Quarter

Average Num Transaction

= Average ([Num Transactions] ForEach ([Portfolio Name]))

Report Average Transactions

= Average ([Num Transactions] ForEach ([Portfolio Name])) In Report

Difference from Report Average

=Average ([Num Transactions] ForEach ([Portfolio Name]) - Average ([Num Transactions] ForEach ([Portfolio Name])) In Report

Combining Context Operators (2)

In the previous exercise, we saw that we didn't really need the *ForEach()* operator, as it added nothing to the context, which is what *ForEach()* operators are supposed to do. In this exercise, we deleted the Portfolio Name column. However, we still want the average portfolio quarterly number of transactions. To do this, we must average the quarters for each portfolio, within the context of the table. For example, the first row of the table is the average of the third quarter, of the year 2000, for each portfolio. The proof of this calculation can be seen in the *Third Quarter 2000 Average* graphic.

We used the *ForEach()* operator to create the context for this calculation by adding Portfolio Name to the context. Without the *ForEach* Operator, the average will equal the sum, because the average will just return the number of transactions, since the transactions will sum first, and then average function will just average one number, which is the sum. Mathematically, it would look like: = *Num Transactions / 1*. The *ForEach()* operator causes the Num Transactions to be divided into their portfolio groups. Mathematically, it would look like *(Num Transactions (P1) + Num Transactions (P2) + ... + Num Transactions (Pn...)) / n*. The number of transactions stay within the Year and Quarter specified on the row, because the ForEach() operator does not override the table's existing contexts.

The Report Average Transactions is the average of all quarters and all years, because the *In Report* expands the context to beyond the current Year and Quarter on the row. This can be seen in the Average for all Quarters graphic.

Exercise: Combining Context Operators

4. Create a query with Portfolio Name, Year Num, Quarter Num, and Num Transactions.
5. Delete the Portfolio Name column.
6. Modify the Num Transactions formula to: = *Average ([Num Transactions] ForEach ([Portfolio Name]))*
7. Modify the Num Transactions header to: Average Num Transactions.
8. Insert two columns to the right of Average Num Transactions.
9. First Column
    a. Header: Report Average Transactions
    b. Formula: = Average ([Num Transactions] ForEach ([Portfolio Name])) In Report
7. Second Column
    a. Header: Difference from Report Average
    b. Formula: = Average ([Num Transactions] ForEach ([Portfolio Name])) - Average([Num Transactions] ForEach ([Portfolio Name])) In Report

Notes

Where() Operator

=[Num Transactions] Where ([Portfolio Name] = "DOW 30")

Portfolio Name	Year Num	Quarter Num	Num Transactions
Alternative Energy	2000	3	42
Alternative Energy	2000	4	36
Alternative Energy	2001	1	49
Alternative Energy	2001	2	36
Alternative Energy	2001	3	11
Biotech	2000	3	43
Biotech	2000	4	48
Biotech	2001	1	37
Biotech	2001	2	45
Biotech	2001	3	11

Data Set for Report

Quarter Num	Year Num	Total Transactions	DOW 30 Transactions	Rest of Transactions	% DOW Transactions
1	2001	645	369	276	57%
2	2001	643	372	271	58%
3	2000	588	322	266	55%
3	2001	167	75	92	45%
4	2000	637	353	284	55%

Comparing DOW 30 Portfolio to Rest of Portfolios

DOW 30 Transactions: = [Num Transactions] **Where** ([Portfolio Name] = "DOW 30")

[DOW 30 Transactions]: = [Num Transactions] **Where** ([Portfolio Name] = "DOW 30")

Rest of Transactions: = [Num Transactions] - [DOW 30 Transactions]

% DOW Transactions: = [DOW 30 Transactions]/[Num Transactions]

Where() Operator

So far, the context operators have operated on dimensions. The Where operator operates on an object's values. For example, we have a document with the data set shown in the upper-right of the graphic. We can see that the data contains Portfolio Name, Year Num, Quarter Num, and Num Transactions. If we delete the Portfolio Name column from the report, the Year Num and Quarter Num will define the new context. Now, instead of five quarters for each Portfolio Name, we have five quarters that contain the transactions for all the portfolios. The Portfolio Name is still in the document's data provider, we are just not showing it in the report.

The Total Transactions column has the total transactions for each quarter for all of the portfolios. In the DOW 30 column, we want to see only the DOW 30 number of transactions. To achieve this, we use the Where operator: *= [Num Transactions] Where ([Portfolio Name] = "DOW 30")*. The *Where()* operator does not override the existing context of the report, so it isolates the DOW 30 transactions within the context of each row, which is the Year - Quarter context.

In the Rest of Transactions formula, we are subtracting the DOW 30 transactions from the total transactions. We simplified the formula by encapsulating the formula for the DOW 30 transactions into a variable. We then use this variable in the *Rest of Transactions* and *% DOW Transactions* formulas.

Exercise: Where Operator

4. Create a query with Portfolio Name, Year Num, Quarter Num, and Num Transactions.
5. Delete the Portfolio Name column.
6. Modify the Num Transactions header to: Total Transactions
7. Insert Three columns to the right of Total Transactions.
8. First Column Header: DOW 30 Transactions
   Formula: = [Num Transactions] Where ([Portfolio Name] = "DOW 30")
9. Create DOW 30 Transactions variable
   a. Click on any value in the DOW 30 Transactions column, and then click the Create Variable button on the Formula Toolbar.
   b. Name the variable DOW 30 Transactions, and qualify as a Measure.
7. Add the Rest of Transactions header and formula (shown in graphic) to the next column.
8. Add the % DOW Transactions header and formula to the last column.

Notes

Where Operator Restrictions

Can Not Do:

Where Statement: Where([Num Transactions] > 50)
Where Statement: Where ([Num Transactions] = ToNumber(UserResponse("Enter Number of Transactions")))

Can Do:

Variable Name: [Is Greater Than 50]
Variable Formula: If [Num Transactions] > 50 Then 1 Else 0
New Where: Where ([Is Greater Than 50] = 1)

Variable Name: [Is Equal to Response]
Variable Formula: If [Num Transactions] = ToNumber(UserResponse("Enter Number of Transactions")) Then 1 Else 0
New Where: Where ([Is Equal to Response] = 1)

Where Operator Restrictions

We can see that the *Where()* operator could be very powerful in reports. However, the logic that we can place in the argument is limited. We can only use the *Equal to* (=) operator and we can only use AND, OR, and NOT logical operators. This greatly limits our creativity when creating the where logic.

Therefore, many report developers do not put any logic in the where argument, except a simple Object = 1 or Object = 2, where 1 is true and 0 is false. Well that seems pretty limited? Well, it seems like that, but the object that we are referring to is a variable that contains any logic that we need. This logic can be simple or complicated, as long as the result of the logic is a simple 1 or 0. We call these kinds of variables flags. I believe this comes from the old fashion mailboxes, where if the mailman delivered mail, he would raise the flag on the mail box. So the flag was either up or down. The variables are either true or false.

For example, in the graphic, we simply want to operate on all Num Transactions that are greater than 50. We cannot use the greater than sign in the *Where* operator's argument. Therefore, we create a variable that will return true (1) when the Num Transactions is greater than 50 and return false (0) when it is 50 or less. We call this variable *Is Greater Than 50*, and we qualify it as a Dimension. It is good to prefix these types of variables with Is, as it returns true when it is and returns false when it is not. Also, many people understand this naming convention. We then use this new variable in the Where operator's argument, as in: *Sum([Revenue]) Where ([Is Greater Than 50] = 1)*.

Notes

_____

Prompted Where Example

Year Num	Quarter Num	Total Transactions	Finance Transactions	Rest of Transactions	Percent Finance Transactions
2000	3	588	24	564	4%
2000	4	637	21	616	3%
2001	1	645	34	611	5%
2001	2	643	32	611	5%
2001	3	167	9	158	5%

Variable Portfolio Table

Finance Transactions: = UserResponse("Enter Portfolio Name:") + " Transactions"
Rest of Transactions: =[Num Transactions] - [Portfolio Transactions]
Percent Finance Transactions:: =[Portfolio Transactions]/[Num Transactions]

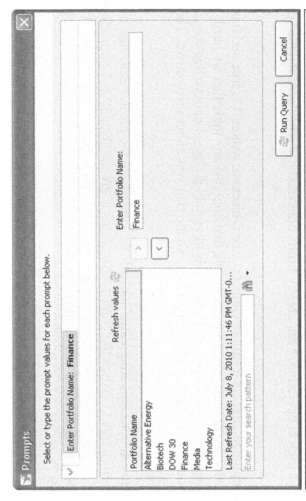

Select Portfolio for Comparison

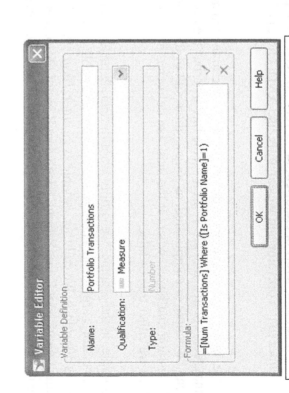

Variable Editor for Portfolio Transactions

Prompted Where Example

In the previous where example, we created the above report with DOW 30 hardcoded into the logic. This means that if we wanted to look at a different portfolio, then we would have to edit all of the formulas with DOW 30 and change DOW 30 to a different portfolio name. This is not very efficient, and it is also error prone, because all formulas may not be edited, which will leave DOW 30 in some and the new portfolio in others.

I have seen people make a tab for each portfolio in a document, which allows a person to just click on a tab to activate a desired portfolio report. However, some people don't like to have so many tabs, or there may be too many values to make the tab solution viable. In this example, we are going to present a method to use a prompt to select a value, and then we will use the prompted value in all of the formulas.

Exercise: Prompted Where Operator

4. Create a query with Portfolio Name, Year Num, Quarter Num, and Num Transactions.

   a. Create a Query Filter by dragging Portfolio Name to the Query Filters section of the Query Panel, select the *Greater Than or Equal to* operator, and select Prompt as the operand.

   b. Create another Query Filter by again dragging Portfolio Name to the Query Filters section, select the Less Than operator, and select Prompt as the operand. Highlight and copy the Prompt text in the filter. Also, double-click on the *And* operator to change it to an *Or*.

2. Delete the Portfolio Name column, and Modify the Num Transactions header to: Total Transactions

3. Create two variables

   a. Name: *Is Portfolio Name*, Qualification: Dimension.
      Formula: = If UserResponse("Enter Portfolio Name:") = [Portfolio Name] Then 1 Else 0

   b. Name: *Portfolio Transactions*, Qualification: Measure.
      Formula: =[Num Transactions] Where ([Is Portfolio Name]=1)

4. Insert three columns to the right of Total Transactions

   a. First inserted column header: = UserResponse("Enter Portfolio Name:") + " Transactions"
      Formula: =[Portfolio Transactions]

   b. Second inserted column header: Rest of Transactions
      Formula: = [Num Transactions] - [Portfolio Transactions]

   c. Third inserted column header: ="Percent" + Char (13) + UserResponse("Enter Portfolio Name:") + Char(13) + "Transactions"
      Formula: = [Portfolio Transactions] / [Num Transactions]

Notes

Section Solution

Alternative Energy

Quarter Num	Year Num	Total Transactions	Rest of Transactions	% Total Transactions
1	2001	49	596	8%
2	2001	36	607	6%
3	2000	42	546	7%
3	2001	11	156	7%
4	2000	36	601	6%

Biotech

Quarter Num	Year Num	Total Transactions	Rest of Transactions	% Total Transactions
1	2001	37	608	6%
2	2001	45	598	7%
3	2000	43	545	7%
3	2001	11	156	7%
4	2000	48	589	8%

DOW 30

Quarter Num	Year Num	Total Transactions	Rest of Transactions	% Total Transactions
1	2001	369	276	57%
2	2001	372	271	58%
3	2000	322	266	55%
3	2001	75	92	45%
4	2000	353	284	55%

Finance

Quarter Num	Year Num	Total Transactions	Rest of Transactions	% Total Transactions
1	2001	34	611	5%
2	2001	32	611	5%
3	2000	24	564	4%
3	2001	9	158	5%

Section Solution

Rest of Transactions: =Sum([Num Transactions] In ([Quarter Num];[Year Num])) - [Num Transactions]

% Total Transactions: =[Num Transactions]/Sum([Num Transactions] In ([Quarter Num];[Year Num]))

Section Solution

The previous two examples compared a selected portfolio to all the other portfolios. The first example hard-coded the portfolio name, while the second allowed the refresher of the report to select the portfolio name to compare. I would be remiss if I didn't show you a solution that compared each portfolio to all portfolios. This solution does not use the *Where()* operator to isolate a portfolio to compare, instead it uses sections to isolate each portfolio in a section. Then, it uses the *In()* operator to look at all portfolio names for the comparison.

Each solution serves basically the same function, which is to compare a portfolio to the rest of the portfolios. However, the presentation differs, and which one to use depends on the need of the people requesting the report. If I am working for somebody, I will sometimes present all three solutions and let them choose which one they would like. Sometimes, I feel very strongly about the one they should use, just to find out that they prefer another. Either way, it's okay, because as report developers, we need to learn that the report requestor has the last say on what reports will be used. Many times I offer up to ten solutions, and the requestor only keeps two. Then, it's on to the next set of reports.

Exercise: Section Solution

4. Create a query with Portfolio Name, Year Num, Quarter Num, and Num Transactions.

2. Drag the Portfolio Name object from the table, and drop it above the default table to create Portfolio Name sections. (Be sure to drag it high enough, so you don't create a crosstab.)

3. Modify the Num Transactions header to: Total Transactions.

4. Insert two columns to the right of Total Transactions
   a. First inserted column header: *Rest of Transactions*

   Formula: = Sum([Num Transactions] In ([Quarter Num];[Year Num])) - [Num Transactions]

   b. Second inserted column header: *% Total Transactions*

   Formula: = [Num Transactions] / Sum ([Num Transactions] In ([Quarter Num];[Year Num]))

Notes

Summary

Alternative Energy

Quarter Num	Year Num	Total Transactions	Rest of Transactions	% Total Transactions
1	2001	49	596	8%
2	2001	36	607	6%
3	2000	42	546	7%
3	2001	11	156	7%
4	2000	36	601	6%

Biotech

Quarter Num	Year Num	Total Transactions	Rest of Transactions	% Total Transactions
1	2001	37	608	6%
2	2001	45	598	7%
3	2000	43	545	7%
3	2001	11	156	7%
4	2000	48	589	8%

DOW 30

Quarter Num	Year Num	Total Transactions	Rest of Transactions	% Total Transactions
1	2001	369	276	57%
2	2001	372	271	58%
3	2000	322	266	55%
3	2001	75	92	45%
4	2000	353	284	55%

Finance

Quarter Num	Year Num	Total Transactions	Rest of Transactions	% Total Transactions
1	2001	34	611	5%
2	2001	32	611	5%
3	2000	24	564	4%
3	2001	9	158	5%

Section Solution

Summary

In the chapter before this one, we learned about formulas and functions. We found that these functions could help us create very powerful and effective reports. However, we also learned that we had to go beyond the current default contexts in a report to get highly effective results. In many of the examples, we used the *In()* operator to go beyond the default contexts, but I offered little explanation as to what it was doing. In this chapter, I hope that you learned why we needed the operator in some of the formulas.

By going outside of the default contexts, we can greatly expand the analytics in our reports, because we can group the values in any context within the report. This allows us to create powerful ratios, variances, and comparisons, as seen in the examples of this chapter. If you have understood the topics up to this point in the book, then you are as capable as many professional Web Intelligence developers, and you should feel quite confident.

Notes

Chapter 8: Drilling

Introduction

Summary Report

Portfolio Name	Revenue	Link to More Detail Report
Alternative Energy	214,665	Details for: Alternative Energy
Biotech	79,426	Details for: Biotech
DOW 30	1,351,453	Details for: DOW 30
Finance	67,462	Details for: Finance
Media	(78,540)	Details for: Media
Technology	(57,270)	Details for: Technology

Detail Report

Portfolio Details

Biotech   Maria Castro 5555551278

Company	Year Num	Quarter Num	Ticker	Revenue
Amgen Inc.	2000	3	AMGN	(25,075)
		4	AMGN	(101,920)
	2000		Sum:	(126,995)
	2001	1	AMGN	8,175
		2	AMGN	75,703
		3	AMGN	45,224
	2001		Sum:	129,101
Amgen Inc.			Sum:	2,106

Company	Year Num	Quarter Num	Ticker	Revenue
Chiron Corporation	2000	3	CHIR	(58,663)
		4	CHIR	10,863
	2000		Sum:	(47,800)
	2001	1	CHIR	(18,097)
		2	CHIR	75,525
		3	CHIR	9,328
	2001		Sum:	66,756
Chiron Corporation			Sum:	18,956

Company	Year Num	Quarter Num	Ticker	Revenue
Deltagen, Inc.	2000	3	DGEN	(27,613)

Introduction

Many times when people are viewing reports, they wonder how the numbers on the report were arrived at. Sometimes, we can determine how numbers evolved by drilling into the dimensions of a report. Drilling means that we can look into a summary dimension, such as year, and look at the hierarchical level detail dimensions, such as quarter, month, and date for year. This allows us to see the quarterly numbers that created the year summary number, or the monthly detail numbers that created the quarter summary numbers.

When we drill down a hierarchy to view the details that created the high levels of summary, we generally simply replace the summary column with a detail column, such as replacing year with quarter. This is helpful, but sometimes it creates more questions that cannot be answered with a simple column replacement. So, Web Intelligence allows document drilling. With document drilling, we can open other documents that contain the details of a summary that we are interested in. This detail document can contain many more dimensions and much more analysis than the summary document.

We will look at both types of drilling in this chapter.

Notes

Hierarchy

Hierarchy of Mothers

4	Mother - 4 Kids
7	Grandma - 3 Kids (+4 Kids)
9	Great Grandma - 2 Kids (+3 +4 Kids)
12	G Great Grandma - 3 Kids (+2 +3 +4 Kids)

Year Num Context in Data

2009	$5,000,000
2009 - 4th Quarter	$2,000,000
2009 - 4th Quarter - November	$600,000
2009 - 4th Quarter - November - 11/20	$22,000

Hierarchy

Hierarchies are levels within data, where each subsequent level is a subset of the preceding level. For example, suppose that there are four kids in a family. That means that the current mother had four kids. Her mother, Grandma, claims that she is responsible for seven kids, because she had three of her own, and her daughter had four. Therefore the current mother's four kids are a subset of grandma's seven kids. This logic can be traced through the generations of mothers in the family, as seen in the *Hierarchy of Mothers* graphic.

Another example could be a business that generated $5,000,000 in revenues in the year 2009. That $5,000,000 can be divided up into quarter amounts, which are subsets of the year 2009. In the graphic, we are showing the 4th Quarter of that year. The revenue in the 4th quarter must be less than or equal to the total for the year (unless there was a negative quarter, which we will assume that there was not), because it is a subset of the year 2009 total. If we divide the 4th quarter into months, then each month will be a subset of the quarter. In the graphic, we are looking at November.

So with hierarchies, we usually start with a general number, a summary. Then, we drill through the levels to look at more detailed information. So, if we start with year, then we may be interested in how the quarters did. If we are at the quarter level, then we may be interested in how the weeks, in a certain month, of that quarter performed.

Hierarchies only make sense when we travel in a direction where each level is a subset (drilling down the hierarchy) or each level is a superset (drilling up the hierarchy) of the preceding level. For example, Year - Quarter - Month - Date or Date - Month - Quarter - Year. Hierarchies do not make sense if the path looks like Year - Month - Quarter - Date. In this example, Month is a subset of Year, and each month has a portion of the yearly total. However, Quarter is not a subset of Month, and now it is impossible for Quarter to gets its total, because it is limited to the month total. If we used this logic and applied it to the hierarchy in the graphic, then we would get the following results:

2009 - $5,000,000, November - $600,000, 4th Quarter - $600,000.

Since the 4th Quarter appears after the Month, then it cannot be larger than the month, as it must be a subset. However, Quarter is not a subset of month, as it owns the month and two other months. The other two months are not visible, since we have limited the path to November. Therefore, the 4th Quarter total has to be the entire set of November, which is obviously incorrect.

Notes

Scope of Analysis

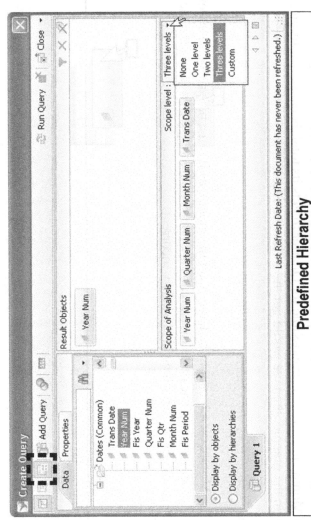

```
SELECT
SIDATE.YEAR_NUM,
SIDATE.QTR_NUM,
SIDATE.MONTH_NUM,
SIDATE.FULL_DATE
FROM
SIDATE
```

Predefined Hierarchy

Default Table

Year Num
2000
2001
2002
2003
2004
2005
2006
2007
2008
2009
2010
2011
2012
2013
2014

All Data in Query

Year Num	Quarter Num	Month Num	Trans Date
2000	1	1	1/1/00
2000	1	1	1/2/00
2000	1	1	1/3/00
2000	1	1	1/4/00
2000	1	1	1/5/00
2000	1	1	1/6/00
2000	1	1	1/7/00
2000	1	1	1/8/00
2000	1	1	1/9/00
2000	1	1	1/10/00
2000	1	1	1/11/00
2000	1	1	1/12/00
2000	1	1	1/13/00
2000	1	1	1/14/00
2000	1	1	1/15/00

Scope of Analysis

Web Intelligence uses *Scope of Analysis* to prepare a document for reports that have pre-populated hierarchy values. In the *Predefined Hierarchy* graphic, we have a query with a single dimension, Year Num, in the Result Objects section of the panel. This particular object has a hierarchy defined for it by the Universe Designer.

The Scope of Analysis section of the Query Panel is opened by clicking the *Show / Hide Scope of Analysis* button in the Query Panel. This section allows for objects to be placed that will define a hierarchy for an object. We have stated that the Year Num object already has a hierarchy defined for it, so there is no need for us to define it again. To take advantage of the pre-definition, we use the *Scope Level* drop list to select how many levels of the hierarchy we want to include in our document. In the graphic, we chose Three Levels, which included the next three levels of dimensions in the Scope of Analysis pane. The included dimensions are Year Num, Quarter Num, Month Num, and Trans Date.

If we look at the SQL for the query, we will see that the scope of analysis has included the hierarchical dimensions in the Select clause of the query, which means that the query will retrieve the additional information. However, when we run the query, the default table created by Web Intelligence will only contain the objects in the Result Objects section of the panel. In this case, fifteen Years - 2000 through 2014. So, if we look at the default table, then we may assume that the query only returned 15 rows. But, the query actually returned 5000 rows, because it included the dates, months, and quarters for each year.

So, why did it return more data then it is going to display in the default table? It did because the extra data will allow the viewer of the report to drill through the hierarchy, without running additional queries to retrieve the next hierarchical level of data.

By the way, you can create any custom hierarchy by dragging dimension objects into the Scope of Analysis pane of the Query Panel. In this example, we used three Levels down, which included the next three levels after the Year Num object in the hierarchy. You can do this, and then delete objects from the pane. For example, suppose that you did not want to include Quarter Num. If this is true, then just remove Quarter Num from the pane. Remember, that if you do create custom hierarchies that each sublevel must be a subset of the level preceding it.

Notes

Drilling Into Hierarchies

Edit Query | Refresh Data | Track | Drill | □ Show BI services

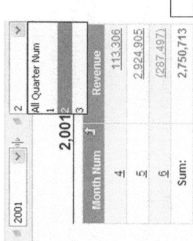

2,001

Quarter Num	⇧	Revenue
1		349,438
2		2,750,713
3		5,410,828
Sum:		8,510,980

2001

Quarter Num	⇧	Revenue
1		349,438
2		2,750,713
3		5,410,828
Sum:		8,510,980

Quarters in Year 2001

Drop objects here to add simple report filters.

Year Num	Revenue
2000	(6,933,784)
2001	8,510,980
Sum:	1,577,196

Drillable Report

2,001 - 2

Month Num	⇧	Revenue
4		
5		2,924,905
6		(287,497)
Sum:		2,750,713

Drill up to Quarter Num

Drilling Up Hierarchy

All Quarter Num — 1 / 2 / 3

2,001

Month Num	⇧	Revenue
4		113,306
5		2,924,905
6		(287,497)
Sum:		2,750,713

2001

Drill Across

2,001 - 2

Month Num	⇧	Revenue
4		113,306
5		2,924,905
6		(287,497)
Sum:		2,750,713

Drill Path on Report

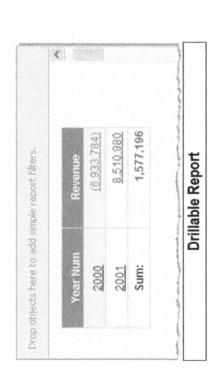

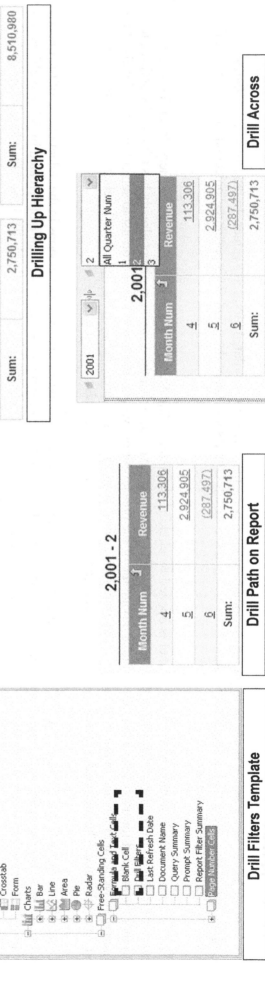

Data | Templates | Map | Properties | Input Controls

Templates
- Report Elements
  - Report
  - Tables
    - Horizontal Table
    - Vertical Table
    - Crosstab
    - Form
  - Charts
    - Bar
    - Line
    - Area
    - Pie
    - Radar
  - Free-Standing Cells
    - Formula and Text Cells
      - Blank Cell
      - Drill Filters
      - Last Refresh Date
      - Document Name
      - Query Summary
      - Prompt Summary
      - Report Filter Summary
    - Page Number Cells

Drill Filters Template

Drilling Into Hierarchies

So why should Web Intelligence bring in more data then the default table will show? The hierarchical data is there so we can drill down the hierarchy - Summary to more detail. I added Revenue to the previous report that we were looking at, and then I clicked the *Drill* toolbar button, which placed the report in drill mode. If we look at the fields in the Drillable Report graphic, then we will notice that the values have hyperlinks. These hyperlinks mean that we can click on these values to drill into the hierarchy associated with the value.

In the *Quarters in Year 2001* graphic, I clicked on Year Num 2001, which cause the year 2001 to be drilled into. Now, the table displays the Quarter Num values that are within the Year Num value of 2001. Notice that the total in the table is equal to the 2001 total in the *Drillable Report* graphic. This means that each quarter in the table is a subset of the year 2001. Also notice that the year 2001 has been placed in a drop list at the top of the report.

If we look at the value in the drop list, then we know that the table has been drilled into on Year Num 2001. If we print the report, this piece of information is not printed, and people may not realize how the quarters in the table were filtered. There is a Drill Filters template that when placed on a report will display the drill path taken through the hierarchies. In the Drill Path on Report graphic, a field created with the template is displaying the drill path, which is Year Num = 2001 and Quarter Num = 2. Notice that when we drill into Quarter that the table is now populated with the month Nums, and since we drilled into the second quarter, these are the Month numbers of the second quarter.

After a column has been drilled into, it may be desired to drill back up the hierarchy. Notice that there is a little upward pointing arrow on the drilled column. If we click on this arrow, then we will drill back up the hierarchy, as can be seen in the *Drilling Up Hierarchy* graphic. Notice that the Drill Filter field changes from 2001 - 2, to 2001.

Now that we have drilled down and up, we now will find out that we can also drill across. Drill across is very similar to a page filter in MS Excel, and in fact many people use this feature as a page filter. To use it as a page filter, we just click the Drill toolbar button, and then drag any dimension to the drill filter bar at the top of the report. A drop list control populated with all of the values of the dimension will appear in the bar. To drill across or filter, we just select values in the drop list. In the *Drill Across* graphic, we can see that we can select any quarter num that is in the currently drilled into year num value.

Notes

Additional Drilling Topics

New Query Drill

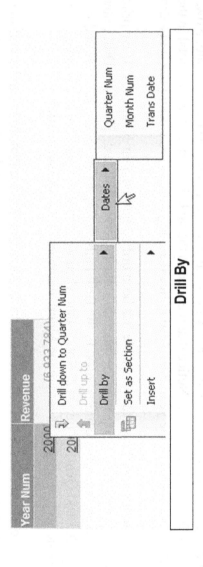

Drill By

Additional Drilling Topics

If a report is drilled into and the Scope of Analysis is not defined, then Web Intelligence will run a new query to retrieve the needed detail data. Many times, report developers will not set the scope of analysis for a document, because the document will contain more data than needed for the summary report. Then, if the report is drilled into, Web Intelligence must run a new query to retrieve the level of detail that the drill is asking for.

If the Scope of Analysis is set, and there is more than one level of the hierarchy included in the query, then the drillable dimension can be right-clicked on to expose the *Drill By* option. The Drill By option allows the next level of the hierarchy to be selected, which can bypass intermediate levels.

Notes

Drilling to New Document

`<a href=http://xaservi:6405/OpenDocument/opendoc/openDocument.jsp?sType=wid&sDocName=Portfolio+Details>`

Basic Syntax to Open a Report

a href: Specifies the destination of a link

xaservi:6405: Web Intelligence Server Name and Port Number

openDocument.jsp: Open Document Function in Java implementations

sType=wid: Web Intelligence Document

sDocName=Portfolio+Details: Document Name with Plus Signs for Spaces (Portfolio Details)

`="<a href=http://xaservi:6405/OpenDocument/opendoc/openDocument.jsp?sType=wid&sDocName=" + URLEncode("Portfolio Details") + ">"`

Formula Version of the Link Using URLEncode to Encode the Document Name

String #1: "<a href=http://xaservi:6405/OpenDocument/opendoc/openDocument.jsp?sType=wid&sDocName="

String #2: URLEncode("Portfolio Details")

String #3: ">"

Portfolio Name	Revenue	Link to More Detail Report
Alternative Energy	214,665	http://xaservi:6405/OpenDocument/opendoc/openDocument.jsp?sType=wid&sDocName=Portfolio+Details
Biotech	79,426	http://xaservi:6405/OpenDocument/opendoc/openDocument.jsp?sType=wid&sDocName=Portfolio+Details
DOW 30	1,351,453	http://xaservi:6405/OpenDocument/opendoc/openDocument.jsp?sType=wid&sDocName=Portfolio+Details

Hyperlink to Another Document in Context of a Table

Drilling to New Document

Drilling into a hierarchy is interesting, but many times we need to adjust the report to reveal more information as we drill into the report. For example, a summary report may contain just the Portfolio Names and Revenues. If we drill into this summary report, then maybe we would see just Companies in the portfolio and Revenues. That is a little interesting, but what if we could see much more information, such as the Year Num, Manager, and Num Transactions? To see more information, we could have the drill open up a detail report.

To open another report from the CMS repository, we can place a hyperlink in the cell of a report structure, and then format the cell: *Read Cell Content as Hyperlink* in the properties for the cell. Then a viewer of the report just needs to click on the link to open the report. The basic syntax for the link is shown in the *Basic Syntax to Open a Report* graphic.

The basic syntax simply uses the *a href* to specify that the content is a link. The link uses the OpenDocument function on the Web Intelligence server. There are two flavors of this function, one for Java (openDocument.jsp) and one for .Net (opendocument.aspx). The link in the example uses the Java version. The OpenDocument function resides in the opendoc directory on the Web Intelligence server. Since it resides on a server, the server name and port are part of the link. In this case, xaservi:6405, where xaservi is my server name and 6405 is the port of the application. Obviously, the name and port number will be different for other servers. So, the first part of the link is pointing to the OpenDocument function on the Web Intelligence server.

> *<a href=http://xaservi:6405/OpenDocument/opendoc/openDocument.jsp*

The second half of the link is specifying the document type, which in this case is a wid (Web Intelligence document). It uses the sType parameter to pass the document type information: *sType=wid*. After the sType argument, there is an ampersand (&), which separates the parameter values in the link. The next parameter is the document name. Notice that there is a plus sign (+) between the words Portfolio and Details. The name of the document is Portfolio Details, but we cannot use this name with a space between the words. Therefore, we replace the space with a plus (+) sign.

A plus sign may or may not be correct for your system. Therefore it may be better to use the URLEncode function to encode the document name in the link. If we use this function, then we must turn the link into a formula, so we can concatenate the components of the link. There are basically three parts to the link, the first of which is the part before the document name, the second in the encoded document name, and the third is the part after the document name. Notice that there are now plus signs and double quotes throughout the syntax for the link. These plus signs are not compensating for spaces in text, they are simply concatenating the sections of the link. The quotes are beginning and terminating the string sections of the link (the first and third sections need quotes). The document name is returned by the URLEncode function and there is no need for quotes for this section.

Notes

Passing Parameters

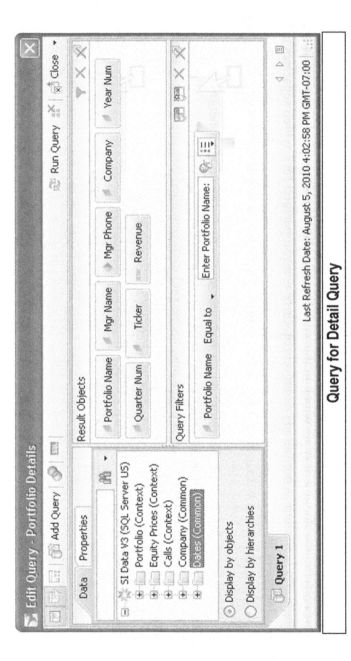

Query for Detail Query

?sType=wid&sDocName=Portfolio+Details&lsSEnter+Portfolio+Name:=Finance>

Hardcoded Parameter Value (Finance)

?&sDocName="+ URLEncode("Portfolio Details")+"&lsS"+URLEncode("Enter Portfolio Name")+":="+URLEncode([Portfolio Name])+">"

Passing Portfolio Name from Active Row

="<a href=http://xaservi:6405/OpenDocument/opendoc/openDocument.jsp?
sType=wid&sDocName=" + URLEncode("Portfolio Details") +
"&lsS" + URLEncode("Enter Portfolio Name") + ":=" + URLEncode([Portfolio Name]) +"
&sRefresh=Y&sWindow=New>"

Hyperlink in our Example

Passing Parameters

The query for a detail report probably will have a parameter, as the query in the graphic. In this query, there is a prompted query filter. The prompt text for the query filter is, "Enter Portfolio Name:". When the link in a summary report is clicked, then we want to pass the name of the portfolio with the open document function. To pass a single value parameter, we us the lsS parameter. We add it to the href string with an ampersand sign, as in the following: ... *?sType=wid&sDocName=Portfolio+Details&lsSEnter+Portfolio+Name:=Finance>*

In this example, we have hardcoded the parameter, which kind of negates the usefulness of the parameter. Therefore, we will instead pass the Portfolio Name value from the row in the report, where the hyperlink was clicked. to do this we will modify the formula to the following: ...*?&sDocName="+URLEncode("Portfolio Details")+"&lsS"+URLEncode("Enter Portfolio Name")+":="+URLEncode([Portfolio Name])+">"*

When we softcode the parameter value, we should use the URLEncode function to correctly format the parameter value for the link. Notice that we use the URLEncode funtion to encode both the prompt text and the value.

Since we are passing a parameter value, then we probably should have the document refresh using the parameter value. Therefore, we should add the sRefresh parameter to our link string. By the way, it seems like the document will refresh anyway, but adding this argument will ensure that the document will refresh using the parameter value. We add the sRefresh as in the following: ... + *"&lsS"+URLEncode("Enter Portfolio Name")+":="+URLEncode([Portfolio Name]) + "&sRefresh=Y>"*.

Many times, we want the detail report to open in its own window, as we don't want it to replace the summary report with the links. To specify a new window, we use the sWindow parameter. We add it to our link, as in the following: + *"&sRefresh=Y&sWindow=New>"*. To allow the new report to replace the report with the links, we use the Same argument, as in + *"&sRefresh=Y&sWindow=Same>"*

A hyperlink can pass multiple parameter values simply by repeating the lsS parameter for each prompt in the detail report.

Notes

Formatting the Link

Summary Report

Portfolio Name	Revenue	Link to More Detail Report
Alternative Energy	214,665	Details for: Alternative Energy
Biotech	79,426	Details for: Biotech
DOW 30	1,351,453	Details for: DOW 30
Finance	67,462	Details for: Finance
Media	(78,540)	Details for: Media
Technology	(57,270)	Details for: Technology

Summary Report

Portfolio Details

Biotech   Maria Castro 555551278

Company	Year Num	Quarter Num	Ticker	Revenue
Amgen Inc.	2000	3	AMGN	(25,075)
	2000	4	AMGN	(101,920)
	2000		Sum:	(126,995)
	2001	1	AMGN	8,175
	2001	2	AMGN	75,703
	2001	3	AMGN	45,224
	2001		Sum:	129,101
Amgen Inc.			Sum:	2,106

Company	Year Num	Quarter Num	Ticker	Revenue
Chiron Corporation	2000	3	CHIR	(58,663)
	2000	4	CHIR	10,863
	2000		Sum:	(47,800)
	2001	1	CHIR	(18,097)
	2001	2	CHIR	75,525
	2001	3	CHIR	9,328
	2001		Sum:	66,756
Chiron Corporation			Sum:	18,956

Company	Year Num	Quarter Num	Ticker	Revenue
Deltagen, Inc.	2000	3	DGEN	(27,613)

Detail Report

Formatting the Link

In our example, we can see the entire text of the link in the report cell. Nobody will understand this text, so it is best to replace it with something simple, as shown in the graphic. We create the link display text by adding the following to our formula:

+"&sRefresh=Y&sWindow=New>" + "Details for: " + [Portfolio Name] + "</a>"

There are many other parameters that can be passed when using the OpenDocument function to create a hyperlink to another report in the InfoView repository. To see these parameters and other details of the link, please see the Web Intelligence user manual for your version of Web Intelligence.

Notes

Summary

Portfolio Details

Biotech Maria Castro 555551278

Company	Year Num	Quarter Num	Ticker	Revenue
Amgen Inc.	2000	3	AMGN	(25,075)
		4	AMGN	(101,920)
	2000		Sum:	(126,995)
	2001	1	AMGN	8,175
		2	AMGN	75,703
		3	AMGN	45,224
	2001		Sum:	129,101
Amgen Inc.			Sum:	2,106

Company	Year Num	Quarter Num	Ticker	Revenue
Chiron Corporation	2000	3	CHIR	(58,663)
		4	CHIR	10,863
	2000		Sum:	(47,800)
	2001	1	CHIR	(18,097)
		2	CHIR	75,525
		3	CHIR	9,328
	2001		Sum:	66,756
Chiron Corporation			Sum:	18,956

Company	Year Num	Quarter Num	Ticker	Revenue
Deltagen, Inc.	2000	3	DGEN	(27,613)

Detail Report

Portfolio Name	Revenue	Link to More Detail Report
Alternative Energy	214,665	Details for: Alternative Energy
Biotech	79,426	Details for: Biotech
DOW 30	1,351,453	Details for: DOW 30
Finance	67,462	Details for: Finance
Media	(78,540)	Details for: Media
Technology	(57,270)	Details for: Technology

Summary Report

Summary

There are two types of drilling: Dimensional and Document. In this chapter, we examined both types of drilling. Dimensional drilling drills down a hierarchy of dimensions. These hierarchies can be defined in the universe or can be custom defined by the report refresher. Dimensional drilling simply replaces a summary column in a report, with a detail column.

Document drilling opens up a new document, when a hyperlink on a report is clicked. The hyperlink is created with the OpenDocument function. Document drilling allows for more detailed information to be presented to the driller.

Notes

_____

Creating Documents with Business Objects Web Intelligence XI V3